CUET

(UG) & Integrated PG
2022

Psychology | English Language

DU | BHU | JNU | JMI | TISS & etc.

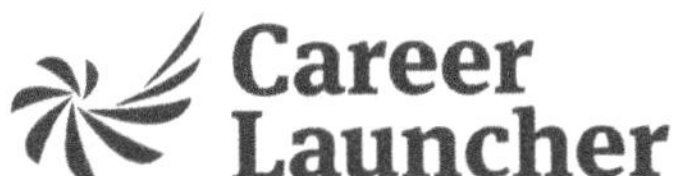

Career Launcher

Title   : CUET 2022 : Psychology and English Guide

Language   : English

Editor's Name   : Pravin Choubey and Shiva Kumar

Copyright ©   : 2022 CLIP

Typeset & Published by :

Career Launcher Infrastructure (P) Ltd.

A-45, Mohan Cooperative Industrial Area, Near Mohan Estate Metro Station, New Delhi - 110044

Marketed by :

G.K. Publications (P) Ltd.

Plot No. 9A, Sector-27A, Mathura Road, Faridabad, Haryana-121003

ISBN   : 978-93-94168-23-7

Printer's Details : Printed in India, New Delhi.

For product information :

Visit ***www.gkpublications.com*** or email to ***gkp@gkpublications.com***

CONTENTS

PSYCHOLOGY

ENGLISH LANGUAGE

Part – I : READING

Part – II : VOCABULARY

Part – III : LANGUAGE

About CUET

A year ago, it would have been unimaginable that cut-offs in Delhi University would skyrocket to 100% for some of the undergraduate courses! While DU has always been known for its high cut-offs, there are several other universities where the story is no different.

However, the National Education Policy 2020 (NEP) aims to do away with the tyranny of the ever-rising cut-offs by introducing a Common Entrance Test for all the Central Universities in the country. NEP not only proposes a holistic approach in evaluating the students by giving them the option to select subjects based on their interest, but it also aims to simplify the process of admission to higher-education institutes.

To start with, there would be a Common Entrance Test for all the Central Universities, which would be conducted twice a year from 2022. While this might sound like a new concept to many, the fact is, there is already a CUET, which is conducted for the Central Universities established in or after 2009. As many as 14 of them already admit students based on their performance in the entrance test. The CUET scores are also accepted by four state universities of the country.

The proposed CUET aims to assess conceptual understanding and application of knowledge; and also, to lessen the burden of appearing in multiple tests.

CUET Eligibility

Getting into a premier University is every student's dream. The brand value of the University not only facilitates securing a seat in a master's program in a national/international institute, but also helps in getting job offers through campus placements.

Entry to a Central University, in most cases earlier, was based on merit, i.e., marks secured in Class XII Board exams. However, from the academic year 2021, all Central Universities will also consider the CUET score for admissions into their Undergraduate programs.

CUET 2022: Eligibility Criteria

While the official criteria will be learnt once the CUET 2021 notification is released, the stipulations are not expected to change much from those of previous years.

- A candidate must have passed Class XII (10+2) or equivalent from a recognized education Board.
- If the respective Board awards grades (or CGPA), the conversion factor given by the Board must be used to compute the percentage of marks.
- Candidates, who have completed their Class XII in 2021, and have passed the Board exams, will also be eligible to apply for CUET 2022.

Eligibility: Class XII Students

While CUET is for students who have passed the Class XII (or equivalent) Board exams, any student who is appearing for the Class XII Board exam in 2022 is also eligible to apply for CUET 2021. The candidate would be required to produce the marksheets and relevant certificates as mandated by the participating Central University, and follow the timelines provided for admissions.

Key Points

- Each participating Central University is free to decide its own eligibility criteria for admissions.

- The weightages for CUET and Class XII Board exam results(if, applicable) will be at the sole discretion of the Central University, to which admission is being sought.

- As of date, CUET does not have an age limit. However, Central Universities can fix minimum & maximum age limit for admissions to all (or any) of the programs on offer.

Reservation of Seats

As CUET is an entrance exam for admissions to Undergraduate courses at the Central Universities, which have been established under an Act of the Parliament, each Central University must follow the norms set by the Government of India, with respect to intake and reservation of seats.

Generally, the following break-up is followed:

Category	Reservation
Scheduled Castes	15%
Scheduled Tribes	7.5%
Other Backward Classes (Non-Creamy)	27%
Persons with Disability	5%

Some institutions might even have provisions for the Economically Weaker Sections, which can account for 10% of the total seats. These EWS seats are carved out from the Open Category.

To avail of the reservation benefit based on caste (or any other category as specified), a candidate must be able to produce valid documents/certificates to support such claims.

Conclusion

It is essential for every candidate to check the validity of their candidature for CUET, as well as the Central University he/she is applying to. The candidate should be aware of the documents that might be required while applying for the exam, or during the admissions.

CUET 2022 notification is expected in March 2022, and registration is also going to start then.

CUET: Exam Pattern

Examination Structure for CUET (UG) -2022:

CUET (UG) –2022 will consist of the following 4 Sections:

> **Section IA** –13 Languages
>
> **Section IB** –19 Languages
>
> **Section II** –27 Domain specific Subjects
>
> **Section III** –General Test

Choosing options from each Section is not mandatory. Choices should match the requirements of the desired University.

Broad features of CUET (UG) -2022 are as follows:

Section	Subjects/ Tests	Questions to be Attempted	Question Type	Duration
Section IA – Languages	There are 13* different languages. Any of these languages may be chosen.	40 questions to be attempted out of 50 in each language	Language to be tested through Reading Comprehension (based on different types of passages–Factual, Literary and Narrative, [Literary Aptitude and Vocabulary]	45 Minutes for each language
Section IB – Languages	There are 19** Languages. Any other language apart from those offered in Section I A may be chosen.			
Section II - Domain	There are 27*** Domains specific subjects being offered under this Section. A candidate may choose a maximum of Six (06) Domains as desired by the applicable University/Universities.	40 Questions to be attempted out of 50	• Input text can be used for MCQ Based Questions • MCQs based on NCERT Class XII syllabus only	
Section III- General Test	For any such undergraduate programme/ programmes being offered by Universities where a General Test is being used for admission.	60 Questions to be attempted out of 75	• Input text can be used for MCQ Based Questions • General Knowledge, Current Affairs, General Mental Ability, Numerical Ability, Quantitative Reasoning (Simple application of basic mathematical concepts arithmetic/algebra geometry/mensuration/s tat taught till Grade 8), Logical and Analytical Reasoning	

* **Languages (13):** Tamil, Telugu, Kannada, Malayalam, Marathi, Gujarati, Odiya, Bengali, Assamese, Punjabi, English, Hindi and Urdu

** **Languages (19):** *French, Spanish, German, Nepali, Persian, Italian, Arabic, Sindhi, Kashmiri, Konkani, Bodo, Dogri, Maithili, Manipuri, Santhali, Tibetan, Japanese, Russian, Chinese.*

*** **Domain Specific Subjects (27):** 1. Accountancy/ Book Keeping 2. Biology/ Biological Studies/ Biotechnology/Biochemistry 3. Business Studies 4. Chemistry 5. Computer Science/ Informatics Practices 6. Economics/ Business Economics 7. Engineering Graphics 8.Entrepreneurship 9. Geography/Geology 10. History 11. Home Science 12.Knowledge Tradition and Practices of India 13. Legal Studies 14. Environmental Science 15. Mathematics 16. Physical Education/ NCC /Yoga 17.Physics 18.Political Science 19. Psychology 20. Sociology 21. Teaching Aptitude 22. Agriculture 23. Mass Media/ Mass Communication 24. Anthropology 25. Fine Arts/Visual Arts (Sculpture/ Painting)/Commercial Arts, 26. Performing Arts – (i) Dance (Kathak/ Bharatnatyam/Oddisi/ Kathakali/Kuchipudi/ Manipuri (ii) Drama- Theatre (iii) Music General (Hindustani/ Carnatic/ RabindraSangeet/ Percussion/ Non-Percussion), 27. Sanskrit *[For all Shastri (Shastri 3 years/ 4 years Honours) Equivalent to B.A./B.A. Honours courses i.e. Shastri in Veda, Paurohitya (Karmakand), Dharamshastra, Prachin Vyakarana, Navya Vyakarana, Phalit Jyotish, Siddhant Jyotish, Vastushastra, Sahitya,Puranetihas, Prakrit Bhasha,Prachin Nyaya Vaisheshik, Sankhya Yoga, Jain Darshan, Mimansa, AdvaitaVedanta, Vishihstadvaita Vedanta, Sarva Darshan, a candidate may choose Sanskrit as the Domain].*

- A Candidate can choose a maximum of **any 3 languages** from Section IA and Section IB taken together. (One of the languages chosen needs to be in lieu of Domain specific subjects)
- Section II offers 27 Subjects, out of which a candidate may choose a **maximum of 6 Subjects.**
- Section III comprises **General Test.**
- For choosing Languages (upto 3) from Section IA and IB and a maximum of 6 Subjects from Section II and General Test under Section III, the Candidate must refer to the requirements of his/her intended University.

Mode of the Test	Computer Based Test-CBT
Test Pattern	Objective type with Multiple Choice Questions
Medium	13 languages (*Tamil, Telugu, Kannada, Malayalam, Marathi, Gujarati, Odiya, Bengali, Assamese, Punjabi, English, Hindi and Urdu)*
Syllabus	**Section IA & IB:** Language to be tested through Reading Comprehension (based on different types of passages–Factual, Literary and Narrative [Literary Aptitude & Vocabulary]
	Section II : As per NCERT model syllabus as applicable to Class XII only
	Section III : General Knowledge, Current Affairs, General Mental Ability, Numerical Ability, Quantitative Reasoning (Simple application of basic mathematical concepts arithmetic/algebra geometry/mensuration/stat taught till Grade 8), Logical and Analytical Reasoning

Level of questions for CUET (UG) -2022:

All questions in various testing areas will be benchmarked at the level of Class XII only. Students having studied Class XII Board syllabus would be able to do well in CUET (UG) – 2022.

Number of attempts:

If any University permits students of previous years of class XII to take admission in the current year also, such students would also be eligible to appear in CUET (UG) – 2022.

Choice of Languages and Subjects:

Generally the languages/subjects chosen should be the ones that a student has opted in his latest Class XII Board examination. However, if any University permits any flexibility in this regards, the same can be exercised under CUET (UG) -2022 also. Candidates must carefully refer to the eligibility requirements of various Central Universities in this regard. Moreover, if the subject to be studied in the Undergraduate course is not available in the list of **27 Domain Specific Subject** being offered, the Candidate may choose the Subject closest to his choice for e.g. For Biochemistry the candidate may choose Biology.

Candidates are advised to visit the NTA CUET (UG)-2022 official website **https://cuet.samarth.ac.in/** for latest updates regarding the Examination.

CUET Syllabus

CUET Syllabus

Before you start your preparation for any entrance exam, it is important to understand the syllabus. Otherwise, your prep will be directionless, and you might be left wondering where things might have gone wrong!

With more than 1.68 lakh seats on offer for the undergraduate courses at the 54 Central Universities, CUET is one the most competitive examinations. For this very reason, while preparing for the exam, you will need to adopt a structured approach. And in doing that, understanding the syllabus is a critical step.

CUET 2022 Overview

CUET 2022 will be a Computer-Based Test (CBT), commonly referred to as an online exam. However, there is a difference between the two terms: CBT and online. In CBT, the questions are kept constant and simply presented in an online format; whereas in an Online Test, questions are stored as a bank, and the system decides which questions are to be presented to the candidate, based on a pre-defined logic.

CUET 2022 is likely to be a General Ability Test, with focus on English Language, Numerical Ability, Logical & Analytical Reasoning, along with General Awareness and Current Affairs.

CUET 2022 Syllabus

The CUET 2022 exam pattern gives a good idea about what is in store for the candidate and how one needs to prepare for the exam.

- **English Language:** The questions in this section will test one's proficiency in the language, based on comprehension passages, fundamentals of grammar, and vocabulary. In the Comprehension section, candidates will be evaluated on their understanding of a passage and its central theme, meanings of words used therein, etc. The Grammar section entails correcting grammatically incorrect sentences, filling of blanks in sentences with appropriate words, etc. Questions on synonyms & antonyms will check one's command over English vocabulary.

- **Numerical Ability:** Questions on Numerical Ability will test the candidate's knowledge of elementary mathematics. Areas like arithmetic, number system, basics of algebra, and modern maths will be central to these types of questions.

- **Logical & Analytical Reasoning:** This section tests the candidate's ability to identify patterns & logical links, and rectify illogical arguments. It can include a variety of Logical Reasoning questions, such as those on syllogisms, logical sequences, analogies, etc., along with Analytical Reasoning questions on series, directions, clocks & calendars, arrangements, and puzzles to name a few.

- **General Awareness and Current Affairs:** The General Awareness section includes static general knowledge, while questions on Current Affairs will gauge a candidate's knowledge of national & international current affairs.

CUET 2022 may or may not have a section on subject knowledge. Once the exam notification is out in March, there will be more clarity on this matter.

While there is no syllabus explicitly mentioned by CUET, the broad idea is always presented. One must look at the previous years' papers and solve the sample papers available to form a basic understanding.

About University of Delhi

University of Delhi (commonly known as DU) was established in 1922 and is one of the largest Universities in the country. With 16 faculties, 86 academic departments, 90 colleges and 540 programs on offer, Delhi University is no doubt one of the sought-after University in the country.

With 1, 96,000 students enrolled in UG programs, Delhi University is a valued university and constantly ranked among the top in the country. DU bagged 11th Rank in NIRF 2020 and ranked 6th in QS India Rankings 2020. The University has two Campuses: North and South.

DU UG Programs

Delhi University offers several programs at the undergraduate level. With more than 60 constituent colleges, the Delhi University offers many undergraduate courses.

Please refer to the table below for the important undergraduate courses offered by the DU and the intake across each program.

Program	Intake
B. A (Pass)	11249
B. A (Hons) Geography	788
B. A (Hons) Economics	2754
B. A (Hons) History	2791
B. A (Hons) Political Science	3657
B. A (Hons) Sociology	596
B. A (Hons) Psychology	670
B. A (Hons) Applied Psychology	252
B. A (Hons) Social Work	133
B. A (Hons) Philosophy	783
B. A (Hons) English	2886
B. A (Hons) Hindi	2829
B. A (Hons) Sanskrit	1407
B. A (Hons) Punjabi	214
B. A (Hons) Urdu	207
BA(Hons) French	49

Program	Intake
BA(Hons) German	49
BA(Hons) Spanish	49
BA(Hons) Italian	49
B. Com (Hons)	7953
B.Com (Pass)	7854
Program	Intake
B.Sc. (H) Biomedical Science	162
B.Sc. (H) Botany	937
B.Sc. (H) Chemistry	1487
B.Sc. (H) Computer Science	1265
B.Sc. (H) Electronics	624
B.Sc. (H) Mathematics	2428
B.Sc. (H) Physics	1659
B.Sc. (H) Zoology	944
B.Sc. Life Sciences	1515
B.Sc. Physical Science with Chemistry	703
B.Sc. Physical Science with Computer Science	553
B.Sc. Physical Science with Electronics	247
B. Sc (Hons.) Statistics	476
B. Sc. (Prog.) Applied Physical Science Industrial Chemistry	96
B.Sc. (Hons.) Home Science	900
B. Sc. (Hons.) Psychology	57
B.Sc. (H) Food Technology	179
B.Sc. (H)Instrumentation	99
B.Sc. (H) Microbiology	238
B.Sc. (H) Polymer Science	59
B.SC. Mathematical Science	224
B.SC. (Hons.) Biochemistry	146
B.SC. Industrial Chemistry	78
B.Sc. (Prog.) Physical Science	940
B.SC. (Hons.) Geology	98

DU UG Programs Eligibility:

As the University offers multiple programs and separate intake for male and female candidates, it is important to check the university official website regularly to keep oneself updated about the eligibility for each program, which can change.

DU UG Admissions:

Until 2021, Delhi University admitted students on the basis of class XII marks. From the academic year 2022, admissions to UG programs offered Delhi University will be based on CUET. CUET will be a common entrance for admissions to UG programs offered by all the Central Universities in the country.

Delhi University UG Programs Reservation:

DU being a Central University offers reservations in admissions according to central government rules.

Schedule Caste (SC): 15% of the total seats are reserved for students who belong to SC category.

Schedule Tribe (ST): 7.5% of the total seats are reserved for students belonging to ST Category.

Other Backward Classes (OBC): 27% of the total intake is reserved for students from Other Backward Classes (OBC), excluding those from creamy layer.

Economically Weaker Section (EWS): The University has reserved 10% seats for EWS category, in accordance with the directive of Ministry of Education.

Persons with Disability (PWD): 5% of the seats are reserved on horizontal basis for students from PWD category.

About BHU

Banaras Hindu University (BHU), situated in the holy city of Varanasi, was founded by Pandit Madan Mohan Malviya in cooperation with Dr. Annie Besant, in 1916 under the act of Parliament-B.H.U Act, 1915. BHU, which is a Central University, comprises of 6 Institutes, 14 Faculties, 144 academic departments, and 4 Inter-disciplinary centers, spread over 1300 acres. The University consists of 15,000 students, 1700 teachers and 8000 non-teaching staff.

BHU was ranked 3rd among the Universities in India in 2020. According to university submissions for NIRF 2021, BHU has 10, 585 students pursuing UG programs, of which 236 students are foreign nationals.

BHU UG Programs

BHU offers a host of undergraduate programs including medical and engineering. Through its various faculties, BHU offers a range of programs which caters to students learning abilities. The University along with its main campus, also offers the undergraduate courses from the following colleges: Mahila Mahavidyalaya (MMV); Arya Mahila Post Graduate College (AMPGC), Vasant Kanya Mahavidyalaya (VKM); Vasanta College for Women (VCW); DAV Post Graduate College (DAVPGC) and Rajiv Gandhi South Campus (RGSC).

Please refer to the table below for the important undergraduate courses offered by BHU and the intake across each program/campuses.

Faculty of Arts				
Course	Campus	Intake	Status	Duration
B.A (Hons) Arts	Faculty of Arts	765	Co-Ed	3 Years
	Mahila Mahavidyalaya	286	Women	3 Years
	Arya Mahila Post Graduate College	383	Women	3 Years
	Vasant Kanya Mahavidyalaya	286	Women	3 Years
	Vasanta College for Women	412	Women	3 Years
	DAV Post Graduate College	309	Co-Ed	3 Years
Faculty of Social Sciences				
Course	Campus	Intake	Status	Duration
B.A (Hons) Social Sciences [incl. B. A (Hons) Economics]	Faculty of Social Sciences	573	Co-Ed	3 Years
	Mahila Mahavidyalaya	193	Women	3 Years
	Arya Mahila Post Graduate College	383	Women	3 Years
	Vasant Kanya Mahavidyalaya	249	Women	3 Years
	Vasanta College for Women	210	Women	3 Years
	DAV Post Graduate College	326	Co-Ed	3 Years

Faculty of Commerce				
Course	Campus	Intake	Status	Duration
B. Com (Hons)	Faculty of Commerce	286	Co-Ed	3 Years
	Vasant Kanya Mahavidyalaya	96	Women	3 Years
	Arya Mahila Post Graduate College	96	Women	3 Years
	DAV Post Graduate College	227	Co-Ed	3 Years
	Rajiv Gandhi South Campus, Mirzapur	114	Co-Ed	3 Years
B. Com (Hons) Financial Markets Management	Faculty of Commerce	62	Co-Ed	3 Years
	Rajiv Gandhi South Campus, Mirzapur	62	Co-Ed	3 Years

Institute of Science				
Course	Campus	Intake	Status	Duration
B.Sc (Hons) Maths Group	Faculty of Science	573	Co-Ed	3 Years
	Mahila Mahavidyalaya	96	Women	3 Years
B.Sc (Hons) Bio Group	Faculty of Science	383	Co-Ed	3 Years
	Mahila Mahavidyalaya	193	Women	3 Years

Faculty of Visual Arts				
Course	Campus	Intake	Status	Duration
B.F.A (Bachelor of Fine Arts)	Faculty of Visual Arts	96	Co-Ed	4 Years
Faculty of Arts				
Bachelor of Vocation (Retail and Logistics Management)	Rajiv Gandhi South Campus	62	Co-Ed	3 Years
Bachelor of Vocation (Hospitality & Tourism Management)	Rajiv Gandhi South Campus	62	Co-Ed	3 Years
Bachelor of Vocation (Fashion Designing and Event Management)	Rajiv Gandhi South Campus	62	Co-Ed	3 Years
Bachelor of Vocation (Modern Office Management)	Rajiv Gandhi South Campus	62	Co-Ed	3 Years
Bachelor of Vocation (Food Processing & Management)	Rajiv Gandhi South Campus	62	Co-Ed	3 Years
Bachelor of Vocation (Medical Lab. & Technology)	Rajiv Gandhi South Campus	62	Co-Ed	3 Years

BHU UG Programs Eligibility:

Each of the courses have different eligibility for admissions. To be eligible for admissions, one must fulfil all the criteria as laid down by the respective faculties of the University.

B.A (Hons) Arts/ B.A (Hons) Social Sciences: Candidate must not be more than 22 years of age and must have passed class XII or equivalent with minimum 50% marks in aggregate.

B.A (Hons) Economics: Candidate must not be more than 22 years of age and must have passed class XII or equivalent with minimum 50% marks in aggregate along with mathematics as one of the papers.

B. Com (Hons)/B. Com (Hons) Financial Markets Management: Candidate must not be more than 22 years of age and must have passed class XII or equivalent with minimum 50% marks in aggregate with Commerce/ Economics/Maths/Computer Science/Finance/Financial Markets Management as one of the subjects.

B. Sc (Hons) Maths Group: Candidate must not be more than 22 years of age and must have passed class XII or equivalent with minimum 50% marks in aggregate in the subjects Physics, Maths plus any one of the following: Chemistry, Statistics, Geology, Computer Science, Information Technology and Geography and must have passed in each of the concerned three subjects.

B. Sc (Hons) Bio Group: Candidate must not be more than 22 years of age and must have passed class XII or equivalent with minimum 50% marks in aggregate in the subjects Physics, Chemistry plus any one of the following: Biology, Geology and Geography and must have passed in each of the concerned three subjects.

B. F. A (Bachelor of Fine Arts): Candidate must not be more than 22 years of age and must have passed class XII or equivalent with minimum 50% marks in aggregate.

Bachelor of Vocation: Candidate must have passed class XII or equivalent in any stream (Science for Food Processing and Medical Lab Technology) or level 4 NSQF certificate.

BHU UG Admissions:

Until 2021, admissions to BHU UG courses were based on Undergraduate Entrance Test (UET) conducted by the University. From the academic year 2022, admissions to UG programs offered by BHU will be based on CUET, which will replace the UET. CUET will be a common entrance for admissions to UG programs offered by all the Central Universities in the country.

BHU UG Programs Reservation:

BHU being a Central University offers reservations in admissions according to central government rules.

Schedule Caste (SC): 15% of the total seats are reserved for students who belong to SC category.

Schedule Tribe (ST): 7.5% of the total seats are reserved for students belonging to ST Category.

Other Backward Classes (OBC): 27% of the total intake is reserved for students from Other Backward Classes (OBC), excluding those from creamy layer.

Economically Weaker Section (EWS): The University has reserved 10% seats for EWS category, in accordance with the directive of Ministry of Education.

Persons with Disability (PWD): 5% of the seats are reserved on horizontal basis for students from PWD category.

About JNU

Ever wondered which University, the cadets from National Defence Academy (NDA) graduate from? Yes. It is Jawaharlal Nehru University (JNU). JNU started in the year 1969, three years after the act of Parliament in 1966. With several academic centres of JNU declared "Centres of Excellence" by the University Grants Commission, JNU has been ranked No. 1 by National Assessment and Accreditation Council (NAAC). JNU has been ranked No. 2 by National Institutional Ranking Framework (NIRF) 2020 and has been awarded the Best University Award by the President of India in 2017. The European Commission has awarded the Jean Monnet Centre of Excellence for European Union Studies in India (CEEUSI) to Jawaharlal Nehru University in 2018. This is one of the highest international recognition for any European Studies programme.

JNU was the first University to start integrated five-year Master of Arts in Language Courses. JNU actively collaborates with National and International Universities for student and faculty exchange programs.

According to university submissions for NIRF 2020, JNU has 1,048 students pursuing UG programs, of which 46 are foreign nationals.

JNU UG Programs

JNU offers a limited program at the undergraduate level, unlike other universities. The focus at undergraduate has been largely on language courses. In 2018, JNU started two programs in engineering and plans to add a few more specializations in future.

Please refer to the table below for the important undergraduate courses offered by JNU and the intake across each program.

School	Program	Intake	Duration
School of Language, Literature and Cultural Studies	B. A (Hons) Pashto	19	3 Years
	B. A (Hons) Persian	39	3 Years
	B. A (Hons) Arabic	39	3 Years
	B. A (Hons) Japanese	48	3 Years
	B. A (Hons) Korean	39	3 Years
	B. A (Hons) Chinese	44	3 Years
	B. A (Hons) French	48	3 Years
	B. A (Hons) German	48	3 Years
	B. A (Hons) Russian	68	3 Years
	B. A (Hons) Spanish	39	3 Years

School of Sanskrit and Indic Studies	B. Sc - M. Sc Integrated Program in Ayurveda Biology	20	5 Years
School of Engineering	B. Tech in Computer Science and Engineering & MS/M. Tech in Social Sciences/Humanities/Science/Technology	25	5 Years
	B. Tech in Electronics and Communication Engineering & MS/M. Tech in Social Sciences/Humanities/Science/Technology	25	5 Years

JNU UG Programs Eligibility:

Each of the courses have different eligibility for admissions. To be eligible for admissions, one must fulfil all the criteria as laid down by the respective faculties of the University.

B.A (Hons) Language Courses: Candidate must not be less than 17 years of age and must have passed Senior School Certificate (10+2) or equivalent examination with minimum of 45% marks.

B. Sc - M. Sc Integrated Program in Ayurveda Biology: Candidate must not be less than 17 years of age and must have passed Senior School Certificate (10+2) or equivalent examination with minimum of 45% marks.

B. Tech-M. Tech: Based on JEE Mains

JNU UG Admissions:

Until 2021, admissions to JNU UG courses were based on JNU Entrance Examination (JNUEE) conducted by the National Testing Agency (NTA). From the academic year 2022, admissions to UG programs offered by JNU will be based on CUET, which will replace the JNUEE. CUET will be a common entrance for admissions to UG programs offered by all the Central Universities in the country.

JNU UG Programs Reservation:

JNU being a Central University offers reservations in admissions according to central government rules.

Schedule Caste (SC): 15% of the total seats are reserved for students who belong to SC category.

Schedule Tribe (ST): 7.5% of the total seats are reserved for students belonging to ST Category.

Other Backward Classes (OBC): 27% of the total intake is reserved for students from Other Backward Classes (OBC), excluding those from creamy layer. Also, Central List of Caste to be followed.

Economically Weaker Section (EWS): The University has reserved 10% seats for EWS category, in accordance with the directive of Ministry of Education.

Persons with Disability (PWD): 5% of the seats are reserved on horizontal basis for students from PWD category.

About Jamia Milia Islamia

Jamia Milia Islamia (JMI) was founded in 1920 in Aligarh and became a Central University in 1988 by the act of Parliament. Jamia in Urdu stands for University and Milia means National, making Jamia Milia Islamia a National University. Jamia Milia Islamia moved to Delhi in 1925 and shifted to its present campus in Okhla in 1935.

Jamia Milia Islamia is a NAAC accredited University with grade "A" and was placed 10th in NIRF Rankings 2020. According to submissions made by University for NIRF 2021, Jamia Milia Islamia has a total of 5,911 students pursuing undergraduate courses at the University, of which 105 are foreign nationals. The University also manage to place a total of 681 UG students with an average salary ranging 4.2 Lacs-6.0 Lacs.

JMI UG Programs

Jamia Milia Islamia (JMI) offers a host of undergraduate programs for students. Through its various faculties, JMI offers a range of programs which caters to students learning abilities.

Please refer to the table below for the important undergraduate courses offered by Jamia Milia Islamia and the intake across each program.

Faculty	Course	Intake	Duration
Faculty of Humanities and Language	B. A (Hons) English	60	3 Years
	B. A (Hons) Hindi	40	3 Years
	B. A (Hons) Mass Media-Hindi	40	3 Years
	B. A (Hons) History	60	3 Years
	Bachelor of Hotel Management (BHM)	40	3 Years
	Bachelor of Tourism and Travel Management	40	3 Years
	B. Voc (Food Production)	40	3 Years
Faculty of Social Sciences	Bachelor of Arts (B. A)	68	3 Years
	B. Com (Hons)	55	3 Years
	BBA (Bachelor of Business Administration)	44	3 Years
	B. A (Hons) Economics	53	3 Years
	B. A (Hons) Sociology	42	3 Years
	B. A (Hons) Political Science	42	3 Years
	B. A (Hons) Psychology	42	3 Years
Faculty of Natural Sciences	B. Sc (Bachelor of Science)	50	3 Years
	B. Sc Biosciences	40	3 Years
	B. Sc Biotechnology	35	3 Years
	B. Sc (Hons) Chemistry	40	3 Years
	B. A/B. Sc (Hons) Geography	60	3 Years
	B. Sc (Hons) Mathematics	45	3 Years
	B. Sc (Hons) Applied Mathematics	45	3 Years
	B. Sc (Hons) Physics	45	3 Years
Faculty of Fine Arts	Bachelor of Fine Arts (Applied Art)	30	4 Years
	Bachelor of Fine Arts (Art Education)	20	4 Years
	Bachelor of Fine Arts (Painting)	20	4 Years
	Bachelor of Fine Arts (Sculpture)	10	4 Years

JMI UG Programs Eligibility:

Each of the courses have different eligibility for admissions. To be eligible for admissions, one must fulfil all the criteria as laid down by the respective faculties of the University.

B. Com (Hons) /BBA /B. A (Hons) Economics: Candidate must have passed class XII or equivalent with a minimum of 50% marks in five subjects.

BHM/BTTM/B. Voc (Food Production): Candidate must have passed class XII or equivalent with a minimum of 45% marks in five subjects.

B. A (Hons) Mass Media/B. A (Hons) Hindi: Candidate must have passed class XII or equivalent with a minimum of 45% marks in five subjects.

B. Sc/B. Sc (Hons): Candidate must have passed class XII or equivalent with minimum 50% marks in each of the science subjects i.e. Physics, Chemistry and Mathematics and 50% marks in aggregate of best 5-subjects.

JMI UG Admissions:

Until 2021, admissions to JMI UG courses were based on Entrance Test (JMI-ET) conducted by the University. From the academic year 2022, admissions to UG programs offered by JMI will be based on CUET, which will replace the JMI-ET. CUET will be a common entrance for admissions to UG programs offered by all the Central Universities in the country.

JMI UG Programs Reservation:

JMI is a minority reservation-based University and accordingly, seats are reserved for candidates as per the norms laid down by the University.

Muslim Minority: 30% of the total seats are reserved for Muslim applicants; 10% of the total seats are reserved for women applicants who are Muslim; 10% of the total intake is for OBC-NC candidates who are Muslims.

Persons with Disability (PWD): 5% of the seats are reserved for students from PWD category.

Jamia Students: 5% seats in all Undergraduate Programs shall be filled by internal students of Jamia who have passed their qualifying examination of the concerned programme (X or XII) from Jamia Schools as regular students.

In addition, Jamia Milia Islamia has supernumerary seats for Kashmiri Migrants and students from Jammu and Kashmir.

About Aligarh Muslim University

Aligarh Muslim University also referred as AMU was established by Sir Syed Ahmad Khan in 1875. The University started as Muhammadan Anglo-Oriental College and became a University (AMU) in 1920. The university has been ranked 801–1000 in the QS World University Rankings of 2021 and 17 in India by the National Institutional Ranking Framework in 2020.

Aligarh Muslim University is institution of national importance, under the seventh schedule of the Constitution of India.

AMU UG Programs

Aligarh Muslim University offers several programs at the undergraduate level. With 7 constituent colleges, the Aligarh Muslim University offers many undergraduate courses.

Please refer to the table below for the important undergraduate courses offered by the AMU and the intake across each program.

Course	Intake	Duration
B. Sc (Hons) Home Science	30*	3 Years
B.Sc (Hons) Agriculture	40	4 Years
B. A (Hons) Arabic	20+10*	3 Years
B. A (Hons) Communicative English	15+20*	3 Years
B. A (Hons) English	40+35*	3 Years
B. A (Hons) Hindi	40+25*	3 Years
B. A (Hons) Geography	50+20*	3 Years
B. A (Hons) Linguistics	20+25*	3 Years
B. A (Hons) Persian	15+25*	3 Years
B. A (Hons) Philosophy	20+10*	3 Years
B. A (Hons) Quaranic Studies	10+10*	3 Years
B. A (Hons) Sanskrit	15+10*	3 Years
B. A (Hons) Urdu	40+50*	3 Years
Bachelor of Fine Arts	15+15*	3 Years
B. Com (Hons)	180+100*	3 Years
B. Voc Production Technology	50	3 Years
B Voc Polymer and Coating Technology	50	3 Years
B. Voc Fashion Design and Garment Technology	50	3 Years
B. A (Hons) Chinese	20	3 Years
B. A (Hons) French	20	3 Years
B. A (Hons) German	20	3 Years

Program	Intake	Duration
B. A (Hons) Russian	20	3 Years
B. A (Hons) Spanish	20	3 Years
B. Sc (Hons) Biochemistry	30+30*	3 Years
B. Sc (Hons) Botany	60+40*	3 Years
B. Sc (Hons) Zoology	60+45*	3 Years
B. Sc (Hons) Physics	120+35*	3 Years
B. Sc (Hons) Chemistry	120+65*	3 Years
B. Sc (Hons) Mathematics	120+40*	3 Years
B. Sc (Hons) Geography	45+30*	3 Years
B. Sc (Hons) Geology	100+30*	3 Years
B. Sc (Hons) Statistics	60+30*	3 Years
B. Sc (Hons) Industrial Chemistry	20+10*	3 Years
B. Sc (Hons) Computer Applications	40+20*	3 Years

AMU UG Programs Eligibility:

As the University offers multiple programs and separate intake for male and female candidates, it is important to check the university official website regularly to keep oneself updated about the eligibility for each program, which can change.

AMU UG Admissions:

Until 2021, AMU conducted its own entrance test to admit students for the UG programs. From the academic year 2022, admissions to UG programs offered by Aligarh Muslim University will be based on CUET. CUET will be a common entrance for admissions to UG programs offered by all the Central Universities in the country.

University of Allahabad UG Programs Reservation:

Allahabad University being a Central University offers reservations in admissions according to central government rules. Kindly check the university website for further details.

PSYCHOLOGY

Variations in Psychological Attributes

Individual Differences in Human Functioning

Variability is a fact of nature, and individuals are no exception to this. The list of variations can be endless. Different traits can exist in varying degrees in an individual.

Situationism, which states that situations and circumstances in which one is placed influence one's behaviour. The situationist perspective views human behaviour relatively more as a result of influence of external factors.

Assessment of Psychological Attributes

Assessment refers to the measurement of psychological attributes of individuals and their evaluation, often using multiple methods in terms of certain standards of comparison.

Our assessment may be informal or formal. Formal assessment is objective, standardised, and organised. On the other hand, informal assessment varies from case to case and from one assessor to another and, therefore, is open to subjective interpretations.

Some Domains of Psychological Attributes

Intelligence is the global capacity to understand the world, think rationally, and use available resources effectively when faced with challenges.

Aptitude refers to an individual's underlying potential for acquiring skills.

Interest is an individual's preference for engaging in one or more specific activities relative to others.

Personality refers to relatively enduring characteristics of a person that make her or him distinct from others.

Values are enduring beliefs about an ideal mode of behaviour.

Intelligence

Intelligence as the power of perceiving, learning, understanding, and knowing.

Theories of Intelligence

Alfred Binet was the first psychologist who tried to formalise the concept of intelligence in terms of mental operations. He, therefore, conceptualised intelligence as consisting of one similar set of abilities which can be used for solving any or every problem in an individual's environment.

In 1927, Charles Spearman proposed a two-factor theory of intelligence employing a statistical method called factor analysis. He showed that intelligence consisted of a general factor (g-factor) and some specific factors (s-factors).

Planning, Attention-arousal, and Simultaneous-successive (PASS) Model of Intelligence

This model has been developed by J.P. Das, Jack Naglieri, and Kirby (1994). According to this model, intellectual activity involves the interdependent functioning of three neurological systems, called the functional units of brain. These units are responsible for arousal/attention, coding or processing, and planning respectively. These PASS processes operate on a knowledge base developed either formally (by reading, writing, and experimenting) or informally from the environment. These processes are interactive and dynamic in nature; yet each has its own distinctive functions.

Individual Differences in Intelligence

In 1912, William Stern, a German psychologist, devised the concept of Intelligence Quotient (IQ). IQ refers to mental age divided by chronological age, and multiplied by 100.

Types of Intelligence Test

Individual or Group Tests: An individual intelligence test is one which can be administered to one person at a time. A group intelligence test can be administered to several persons simultaneously.

Verbal, Non-Verbal, or Performance Tests: Verbal tests can be administered only to literate people. Raven's Progressive Matrices (RPM) Test is an example of a non-verbal test. In this test, the subject examines an incomplete pattern and chooses a figure from the alternatives that will complete the pattern

Culture-Fair or Culture-Biased Tests: Psychologists have tried to develop tests that are culture-fair or culturally appropriate, i.e. one that does not discriminate against individuals belonging to different cultures.

Intelligence Testing in India: S.M. Mohsin made a pioneering attempt in constructing an intelligence test in Hindi (NCERT) has documented Indian tests.

Culture and Intelligence

The cultural environment provides a context for intelligence to develop. A person's intelligence is likely to be tuned by these cultural parameters. Many theorists have regarded intelligence as attributes specific to the person without regard to their cultural background.

Emotional Intelligence

Emotional intelligence is a set of skills that underlie accurate appraisal, expression, and regulation of emotions. It is the feeling side of intelligence.

Emotional Quotient (EQ) is used to express emotional intelligence in the same way as IQ is used to express intelligence.

Special Abilities

Aptitude refers to special abilities in a particular field of activity. It is a combination of characteristics that indicates an individual's capacity to acquire some specific knowledge or skill after training.

Interest is a preference for a particular activity; aptitude is the potentiality to perform that activity.

Creativity

Einstein's theory of relativity is an example of the highest level of creativity which implies bringing out altogether new ideas, facts, theory, or a product. Another level of creativity is working on what has already been established earlier by way of modifications, by putting things in new perspectives or to new use

Creativity and Intelligence: Researchers have found that the relationship between creativity and intelligence is positive. All creative acts require some minimum ability to acquire knowledge and capacity to comprehend, retain, and retrieve.

Creativity tests came into existence to assess variations in terms of the potential for creativity in contrast to intelligence.

Exercise

1. _______________ approach considers intelligence as an aggregate of abilities.

   (a) Psychmetric   (b) Emotional Intelligence

   (c) Values   (d) Aptitude

2. The concept of "Two factor theory of Intelligence" proposed by

   (a) Charles Spearman   (b) J. P Guilford

   (c) Alfred Binet   (d) Arthur Jensen

3. _______________ ability to understand of one's own feelings, motives, and desires.

   (a) Interpersonal   (b) Intrapersonal

   (c) Naturalistic   (d) Spatial

4. Triarchic Theory of Intelligence was proposed by?

   (a) Jack Naglieri   (b) Kirby

   (c) Robert Sternberg   (d) Alfred Binet

5. _______________ refers to an individual's underlying potential for acquiring skills.

   (a) Intelligence   (b) Aptitude

   (c) Interest   (d) Personality

6. Name the psychologist who proposed the concept of Intelligence Quotient.

   (a) Alfred Binet   (b) Theodore Simon

   (c) William Stern   (d) Jack Naglieri

7. _______________ refers to the abilities involved in forming, using, and transforming mental images.

   (a) Spatial   (b) Musical

   (c) Naturalistic   (d) Intrapersonal

8. Who among the following is not associated with PASS model?

   (a) J. P. Das   (b) Jack Naglieri

   (c) Kirby   (d) Theodore Simon

9. The knowledge of _______________ can help us to predict an individual's future performance.

   (a) Emotional Intelligence

   (b) Interest

   (c) Creativity

   (d) Aptitude

10. Identify the formula for calculating intelligence quotient.

   (a) $IQ = \dfrac{MA}{CA} \times 100$

   (b) $IQ = \dfrac{CA}{MA} \times 100$

   (c) $IQ = MA + CA \times 100$

   (d) $IQ = MA \times CA \times 100$

Answers

1. (a)   2. (a)   3. (b)   4. (c)   5. (b)   6. (c)   7. (a)   8. (d)   9. (d)   10. (a)

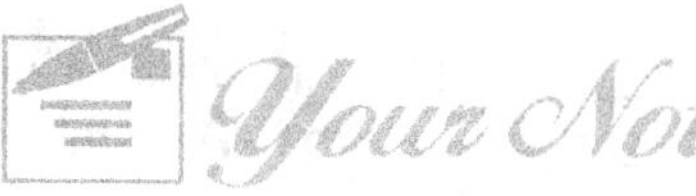
Your Notes :

CHAPTER 2

Self and Personality

Self and personality refer to the characteristic ways in which we define our existence.

Self refers to the totality of an individual's conscious experiences, ideas, thoughts and feelings with regard to herself or himself.

Personal identity refers to those attributes of a person that make him/her different from others.

Kinds of Self

The personal self leads to an orientation in which one feels primarily concerned with oneself.

The social self emerges in relation with others and emphasises such aspects of life as cooperation, unity, affiliation, sacrifice, support or sharing.

Cognitive and Behavioural Aspects of Self

The way we perceive ourselves and the ideas we hold about our competencies and attributes is also called self-concept.

Self-esteem is an important aspect of our self. As persons we always make some judgment about our own value or worth. This value judgment of a person about herself/himself is called self-esteem.

Self-efficacy is the extent to which a person believes they themselves control their life outcomes or the outcomes are controlled by luck or fate or other situational factors.

Self-regulation refers to our ability to organise and monitor our own behavior.

Self-control is learning to delay or refer the gratification of needs.

Techniques of self-control:

1. Observation of own behaviour: provides necessary information that may be used to change, modify or strengthen certain aspects of self.

2. Self-instruction: instructs ourselves to do something and behave the way we want to.

3. Self-reinforcement: rewards behaviours that have pleasant outcomes.

Concept of Personality

In psychological terms, personality refers to our characteristic ways of responding to individuals and situations.

Features of Personality:

1. Personality has both physical and psychological components.

2. Its expression in terms of behaviour is fairly unique in a given individual.

3. Its main features do not easily change with time.

4. It is dynamic in the sense that some of its features may change due to internal or external situational demands; adaptive to situations.

Major Approaches to the Study of Personality

The type approaches attempts to comprehend human personality by examining certain broad patterns in the observed behavioural characteristics of individuals. n India also, CharakSamhita, a famous treatise on Ayurveda, classifies people into the categories of vata, pitta and kapha on the basis of three humoural elements called tridosha.

In contrast, the trait approach focuses on the specific psychological attributes along which individuals tend to differ in consistent and stable ways.

Five-Factor Model of Personality:

- Openness to experience :
- Extraversion :
- Agreeableness :
- Neuroticism :
- Conscientiousness :

Allport's Trait Theory: Gordon Allport is considered the pioneer of trait approach. He proposed that individuals possess a number of traits, which are dynamic in nature.

Eysenck's Theory: H.J. Eysenck proposed that personality could be reduced into two broad dimensions.

1. Neuroticism vs. emotional stability : It refers to the degree to which people have control over their feelings.

2. Extraversion vs. introversion : It refers to the degree to which people are socially outgoing or socially withdrawn.

Stages of Personality Development

- **Oral Stage:** A newborn's instincts are focused on the mouth. This is the infant's primary pleasure seeking centre

- **Anal Stage:** It is found that around ages two and three the child learns to respond to some of the demands of the society.

- **Phallic Stage:** This stage focuses on the genitals. At around ages four and five children begin to realise the differences between males and females.

- **Latency Stage:** This stage lasts from about seven years until puberty. During this period, the child continues to grow physically, but sexual urges are relatively inactive.

- **Genital Stage:** During this stage, the person attains maturity in psychosexual development. The sexuality, fears and repressed feelings of earlier stages are once again exhibited.

Behavioural Approach: This approach does not give importance to the internal dynamics of behaviour. The behaviourists believe in data, which they feel are definable, observable, and measurable.

Cultural Approach: This approach attempts to understand personality in relation to the features of ecological and cultural environment.

Humanistic Approach: The humanistic theories are mainly developed in response to Freud's theory. Carl Rogers and Abraham Maslow have particularly contributed to the development of humanistic perspective on personality.

Assessment of Personality

A formal effort aimed at understanding personality of an individual is termed as personality assessment.

The Minnesota Multiphasic Personality Inventory (MMPI): This inventory is widely used as a test in personality assessment. Hathaway and McKinley developed this test as a helping tool for psychiatric diagnosis, but the test has been found very effective in identifying varieties of psychopathology.

Eysenck Personality Questionnaire (EPQ)

Developed by Eysenck this test initially assessed two dimensions of personality, called introverted-extraverted and emotionally stable-emotionally unstable.

Behavioural Analysis: An observer's report may contain data obtained from interview, observation, ratings, nomination, and situational tests.

Exercise

1. _______________ refers to those attributes of a person that make her/him different from others.
   - (a) Self
   - (b) Personal identity
   - (c) Trait
   - (d) Habbit

2. Value judgment of a person about herself/himself is called _______________.
   - (a) Self-esteem
   - (b) Personal self
   - (c) Self concept
   - (d) Self regulation

3. _______________ refers to our ability to organise and monitor our own behavior.
   - (a) Self-esteem
   - (b) Personal self
   - (c) Self concept
   - (d) Self regulation

4. The Thematic Apperception Test (TAT) was developed by _______________
   - (a) Morgan and Murray
   - (b) Hathaway and McKinley
   - (c) Hermann Rorschach and Cattel
   - (d) H. J. Eysenck

5. _______________ refers to our characteristic ways of responding to individuals and situations.
   - (a) Personality
   - (b) Self
   - (c) Self esteem
   - (d) Ego

6. The _______________ are stable, and are considered as the building blocks of personality.
   - (a) source traits
   - (b) surface traits
   - (c) cardinal traits
   - (d) central traits

7. Which of the following is not the part of Five-Factor Model of Personality?
   - (a) Conscientiousness
   - (b) Neuroticism
   - (c) Agreeableness
   - (d) Preconscious

8. Which of the following test consists of 10 inkblots?
   - (a) Rorschach Test
   - (b) Thematic Apperception Test
   - (c) Self esteem Test
   - (d) Draw-a-Person Test

9. Sixteen Personality Factor (16 PF) Questionnaire was developed by _______________.
   - (a) Hathaway
   - (b) McKinley
   - (c) Cattell
   - (d) Eysenck

10. P-F Study was developed by _______________?
    - (a) Mckinley
    - (b) Rosenzweig
    - (c) Morgan and Murray
    - (d) Cattell

11. Who among the following developed Client-centred therapy?
    - (a) Rogers
    - (b) Alfred Adler
    - (c) Erik Erikson
    - (d) Erich Fromm

12. Analytical psychology one of the theory of personality is developed by _______________?
    - (a) Carl Jung
    - (b) Karen Horney
    - (c) Erich Fromm
    - (d) Erik Erikson

13. The Minnesota Multiphasic Personality Inventory (MMPI) is developed by _______________?
    - (a) Hathaway and McKinley
    - (b) Eysenck
    - (c) Cattell
    - (d) Morgan and Murray

14. Five-stage theory of personality developed by _______________?
    - (a) Erik Erikson
    - (b) Mckinley
    - (c) Murray
    - (d) Freud

15. Which of the following is not one of the stage of Stages of Personality development?
    - (a) Oral
    - (b) Anal
    - (c) Mature
    - (d) Phallic

Answers

1. (b)   2. (a)   3. (d)   4. (a)   5. (a)   6. (a)   7. (d)   8. (a)   9. (c)   10. (b)

11. (a)   12. (a)   13. (a)   14. (d)   15. (c)

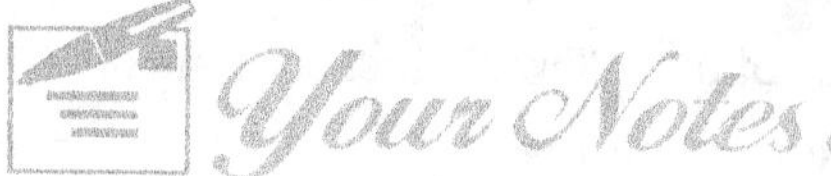 *Your Notes:* ....

Meeting Life Challenges

Nature, Types and Sources of Stress

All the challenges, problems, and difficult circumstances put us to stress. It is important to remember that not all stress is inherently bad or destructive.

Stress have two levels: 'Eustress' is the term used to describe the level of stress that is good for you and is one of a person's best assets for achieving peak performance and managing minor crisis.

Distress: It is negative, unhealthy demotivating and causes our body's wear and tear.

Nature of stress: The word stress has its origin in the Latin word 'strictus', meaning tight or narrow and stringer, the verb meaning to tighten.

Psychological characteristics like mental health, temperament, and self-concept are relevant to the experience of stress.

Signs and Symptoms of Stress: Symptoms of stress can be physical, emotional and behavioral. Any of the symptoms can indicate a degree of stress which, if left unresolved, might have serious implications.

Types of Stress

Physical and Environmental Stress: Physical stresses are demands that change the state of our body. Environmental stresses are aspects of our surroundings that are often unavoidable such as air pollution, crowding, noise, heat of the summer, winter cold, disasters.

Psychological Stress: Some of the important sources of psychological stress are frustration, conflicts, internal and social pressures, etc.

Social Stress: These are induced externally and result from our interaction with other people. Social events like death or illness in the family, strained relationships, trouble with neighbours are some examples of social stresses.

Sources of Stress: Among the most important of these are major stressful life events, such as death of a loved one or personal injury, the annoying frequent hassles of everyday life and traumatic events that affect our lives.

Effects of Stress on Psychological Functioning and Health

There are four major effects of stress associated with the stressed state, viz. emotional, physiological, cognitive, and behavioural.

When stress is prolonged, it affects physical health and impairs psychological functioning. People experience exhaustion and attitudinal problems when the stress due to demands from the environment and constraints are too high and little support is available from family and friends.

General Adaptation Syndrome: According to Selye, GAS involves three stages: alarm reaction, resistance, and exhaustion. Selye's model has been criticised for assigning a very limited role to psychological factors in stress.

Copping with Stress: Coping is a dynamic situation-specific reaction to stress. Coping refers to constantly changing cognitive and behavioural efforts to master, reduce or tolerate the internal or external demands that are created by the stressful transaction.

Stress Management Techniques: Some of these techniques are: Relaxation Techniques, Meditation Procedures, Biofeedback.

Creative Visualisation: It is an effective technique for dealing with stress.

Promoting Positive Health and Well Being

Stress Resistant Personality : Recent studies by Kobasa have shown that people with high levels of stress but low levels of illness share three characteristics, which are referred to as the personality traits of hardiness. It consists of 'the three Cs', i.e. commitment, control, and challenge.

Life Skills Life skills are abilities for adaptive and positive behaviour that enable individuals to deal effectively with the demands and challenges of everyday life.

Exercise

1. The reaction to external stressors is called_____.
   - (a) Eustress
   - (b) Distress
   - (c) Strain
   - (d) Stimulus

2. __________ results from the blocking of needs and motives by something or someone that hinders us from achieving a desired goal.
   - (a) Social Pressure
   - (b) Internal Pressure
   - (c) Conflict
   - (d) Frustration

3. Which one of the following are not the effects of stress?
   - (a) Emotional
   - (b) Behavioral
   - (c) Cognitive
   - (d) Social

4. General Adaptation Syndrome(GAS) was studied by _________?
   - (a) Selye
   - (b) Endler
   - (c) Parker
   - (d) Kobasa

5. Stress Resistant Personality studied is done by _________?
   - (a) Endler
   - (b) Kobasa
   - (c) Parker
   - (d) Selye

6. Which of the following techniques aim to inoculate people against stress?
   - (a) Stress Resistant Personality
   - (b) Creative Visualisation
   - (c) Cognitive Behavioural Techniques
   - (d) Assertiveness

7. The state of physical, emotional and psychological exhaustion is known as :
   - (a) Resistance
   - (b) Stress
   - (c) Burnout
   - (d) coping

8. __________ are abilities for adaptive and positive behaviour that enable individuals to deal effectively with the demands and challenges of everyday life.
   - (a) Assertiveness
   - (b) Life Skill
   - (c) Self-care
   - (d) Time management

9. Coping concept is conceptualized by _______?
   - (a) Lazarus
   - (b) Folkman
   - (c) Both A and B
   - (d) None

10. Which of the following is not the part of personality traits of hardiness?
    - (a) Conflict
    - (b) Commitment
    - (c) Control
    - (d) Challenge

Answers

1. (c)   2. (d)   3. (d)   4. (a)   5. (b)   6. (c)   7. (c)   8. (b)   9. (c)   10. (a)

Psychological Disorders

Concepts of Abnormality and Psychological Disorders

Since the word 'abnormal' literally means "away from the normal", it implies deviation from some clearly defined norms or standards.

The first approach views abnormal behaviour as a deviation from social norms. The second approach views abnormal behaviour as maladaptive.

Classification of Psychological Disorders

The American Psychiatric Association (APA) has published an official manual describing and classifying various kinds of psychological disorders.

The current version of it, the Diagnostic and Statistical Manual of Mental Disorders, 5 th Edition (DSM-5), presents discrete clinical criteria which indicate the presence or absence of disorders.

Factors Underlying Abnormal Behaviour

Biological factors influence all aspects of our behaviour. A wide range of biological factors such as faulty genes, endocrine imbalances, malnutrition, injuries and other conditions may interfere with normal development and functioning of the human body.

Genetic factors have been linked to bipolar and related disorders, schizophrenia, intellectual disability and other psychological disorders.

The psychological models include the psychodynamic, behavioural, cognitive, and humanistic-existential models. The psychodynamic model is the oldest and most famous of the modern psychological models.

Major Psychological Disorders

The term anxiety is usually defined as a diffuse, vague, very unpleasant feeling of fear and apprehension.

A panic attack denotes an abrupt surge of intense anxiety rising to a peak when thoughts of a particular stimuli are present.

Separation anxiety disorder (SAD) is another type of anxiety disorder.

Obsessive-Compulsive and Related Disorders

People affected by obsessivecompulsive disorder are unable to control their preoccupation with specific ideas or are unable to prevent themselves from repeatedly carrying out a particular act or series of acts that affect their ability to carry out normal activities.

Trauma- and Stressor-Related Disorders: Very often people who have been caught in a natural disaster (such as tsunami) or have been victims of bomb blasts by terrorists, or been in a serious accident or in a war-related situation, experience post-traumatic stress disorder (PTSD).

Dissociative Disorders

Dissociation involves feelings of unreality, estrangement, depersonalisation, and sometimes a loss or shift of identity.

Schizophrenia Spectrum and Other Psychotic disorders

Schizophrenia is the descriptive term for a group of psychotic disorders in which personal, social and occupational functioning deteriorate as a result of disturbed thought processes, strange perceptions, unusual emotional states, and motor abnormalities.

Many people with schizophrenia develop delusions.

People with schizophrenia may have hallucinations, i.e. perceptions that occur in the absence of external stimuli.

Neurodevelopmental Disorders A common feature of the neurodevelopmental disorders is that they manifest in the early stage of development. Often the symptoms appear before the child enters school or during the early stage of schooling.

Autism Spectrum Disorder is characterised by widespread impairments in social interaction and communication skills, and stereotyped patterns of behaviours, interests and activities.

Disruptive, Impulse-Control and Conduct Disorders: The disorders included under this category are Oppositional Defiant Disorder, Conduct Disorder and others.

Substance-Related and Addictive Disorders: Addictive behaviour, whether it involves excessive intake of high calorie food resulting in extreme obesity or involving the abuse of substances such as alcohol or cocaine, is one of the most severe problems being faced by society today.

Exercise

1. Psychological conflict and disturbed interpersonal relationships as causes of psychological disorders is said by ______________ ?
   - (a) Johann Weyer
   - (b) Hippocrates
   - (c) Plato
   - (d) Socrates

2. The seventeenth and eighteenth centuries were known as the ______________ .
   - (a) Renaissance Period
   - (b) Reform Movement
   - (c) Age of Reason and Enlightenment
   - (d) Deinstitutionalisation

3. ______________ defined as a diffuse, vague, very unpleasant feeling of fear and apprehension.
   - (a) Phobia
   - (b) Anxiety
   - (c) Conversion disorder
   - (d) Dissociative disorder

4. Paralysis, blindness, deafness and difficulty in walking are generally among the symptoms of ______________ ?
   - (a) Dissociative disorder
   - (b) Anxiety
   - (c) Conversion disorder
   - (d) Phobia

5. ______________ is a false belief that is firmly held on inadequate grounds.
   - (a) Schizophrenia
   - (b) Delusions
   - (c) Avolition
   - (d) Alogia

6. Perceptions that occur in the absence of external stimuliis called ______________ ?
   - (a) Hallucinations
   - (b) Alogia
   - (c) Delusions
   - (d) Avolition

7. In ______________ there are frequent episodes of out-of-control eating.
   - (a) Binge Eating
   - (b) Bulimia nervous
   - (c) Anorexia nervosa
   - (d) Hyperactivity

8. Which of the following is not Commonly Abused Substances?
   - (a) Caffeine
   - (b) Tobacco
   - (c) Stimulants
   - (d) Neem

9. ______________ is characterized by extensive but selective memory loss that has no known organic cause.
   - (a) Dissociative amnesia
   - (b) Dissociative fugue
   - (c) Dissociative identity disorder
   - (d) None of the above

10. ______________ is the term used when people develop a fear of entering unfamiliar situations.
    - (a) Social phobias
    - (b) Agoraphobia
    - (c) Specific phobias
    - (d) None of the above

Answers

1. (a)   **2.** (c)   **3.** (b)   **4.** (c)   **5.** (b)   **6.** (a)   **7.** (a)   **8.** (d)   **9.** (a)   **10.** (b)

CHAPTER 5

Therapeutic Approaches

Psychotherapy is a voluntary relationship between the one seeking treatment or the client and the one who treats or the therapist. The purpose of the relationship is to help the client to solve the psychological problems being faced by her or him.

Therapeutic Relationship

The special relationship between the client and the therapist is known as the therapeutic relationship or alliance. Two components of the therapeutic relationship are:

- Contractual nature of the relationship in which two willing individuals, the client, and the therapist, enter into a partnership that is propelled by the aim of resolving the problems of the client
- Limited duration of the psychotherapy

Types of Therapies

Psychodynamic Therapy: Psychodynamic therapy is considered as the oldest form of therapy which was given by Dr. Sigmund Freud and this therapy explained the sources of psychological distress, conceptualized the structure of the psyche, dynamics between different components of the psyche

Behavior Therapy: Behavior Therapies lay focus on the fact that Psychological distress arises because of faulty thinking or behavioral patterns. The ultimate focus is laid on present thinking patterns and thoughts and the past is just relevant for understanding the cause of clients' maladaptive behavior. The past is not relived, unlike Psychodynamic Therapy.

Various techniques of behavioral therapy are discussed below:

1. **Aversive Conditioning**– Here an association is made between an undesirable response and an unfavorable consequence and this Technique is used in rehabilitation centers

2. **Positive Reinforcement-** When the adaptive Behaviour occurs rarely, positive reinforcement is used to cover up the deficit

3. **Negative Reinforcement-** It is provided in order to escape the painful stimulus in the environment.

4. **Modeling –** In order to bring the desired change in the behavior, the client will try to imitate or shadow the movements of the person whom they consider as their role model

5. Other techniques of behavioural therapy are token economy, differential reinforcement, principle of reciprocal inhibition, and systematic desensitisation

Albert Ellis formulated rational-emotive therapy. The first step in this therapy is ABC (Antecedent-Behaviour-Consequence) analysis where Antecedent events are the causal factors of Psychological distress, Irrational beliefs are found out by interviewing the client and these beliefs distort the reality.

Cognitive Therapy by Aaron Beck

Society, peers, and parents shape up the Beliefs of an individual and as per the cognitive therapy given by Aaron Beck, these beliefs are known as core schemas.

Cognitive Behaviour Therapy

CBT is considered as a short and efficacious treatment for a plethora of Psychological Disorders like anxiety, panic attacks, borderline personality, etc. It combines Techniques of Behaviour Therapy along with Cognitive Therapy and it is based on the BioPsychosocial approach.

Humanistic-Existential Therapy

The main cause of Psychological distress is feelings of loneliness, alienation, and inability to find meaning and responsibility in life.

Client-Centered Therapy

This Therapy was given by Carl Rogers. The main focus is to provide a warm relationship so that the client can reconnect and understand his/her disintegrated feelings. In client-centered therapy, the Therapist provides unconditional positive regard which means total acceptance of what the client actually is, empathy which means understanding the client's problems from their perspective, and that helps clients feel secure.

Biomedical Therapy

In some cases, medicines are used to treat mental Disorders and these medicines can be given by professional doctors called Psychiatrists.

Factors Contributing to Healing in Psychotherapy

The technique adopted by the therapist and its execution is a major factor that contributes to healing in Psychotherapy. Factors contributing to healing in Psychotherapy are given as follows:

1. The therapeutic alliance between the Therapist and client is also an important factor as the healing of the client depends on warmth and empathy provided by the Therapist.

2. The process of complete emotional expression which is called catharsis is important for healing.

3. Some non-specific factors like patient variables like motivation for change, the expectation of improvement due to therapy, and therapist variables like warmth, positive nature, etc

Ethics in Psychotherapy

Just like every job role, psychotherapy also has some ethics to be followed by every individual. Ethical standards that need to be adhered to by psychologists are mentioned below:

1. Informed Consent needs to be taken

2. Respect for human rights and dignity

3. Confidentiality of the client's problem must be maintained

4. Professional competence and skills are musts

5. Alleviating the personal distress of the client must be the goal of therapy

6. The integrity of the practitioner-client relationship must be there

Exercise

1. _______________ is the case in which the client idolises, or falls in love with the therapist, and seeks the therapist's approval.
   (a) Transference neurosis
   (b) Positive transference
   (c) Negative transference
   (d) None of the above

2. Which of the following are inventions for for eliciting the intrapsychicconflicts.?
   (a) Dream interpretation (b) Transference
   (c) Psychodynamic   (d) Existential

3. Who among the following invented Rational Emotive Therapy?
   (a) Aaron Beck   (b) Albert Ellis
   (c) Freiderick   (d) Simon hard

4. Client-centred therapy was given by ___________.
   (a) Freiderick   (b) Victor Frankl
   (c) Carl Rogers   (d) None of the above

5. Which of the following therapy is used for the treatment of soul?
   (a) Existential anxiety (b) Gestalt Therapy
   (c) Logotherapy   (d) Biomedical Therapy

6. The central thesis of this therapy is that irrational beliefs mediate between the antecedent events and their consequences. Name the therapy.
   (a) Cognitive Behaviour Therapy (CBT)
   (b) Rational Emotive Therapy (RET)
   (c) Humanistic-existential Therapy(HET)
   (d) None of the above

7. The repeated process of using confrontation, clarification, and interpretation is known as___________
   (a) Working through.   (b) Insight
   (c) Resistance   (d) Confrontation

8. _____________ are those causes which predispose the person to indulge in that behaviour.
   (a) Malfunctioning behaviours
   (b) Antecedent factors
   (c) Maintaining factors
   (d) Consequent operations

9. Who among the following given theory Psychological distress ?
   (a) Freiderick   (b) Victor Frankl
   (c) Carl Rogers   (d) Aaron Beck

10. The goal of___________is to increase an individual's self-awareness and selfacceptanc.
    (a) Gestalt therapy
    (b) Biomedical Therapy
    (c) Client-centred Therapy
    (d) Logotherapy

Answers

1. (b)   **2.** (a)   **3.** (b)   **4.** (c)   **5.** (c)   **6.** (b)   **7.** (a)   **8.** (b)   **9.** (d)   **10.** (a)

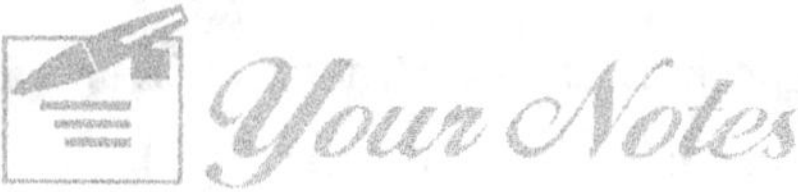 *Your Notes:* ....

CHAPTER 6

Attitude and Social Cognition

Social behaviour is a necessary part of human life, and being social means much more than merely being in the company of others.

When we meet people, we make inferences about their personal qualities. This is called impression formation.

Nature and Components of Attitudes

An attitude is a state of the mind, a set of views, or thoughts, regarding some topic (called the 'attitude object'), which have an evaluative feature (positive, negative or neutral quality).

The thought component is referred to as the cognitive aspect, the emotional component is known as the affective aspect, and the tendency to act is called the behavioural (or conative) aspect.

Attitudes have to be distinguished from two other closely related concepts, namely beliefs and values. Beliefs refer to the cognitive component of attitudes, and form the ground on which attitudes stand, such as belief in God, or belief in democracy as a political ideology. Values are attitudes or beliefs that contain a 'should' or 'ought' aspect, such as moral or ethical values.

Four significant features of attitudes are: Valence (positivity or negativity), Extremeness, Simplicity or Complexity (multiplexity), and Centrality.

Valence (positivity or negativity): The valence of an attitude tells us whether an attitude is positive or negative towards the attitude object.

Extremeness: The extremeness of an attitude indicates how positive or negative an attitude is.

Simplicity or Complexity (multiplexity): This feature refers to how many attitudes there are within a broader attitude.

Centrality: This refers to the role of a particular attitude in the attitude system.

Attitude Formation and Change

In general, attitudes are learned through one's own experiences, and through interaction with others.

Factors that Influence Attitude Formation:

1. **Family and School Environment:** Particularly in the early years of life, parents and other family members play a significant role in shaping attitude formation.

2. **Reference Groups:** Reference groups indicate to an individual the norms regarding acceptable behaviour and ways of thinking.

3. **Personal Experiences:** Many attitudes are formed, not in the family environment or through reference groups, but through direct personal experiences which bring about a drastic change in our attitude towards people and our own life.

4. **Media-related Influences:** Technological advances in recent times have made audio-visual media and the Internet very powerful sources of information that lead to attitude formation and change.

Attitude Change: During the process of attitude formation, and also after this process, attitudes may be changed and modified through various influences.

Factors that Influence Attitude Change: Characteristics of the existing attitude : All four properties of attitudes mentioned earlier, namely, valence (positivity or negativity), extremeness, simplicity or complexity (multiplexity), and centrality or significance of the attitude, determine attitude change.

In addition, one must also consider the direction and extent of attitude change. An attitude change may be congruent - it may change in the same direction as the existing attitude.

Source characteristics: Source credibility and attractiveness are two features that affect attitude change. Attitudes are more likely to change when the message comes from a highly credible source rather than from a low-credible source.

Target characteristics: Qualities of the target, such as persuasibility, strong prejudices, self-esteem, and intelligence influence the likelihood and extent of attitude change.

Attitude-Behaviour Relationship: Psychologists have found that there would be consistency between attitudes and behaviour when:

- the attitude is strong, and occupies a central place in the attitude system,
- the person is aware of her/his attitude,
- there is very little or no external pressure for the person to behave in a particular way. For example, when there is no group pressure to follow a particular norm,

Pro-Social Behaviour

Throughout the world, doing good to others and being helpful is described as a virtue. All religions teach us that we should help those who are in need. This behaviour is called helping or pro-social behaviour.

Pro-social behaviour is more likely to be shown by individuals who have a high level of empathy, that is, the capacity to feel the distress of the person who is to be helped, such as Baba Saheb Amte and Mother Teresa.

Exercise

1. If we are interested to know why people behave in the ways they do is known as ___________.
   - (a) Attribution
   - (b) Empathy
   - (c) Schema
   - (d) Impress formation

2. Schemas that function in the form of categories are called ___________.
   - (a) Stereotypes
   - (b) prototypes
   - (c) perceivers
   - (d) None of the above

3. The ___________ of an attitude tells us whether an attitude is positive or negative towards the attitude object.
   - (a) Centrality
   - (b) valence
   - (c) extremeness
   - (d) simplicity

4. The ___________ of an attitude indicates how positive or negative an attitude is.
   - (a) Simplicity
   - (b) Extremeness
   - (c) Centrality
   - (d) Complexity

5. The 'P-O-X' triangle concept is given by ___________?
   - (a) Fritz Heider
   - (b) S.M. Mohsin
   - (c) Festinger
   - (d) Bernard Wiener

6. The two-step concept was proposed by ___________.
   - (a) Festinger
   - (b) Carlsmith
   - (c) S.M. Mohsin
   - (d) Richard LaPiere

7. ___________ refers to all those mental processes that deal with obtaining and processing of information.
   - (a) Cognition
   - (b) Empathy
   - (c) Value
   - (d) Attitude

8. The person who forms the impression is called the ___________.
   - (a) Perceiver
   - (b) Target
   - (c) Steroyotypes
   - (d) Schema

9. The individual about whom the impression is formed is called the ___________.
   - (a) Perceiver
   - (b) Target
   - (c) Steroyotypes
   - (d) Schema

Answers

1. (a)   **2.** (b)   **3.** (b)   **4.** (b)   **5.** (a)   **6.** (c)   **7.** (a)   **8.** (a)   **9.** (b)

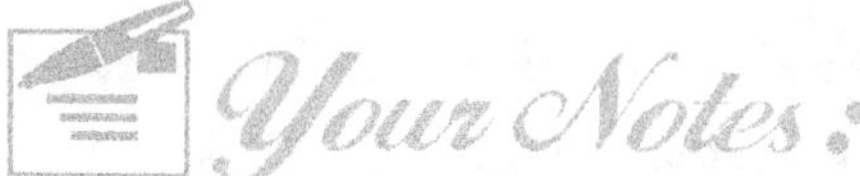 Your Notes : ....

CHAPTER 7

Social Influence and Group Processes

What is a Group?

A group may be defined as an organized system of two or more individuals, who are interacting and interdependent, who have common motives, have a set of role relationships among its members, and have norms that regulate the behaviour of its members.

Teams are special kinds of groups. Members of teams often have complementary skills and are committed to a common goal or purpose.

Group Formation:

Proximity: Common interests, attitudes, and background are important determinants of your liking for your group members.

Similarity: Being exposed to someone over a period of time makes us assess our similarities and paves the way for formation of groups.

Common motives and goals: When people have common motives or goals, they get together and form a group which may facilitate their goal attainment.

Four important elements of group structure are:

Roles are socially defined expectations that individuals in a given situation are expected to fulfil. Roles refer to the typical behaviour that depicts a person in a given social context.

Norms are expected standards of behaviour and beliefs established, agreed upon, and enforced by group members.

Status refers to the relative social position given to group members by others. This relative position or status may be either ascribed (given may be because of one's seniority) or achieved (the person has achieved status because of expertise or hard work).

Cohesiveness refers to togetherness, binding, or mutual attraction among group members.

Influence of Group on Individual Behaviour

Social Loafing: Social facilitation research suggests that presence of others leads to arousal and can motivate individuals to enhance their performance if they are already good at solving something.

Group Polarisation: Groups show another tendency referred to as 'group polarisation'.

Conformity, Compliance, and Obedience

The term 'social influence' refers to those processes whereby our attitudes and behaviours are influenced by the real or imagined presence of other people.

Kelman distinguished three forms of social influence, viz. compliance, identification, and internalisation.

Conformity: The pioneering experiments on conformity were carried out by Sherif and Asch. They illustrate some of the conditions that determine the extent of conformity, and also methods that may be adopted for the study of conformity in groups. These experiments demonstrate what Sherif called the 'autokinetic effect'.

Compliance: It was stated earlier that compliance refers simply to behaving in response to a request from another person or group even in the absence of a norm. A good example of compliance is the kind of behaviour shown when a salesperson comes to our door.

Obedience: When compliance is shown to an instruction or order from a person in authority, such as parents, teachers, leaders, or policemen, that behaviour is called obedience.

Cooperation and Competition

Behaviours in most social situations are characterised by either 'cooperation' or 'competition'.

Prisoner's Dilemma Game, which is a two person game in which both parties are faced with cooperation or competition, and depending upon their choices both can win or lose, is often used to study cooperation or competition.

Conflict Resolution Strategies

Introduction of superordinate goals: Sherif's study, already mentioned in the section on cooperation and competition, showed that by introducing superordinate goals, intergroup conflict can be reduced.

Structural solutions: Conflict can also be reduced by redistributing the societal resources according to principles based on justice. Research on justice has identified several principles of justice.

Exercise

1. ___________ have complementary skills and are committed to a common goal or purpose.
   - (a) Goal
   - (b) Team
   - (c) Crowd
   - (d) Audience

2. Which of the following is not related to group formation?
   - (a) Proximity
   - (b) Similarity
   - (c) Storming
   - (d) Norming

3. ___________ refers to togetherness, binding, or mutual attraction among group members.
   - (a) Cohesiveness
   - (b) Status
   - (c) Roles
   - (d) Norms

4. 'Auto kinetic effect' was suggested by ___________.
   - (a) Kelman
   - (b) Sherif
   - (c) Milgram
   - (d) Freud

5. Who wrote the book 'In the Minds of Men'?
   - (a) Gardner Murphy
   - (b) Deutsch
   - (c) Milgram
   - (d) Henry stew

6. Which of the following are not the important forms of social influence?
   - (a) Conformity
   - (b) Compliance
   - (c) Obedience
   - (d) Empathy

7. Which of the following are not facilitate group formation?
   - (a) Proximity
   - (b) Similarity
   - (c) Goal
   - (d) Self esteem

8. Who among the following distinguish three forms of social influence?
   - (a) Kelman
   - (b) Sherif
   - (c) Milgram
   - (d) Freud

9. Which of the following are not the types of groups?
   - (a) Primary
   - (b) Secondary
   - (c) Formal
   - (d) Tertiary

Answers

1. (b) **2.** (a) **3.** (a) **4.** (b) **5.** (a) **6.** (d) **7.** (d) **8.** (a) **9.** (d)

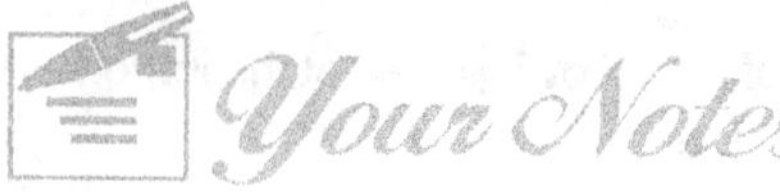 Your Notes : ....

CHAPTER 8

Psychology and Life

A branch of psychology called environmental psychology deals with various psychological issues pertaining to the human-environment interaction in a very broad sense of the term.

The minimalist perspective assumes that the physical environment has minimal or negligible influence on human behaviour, health and well being.

The instrumental perspective suggests that the physical environment exists mainly for use by human beings for their comfort and well-being.

The spiritual perspective refers to the view of the environment as something to be respected and valued rather than exploited.

Environmental Effects on Human Behaviour

Environmental influences on perception: Some aspects of the environment influence human perception.

Environmental influences on emotions: The environment affects our emotional reactions as well. Watching nature in any form, whether it is a quietly flowing river, a smiling flower, or a tranquil mountain top, provides a kind of joy that cannot be matched by any other experience.

Ecological influences on occupation, living style and attitudes: The natural environment of a particular region determines whether people living in that region rely on agriculture (as in the plains), or on other occupations such as hunting and gathering (as in forest, mountainous or desert regions), or on industries (as in areas that are not fertile enough for agriculture).

Three characteristics of noise have been found to determine its effect on task performance, namely, intensity, predictability, and controllability of noise.

The experience of crowding has the following features:

- Feeling of discomfort,
- Loss or decrease in privacy,
- Negative view of the space around the person, and
- Feeling of loss of control over social interaction.

Natural Disasters: Environmental stressors such as noise, various forms of pollution and crowding are the result of human behaviour.

Common examples of natural disasters are earthquakes, tsunamis, floods, cyclones, and volcanic eruptions. One finds examples of other disasters also, such as wars, industrial accidents such as the leaking of poisonous or radioactive elements in industrial plants, or epidemics (e.g., the plague that affected some parts of our country in 1994).

Promoting Pro-environmental Behaviour

Pro-environmental behaviour includes both actions that are meant to protect the environment from problems, and to promote a healthy environment.

An American psychologist, John Dollard along with his collaborators, conducted research specifically to examine the frustration-aggression theory. This theory proposes that it is frustration that leads to aggression.

Exercise

1. Who describes three approaches that may be adopted to describe the humanenvironment relationship?
   - (a) Gorge stew
   - (b) Stokols
   - (c) Andrew freud
   - (d) Muller

2. In Intimate distance how much distance is maintained?
   - (a) 18 inches
   - (b) 4 feet
   - (c) 10 feet
   - (d) Infinity

3. Which of the following is not the features of Post-traumatic stress disorder (PTSD)?
   - (a) Immediate reaction
   - (b) Physical reaction
   - (c) Cognitive disorder
   - (d) Social reactions

4. Which of the following are not the causes of aggression?
   - (a) Inborn tendency
   - (b) Frustration
   - (c) Child rearing
   - (d) Schema

5. Frustration-aggression theory was given by _________________.
   - (a) John dollard
   - (b) Stokols
   - (c) Andrew freud
   - (d) Muller

6. Which of the following are not affected by Noise?
   - (a) Thinking
   - (b) Memory
   - (c) Learning
   - (d) Intelligence

7. _______ is the psychological feeling of not having enough space available.
   - (a) Group
   - (b) Team
   - (c) Crowding
   - (d) Conjust

8. _________ and violence are among the major problems in today's society.
   - (a) Poverty
   - (b) Crowding
   - (c) Aggression
   - (d) Accident

9. The distance you maintain in a formal setting is called ____________.
   - (a) Social distance
   - (b) Public distance
   - (c) Personal distance
   - (d) Intimate disatence

10. Which of the following is not environmental stressor?
    - (a) Noise
    - (b) Pollution
    - (c) Crowding
    - (d) Chronic Disease

Answers

1. (b) **2.** (a) **3.** (c) **4.** (d) **5.** (a) **6.** (d) **7.** (c) **8.** (c) **9.** (b) **10.** (d)

CHAPTER 9

Developing Psychological Skills

The term 'skill' may be defined as proficiency, facility or dexterity that is acquired or developed through training and experience. The Webster dictionary defines it as "possession of the qualities required to do something or get something done".

Developing as an Effecive Psychologis

Generally people pick up such terms from popular writings and media. There are a lot of common sense notions about human behaviour that one develops in the course of their lives.

The basic skills or competencies which psychologists have identified for becoming an effective psychologist fall into three broad sections, namely,

(a) General Skills,

(b) Observational Skills, and

(c) Specific Skills.

Observational Skills

A psychologist engages in observing various facets of surroundings including people and varying events.

Naturalistic Observation is one of the primary ways of learning about the way people behave in a given setting.

Participant Observation is the variation of the method of naturalistic observation.

Specific Skills

(a) Communication Skills

  • Speaking

  • Active listening

  • Body language or non-verbal skills

(b) Psychological Testing Skills

(c) Interviewing Skills

(d) Counselling Skills

  • Empathy

  • Positive regard

  • Authenticity

Intrapersonal communication involves communicating with yourself. It encompasses such activities as thought processes, personal decision making, and focusing on self.

Interpersonal communication refers to the communication that takes place between two or more persons who establish a communicative relationship.

Public communication is characterised by a speaker sending a message to an audience.

Components of Human Communication

Speaking: One important component of communication is speaking with the use of language.

Listening: Listening is an important skill that we use daily. Your academic success, employment achievement, and personal happiness, to a large extent, depend upon your ability to listen effectively.

Reception: The initial step in the listening process is the reception of a stimulus or message.

Attention: Once the stimulus, i.e. the word or visual, or both, is received, it reaches the attention stage of the human processing system.

Assignment of Meaning: The process of putting the stimulus we have received into some predetermined category develops as we acquire language

Psychological Testing Skills: The next set of competencies which psychologists require is concerned with the knowledge base of the discipline of psychology.

Interviewing Skills

An interview is a purposeful conversation between two or more people that follows a basic question and answer format.

Body of the Interview: The body of the interview is the heart of the process.

Meaning and Nature of Counselling: Counselling provides a system for planning the interview, analysing the counsellor's and client's behaviour, and determining the developmental impact on the client.

Characteristics of Effective Helper: Authenticity : Your image or perception of yourself makes up your "I". The selfperceived "I" is revealed through ideas, words, actions, clothing, and your life-style.

Positive Regard for Others: In a counselling-counsellor relationship, a good relationship allows freedom of expression.

Empathy: This is one of the most critical competencies that a counsellor needs to have.

Exercise

1. __________ is one of the primary ways of learning about the way people behave in a given setting.
   (a) Naturalistic Observation
   (b) Participant Observation
   (c) Empathy
   (d) Authenticity

2. Which of the following are not the characteristics of communication?
   (a) Dynamic
   (b) Continuous
   (c) Irreversible
   (d) Unpredictable

3. The consistency between current and past patterns of behaviour, as well as harmony between verbal and non-verbal communication, is termed as__________:
   (a) Cluster
   (b) Congruency
   (c) Interpretation
   (d) Attitude

4. Which of the following is not one types of interview questions?
   (a) Direct Question
   (b) Open ended Question
   (c) Bipolar question
   (d) Closed ended Question

5. __________ means that your behavioural expressions are consistent.
   (a) Empathy
   (b) Authenticity
   (c) Paraphrasing
   (d) Ability to empathise

6. Which of the following are bot the characteristics of Effective helper?
   (a) Authenticity
   (b) Paraphrasing
   (c) Positive regard for others
   (d) Schema

7. Ability to examine and consider one's own motives, attitudes, behaviours is called __________.
   (a) Expressive skills
   (b) Reflective skills
   (c) Personal skills
   (d) Affective skills

8. Desire to help others, openness to new ideas, honesty is called __________.
   (a) Affective skills
   (b) Reflective skills
   (c) Personal skills
   (d) Expressive skills

Answers

1. (a)   **2.** (d)   **3.** (b)   **4.** (d)   **5.** (b)   **6.** (d)   **7.** (b)   **8.** (c)

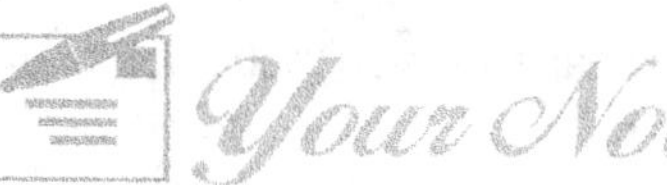
Your Notes: ....

ENGLISH LANGUAGE

PART – I : READING

Reading Comprehension

In this section, a passage is given and you are asked to answer questions based on information that is specifically given in the passage. So, do not rely on your own judgement based on matter you are familiar with.

Why do we need to pay specific attention to RC, Reading Comprehension? It is because we are being tested on what we have understood after reading the passage under a time constraint. The reading style for RC varies from the reading style we generally use. We do not read a passage as we read our text books while studying. In a text book we cannot afford to skip a point here or a line there, lest we miss out on that crucial one mark. Nor do we read a passage as we read an Agatha Christie novel, from page to page, word by word, curled up in bed on a nice wintry day.

In RC, we need to finish off our task within the allotted time. So, it is seldom advised to take more than 4 or 5 minutes for a passage– this includes the time to answer the questions. We get marks for answering questions and not for reading the passage. But we must bear in mind that if we read the passage smoothly and speedily, we can answer almost all the questions confidently.

Is it possible for us to answer the questions without reading the passage? Yes. We should just search for the answers if we have just a minute or so to read the passage. But we must understand the importance of reading fast and understanding important points without dilly-dallying.

There are a few techniques that we can apply to read faster and comprehend better:

- Do not regress while reading. Read right the first time round, instead of re-reading and re-re-reading and re-re-... Always move forward while reading, do not look back at all.
- Completely concentrate on what you are reading.
- Read fast, as if you have an express train running after you.
- Place the passage details roughly in your mind so that you can search for the answer quickly instead of going on a treasure hunt.

- Do not read aloud or word-by-word in your mind, this is because there is really no need to read everything, you can skip a point here and there if you feel that it is not important enough.
- Try to have a map of what you read so that you can get the whole picture.
- Try to take in more than one word than at a glance.
- If you can't figure out the meaning of a word, try to guess its contextual meaning by reading the whole sentence.
- Read the editorials in the middle page of your newspaper, they are more or less of the same type as passages and help enhance your general knowledge as well.
- Mark the right answer! Do not answer half-heartedly, verify!

Approaches to Reading Comprehension

There are several methods of attempting a Reading Comprehension passage. They are as given below:

- Read the passage and answer the questions. This is a good method and can help you get all the answers right, or at least help you guess intelligently.
- Take a glance at the questions first, and then read the passage and answer the questions. This is a smart way to work since you can answer questions as you read the passage and not waste time reading unnecessary material.
- Just read the questions and search for the answers. If you do not have any time to read the passage, just go and mark answers to whatever questions you can trace in the passage.
- Read two paragraphs, look up if there are any questions based on it and answer them. Then read two more paragraphs and answer any questions based on them and so on...This is a good method too as whatever you have read remains fresh in your mind and you can immediately answer questions related to it.

There are various methods that help you to improve your reading speed. Some of these are:

Underlining Hand Method

In this method, we move our finger or pencil in the forward direction under the line that we are reading. This helps us to concentrate and keep reading forward.

Vertical Page Motion

In this method, you get focus and concentration by placing your hands on either side of the passage and moving it down as you read along. This method helps you to read more as compared to the previous method as using this you can take a look at the entire line and the portion below it too.

The Brush Technique

This is quite an advanced technique. Here you have to brush your hands diagonally from the north-west corner of the page right to the bottom. It requires a lot of concentration and an attention to detail.

The Mapping Technique

Read paragraph by paragraph and make a mental map of what you have read in each paragraph so that you can search in the exact paragraph, should you wish to search for an answer. Also, you must keep in mind how each paragraph links to the previous one and the one after.

Finally, read with enthusiasm, instead of boredom. Positive thinking always leads to outstanding results!

Exercise

Passage – 1

San Francisco, America's romantic city by the bay, has always been for the artists, writers and lovers who have left at least part of their hearts there. One of the great American romantics, who wrote in San Francisco, was Jack Kerouac. Kerouac rewrote the history of an entire post-war era in *On the Road*.

Born on March 12, 1922, in Lowell, Massachusetts, to a working class Catholic, French-Canadian family, Kerouac had a typically all American childhood. He played baseball, read Pulp Fiction and became a high school football star. He entered Columbia University on a football scholarship but when a leg injury put him out of action on the grid iron, he chose the literary field of work. American literature would never be the same anymore. His romanticized autobiographical novels and wayward travels, which were often the basis of his work, made him the unquestioned king of the Beat Generation writers.

Before becoming the father of the San Francisco-based Beat Generation, Kerouac was writing in the bars and basement apartments of New York City's Lower East and Lower West sides. Here he met and worked with William S. Burroughs and Allen Ginsberg before they all took their restless spirits West and started a literary and cultural revolution.

Kerouac first landed in the San Francisco Bay area in 1947, hoping to get a berth on a merchant marine ship. Here he soon met his kindred spirit, Neal Cassady, whose frenetic letters and cross-country travels spurred Jack to write *On the Road*, perhaps his pre-eminent work, in one long paragraph during the month of April 1951.

Since the book was written as a simple personal testament "in search of his writing soul", Kerouac had no idea that *On the Road* would spur a generation onto the highways and into the tumultuous activism of the Vietnam era, a decade later.

Almost overnight, Kerouac became a media superstar and even a mythical figure himself. But in the end, he could not live with the myth he created. He split from the ranks of his fellow beat writers, like Ginsberg, and actually voiced support for America's war effort in Vietnam. Later in his life, he moved in back with his mother, drank too much, and became more and more reactionary. His later years wer e an ironic turn on the life of freedom he wrote about and lived to a great extent. Still, the stories he created live on within the souls of American youth, the lingering American romantics.

1. Jack Kerouac was born

    (a) to a working class family in Massachusetts.

    (b) to a Canadian family.

    (c) to Irish Catholic parents.

    (d) in a sandlot.

2. Jack Kerouac relocated to San Francisco in

    (a) 1922

    (b) 1951

    (c) 1947

    (d) the midst of the Vietnam War

3. Kerouac met Neal Cassady

    (a) in the French Canadian Massachusetts.

    (b) in San Francisco.

    (c) in New York.

    (d) in Vietnam.

4. *On the Road* was

    (a) not important to the youth of America.

    (b) one long paragraph.

    (c) Alan Ginsberg's poem.

    (d) Kerouac's autobiography.

5. Which of the following is NOT mentioned about Kerouac's life?

   (a) His support for the US war effort in Vietnam

   (b) His French-Canadian upbringing

   (c) His leading role in the beat generation

   (d) His unsuccessful marriage

6. The best title for this passage would be

   (a) *Post-war Literature and a New Beginning*

   (b) *Kerouac: King of the Beats Opens a New Road*

   (c) *San Franciso Writers*

   (d) *Vietnam Protests: The Early Years*

Passage – 2

Rock, or rock-and-roll is a form of music that was invented in the United States in the 1950s. It has become popular in the US, Europe, and many other parts of the world. African-American performers like Little Richards, Fats Domino, Ray Charles, and Big Joe Turner were among the first people to come up with true rock-and-roll, a combination of various elements from country, western, gospel, rhythm and blues and jazz. The influences of blues man Muddy Waters, gospel performer Ruth Brown, jazz musician Louis Jordan, on rock-and-roll, are still felt today. For example, the songs of early country legend Hank Williams affected musicians ranging from early rock star Buddy Holly to 1980s rocker Bruce Springsteen.

In the segregated 1950s, African-American musical forms were not considered appropriate for White audiences. Much of the US population had not been exposed to them. All that changed, when in 1953, Cleveland based disc jockey Alan Freed began to play rhythm and blues to a largely non African-American audience. Freed was successful and a lot of records were sold. The music spread, and the term that Freed had adopted for the music — rock-and-roll, began to spread as well.

Teenagers and the money they were willing to spend on records provided an impetus for rock-and-roll. On their way to becoming rock stars, many performers copied songs from the original artists. For instance, Pat Boone scored a hit with a toned-down version of Little Richards' song, 'Tutti Frutti', prompting Little Richard to comment, "He goes and outsells me with my song that I wrote." In 1955-56, Chuck Berry, Bill Haley and the Comets, and particularly Elvis Presley became famous for their version of traditional rhythm and blues. Elvis Presley's first television appearance in January 1956 marked rock-and roll's ascendancy into the world of pop music.

1. What is the main topic of this passage?

   (a) American Popular Music

   (b) The Careers of Successful Rock Musicians

   (c) The Musical Elements that Distinguish Pop from Classical Music

   (d) The Origins of the Music that Came to be Called Rock-and-Roll

2. Who is NOT mentioned as an African-American performer who was amongst the first to come out with rock-and-roll?

   (a) Fats Domino   (b) Little Richards

   (c) Elvis Presley   (d) Ray Charles

3. According to the passage, true rock-and-roll is characterized by a combination of which of the following?

   (a) The music of Bruce Springsteen and Hank Williams

   (b) Musical influences from Europe and Asia

   (c) Forms of music heard on most radio stations in the early 1950s

   (d) Country, western, gospel, rhythm and blues and jazz

4. In the 1950s rock-and-roll

   (a) was invented.

   (b) was not considered appropriate for White audiences.

   (c) sold few records.

   (d) was the property of Buddy Holly.

5. Many performers copied songs from

   (a) classical music   (b) Pat Boone

   (c) original artists   (d) 'Tutti Frutti'

6. Which of the following is not mentioned in the passage as being a factor in the commercial success of early rock-and-roll?

   (a) The purchasing power of early rock enthusiasts.

   (b) The charismatic personality of disc jockey Alan Freed.

   (c) The exposure of a non African-American audience to African-American musical forms.

   (d) Rock's popularity with teenage audiences

Passage – 3

Primitive mammals called monotremes are the only living representatives of the subclass Prototheria. This makes them the most likely living representatives of the creatures that were part of the evolutionary transition from reptiles to mammals. They share some qualities with reptiles and birds, but are nevertheless true mammals. Like birds and reptiles, monotremes lay eggs rather than give birth. But like other mammals, they have hair, large brains and mammary glands that produce milk to nourish their offspring.

Their primitive organization and close relation to reptiles is manifested in their uncomplicated brain structure, egg-laying habits and cloaca. (A cloaca is found in amphibians, reptiles, birds, certain fish and monotremes, but not in placental mammals or most bony fishes. The animal's intestinal, urinary and genital tracts open into this common cavity, which also functions as an outlet.)

Another feature that indicates they may be related to reptiles is their egg-laying behaviour. Monotremes lay shelled eggs, which are predominantly yolk, like those of reptiles and birds. The young are born in a relatively early stage of development and remain dependent upon the parents. The females have no teats; the milk that they secrete from their mammary glands passes directly through their skin.

There are only three types of monotremes in existence: the duck-billed platypus and two species of spiny echidna or anteater. The platypus has webbed feet, a flat tail, and a 'bill' like a duck's. The short and the long-nosed echidnas have spines and tube-like noses. The female echidna lays one egg at a time into a pouch that she develops in her abdomen. Her young will hatch in it and develop for several months.

1.   The passage focuses on which of the following aspects of monotremes?

     (a) The food they eat and their behaviour in the wild.

     (b) The times of day when they are most active.

     (c) Their relationship to both reptiles and mammals.

     (d) Their mating behaviour and reproductive organs.

2.   Which of the following is NOT mentioned as a quality that monotremes share with other mammals?

     (a) Hair on the body

     (b) Development of mammary glands

     (c) Egg-laying

     (d) A large brain

3.   The passage states that monotremes are

     (a) extinct

     (b) reptiles and birds

     (c) egg-laying mammals that are related to reptiles and birds

     (d) highly intelligent

4.   Monotreme babies are born

     (a) in the early stages of development and must rely on their mothers.

     (b) fully developed and quickly become independent.

     (c) live like the babies of other mammals.

     (d) without mammary glands.

5.   The duck-billed platypus is

     (a) the tube-like nose of a monotreme.

     (b) a subspecies of anteater.

     (c) a portion of the monotreme reproductive system.

     (d) one of the few surviving species of monotreme.

6.   According to the passage, where do young echidnas live right after they are hatched?

     (a) In a pouch on their mother's abdomen

     (b) In their mother's cloaca

     (c) In amphibians, birds, reptiles, and certain fish

     (d) In an egg that has a shell and that is predominantly yolk

Passage – 4

Asteroids are rocky, metallic objects that orbit around the sun, but are too small to be considered planets. The largest known asteroid, Ceres, has a diameter of about 1,000 kilometres. The smallest asteroids are the size of pebbles. Millions are the size of boulders. Most are irregularly shaped — only a few are large enough for gravity to have made them into spheres. About 250 asteroids in the solar system are 100 kilometres in diameter, and at least 16 have a diameter of 240 kilometres or greater. Their orbits lie in a range that stretches from earth's orbit to beyond Saturn's orbit. Tens of thousands of asteroids exist in a belt between the orbits of Mars and Jupiter. An asteroid that hits earth's atmosphere is called a meteor or shooting star, because it burns and gives off a bright flash of light. Whatever does not completely burn falls to earth as a meteorite. Between 1,000 and 10,000 tonnes of this material fall to earth daily. Much is in the form of small grains of dust, but about 1,000 metallic or rocky bits fall to earth each year.

There has been much speculation about large meteors hitting the earth. A large asteroid or comet is thought to have landed in Mexico about 65 million years ago. The impact may have led to the extinction of many species, including the dinosaurs, by throwing dust into the atmosphere, blocking the sunlight, and causing a climate change. The period of time between such a large meteor impacts is probably in the millions of years, but smaller meteors such as the one that caused the Metro's Crater in Arizona (about 1.2 kilometres in diameter), may hit the earth every 50,000 to 100,000 years. There's no historical record of a person being killed by a meteorite. The only reported injury occurred on November 30, 1954, when an Alabama woman was bruised by an eight-pound meteorite that fell through the roof of her house.

1.   The milions of asteroids are

     (a) the size of boulders

     (b) symmetrical

     (c) about 1,000 kilometres in diameter

     (d) regular in shape

2. Which of the following explains why a meteor is called a shooting star?

   (a) It may have caused the extinction of dinosaurs.

   (b) No one is known to have been killed by one.

   (c) It burns in a flash of light.

   (d) It can be rocky or metallic.

3. In the passage, why does the author mention the Metro's Crater in Arizona?

   (a) To give an example of the impact of a smaller meteor.

   (b) To increase interest in astronomy.

   (c) To close the passage on an interesting note.

   (d) To show how meteors can wipe out animal species.

4. The Alabama woman in the passage is mentioned to

   (a) show that meteorites can kill.

   (b) illustrate the only documented injury of a human being by a meteorite.

   (c) show that meteorites can damage homes.

   (d) summarize the historical records.

Passage – 5

A highly-acclaimed motion picture of 1979 concerned a nearly disastrous accident at a nuclear power plant. Within a few weeks of the film's release, in a chilling coincidence, a real-life accident startlingly similar to the fictitious one occurred at the Three Mile Island plant near Harrisburg, Pennsylvania. The two incidents even corresponded in certain details, for instance, both in the film and in real life, one cause of the mishap was a false metre reading caused by a jammed needle.

Such similarities led many to wonder whether the fictional movie plot had been prophetic in other ways. The movie depicted officials of the power industry as seriously corrupt, willing to lie, bribe, and even kill to conceal their culpability in the accident. Did a similar cover-up occur in the Three Mile Island accident? Perhaps we will never know. We do know that, despite the endeavours of reporters and citizen groups to uncover the cause of the accident, many of the facts remain unknown. Although they declare that the public is entitled to the truth, many of the power industry leaders responsible have been reluctant to cooperate with independent, impartial investigators.

1. The nuclear accident described in the movie

   (a) was successfully concealed by power industry leaders and officials.

   (b) was caused by a series of coincidences.

   (c) was a surprisingly accurate foreshadowing of actual events.

   (d) took place at the Three Mile Island.

2. Officials of the nuclear power industry

   (a) have committed murders to make possible a cover-up of the incident at Harrisburg.

   (b) had predicted that nuclear accidents were likely to occur.

   (c) have been reluctant to reveal the full story about the Three Mile Island incident.

   (d) have tried to make all the facts freely accessible to those concerned.

3. According to the passage, public concern over the accident near Harrisburg

   (a) had no effect on the subsequent investigation.

   (b) was lessened by the quick response of industry leaders and officials.

   (c) prompted widespread panic throughout Pennsylvania.

   (d) persisted as many questions were left unanswered.

4. Reporters looking into the accident at Three Mile Island

   (a) uncovered more facts than did citizen groups.

   (b) did not succeed in uncovering all the facts about the cause of the accident.

   (c) cooperated closely with power industry officials.

   (d) kept documented information from the public.

5. All of the following are true, except

   (a) the movie about a nuclear accident had been praised.

   (b) the press had sought information about the Three Mile Island mishap.

   (c) a mechanical breakdown was a partial cause of the Harrisburg accident.

   (d) the release of the movie came only weeks after the Three Mile Island accident.

Passage – 6

Aristotle Onassis was religious. As a child, he sang in the church choir, learned his catechism, and was drilled in theology at his local church for two hours a week. As a man, he never broke away from the church. He was far from outstanding in school, yet he tried to shine at everything he undertook, whether it was swimming, or water polo, or sailing, or making a fortune. Disaster came to him and his family in 1922, when the Turks ran the Greeks out of Turkey, chased them into the sea, and slaughtered them. Thousands of Greek refugees poured into Smyrna ahead of the Turkish army, with dreadful tales of savagery and horror that echoed the bloody history of the Turkish massacres of centuries before. The Turks were taking a horrible revenge for the Greek atrocities of 1919 on the Turkish population. The old and the beautiful city was burned on September 13,1922. The horror was unbelievable, with a pall of black smoke rising from the ruins, the dreadful smell of burning flesh, and hundreds of men, women and children crowding into every available craft, even small rowing boats, in order to escape. Not least in horror was the cruelty with which the escaping Greeks broke the legs of the mules in order to keep them from being useful to the Turks. When the Greeks had been in power, they had burned the most prosperous towns in the west of Turkey. Now the innocent Greek population of Smyrna were paying with their blood.

Aristotle Onassis's father was thrown into a Turkish prison, and his new wife and three daughters were sent to an evacuation centre, to await transportation from Smyrna to Greece. Only the 16-year-old Aristotle and his grandmother were left at home, but not for long. Soon the Turkish general requisitioned the house and the old lady had to get out. The boy had to grow up overnight — somehow to rescue what was left of the family; somehow to save what was left of the family; somehow to survive against dreadful odds; somehow to get them all out of Turkish Smyrna; and somehow to start again. Almost incredibly, he succeeded in all these aims. He made up to the Turks, and to the Americans, supplying the Turks with information, the Americans with liquor, for he hid bottles of raki, ouzo and even French brandy, and supplied them to the Americans. His commission would be a single bottle, and he would give that to his friend, the Turkish general. From the Americans, he obtained an identification pass to take him in and out of the United States marine zone; and from the Turks, a Turkish army pass to enter and leave the still smoldering city. Now he could operate, but first he must find his family. His grandmother had disappeared, and his father was in a Turkish prison for summary trial as a political offender — his death by hanging dead. His brothers were also arrested, and one of them Alexander had been burned alive in a church.

Miraculously, Aristotle managed to rescue his relatives. Through the American Vice Consul's intercession, he obtained the release of his half-sister and his stepmother from their camp, and they were put on an American ship and dispatched to Lesbos. For his father, he needed a great deal of money. His father had run a one-man banking business, and at his offices, on Grand Vizier Han Street, there were valuables belonging to Turkish friends in an old-fashioned black safe. Going with a Turkish friend of his father's to retrieve a parcel of papers

and valuables left with his father for safe-keeping, Aristotle opened the safe, secured the parcel for his friend and emptied the safe of his father's fortune in Turkish pounds. Next, he organized a march of 50 leading Turkish businessmen waving a banner, shouting against the arrest of Socrates Onassis, and demanding his release. This almost certainly saved his father's life.

1.	What was the prime objective of Aristole Onassis after the Turkish attack?

	(a) Trying to shine in making a fortune

	(b) Trying to get his father out on bail

	(c) Trying to rescue as many relatives as he could

	(d) Trying to get his family together

2.	What led the Greeks to resort to cruelty to the mules?

	(a) They wanted to ensure that mules could not be used by anyone else.

	(b) They wanted to ensure that they retaliate to the atrocities of the Turks.

	(c) They wanted to prove that they could hit back.

	(d) They could no longer contain their vengeance.

3.	What is the meaning of the word catechism?

	(a) Religious revelatory prophecies

	(b) A questionnaire based on facts of life

	(c) A new world order

	(d) A religious sermon

4.	Why was Socrates imprisoned?

	(a) Because he had led a rebellion.

	(b) Because he was considered a political offender.

	(c) Because he had headed a maverick firm.

	(d) Because he was on good terms with the Americans.

5.	What was the probable reason of the Turk rally?

	(a) It was a step to siege the neighbouring territory.

	(b) It was a step taken out of revenge.

	(c) It was done to torture the Greeks for nothing.

	(d) It was done to pillage the neighbours.

6.	What could be the only solution for Socrates's release?

	(a) To pay the people who had captured him.

	(b) To escape from the jail and run away from the country.

	(c) To overthrow the power of the Turks.

	(d) To befriend the Turkish officers and then ask for a favour.

Passage – 7

I am sitting at an airport watching people in the final moments before their loved ones arrive or depart. They are pacing nervously, looking at one another, touching and not touching. The emotion is intense.

A woman, speaking Spanish, is running in circles trying to gather family members together for a goodbye. Her voice is high-pitched. When the final moment comes before boarding, she wraps her arms around her son, giving him a powerful embrace that should protect him until he returns.

A grandmother and grandson stand at the rail where I am waiting; the people who were supposed to pick them up are late. Two ladies, next to them but unrelated, look up and down the corridor as if scanning an open sea. They probably want to help the grandmother. A mother holds a baby as she kisses her husband. Tears dampen her cheeks. The moment is charged.

At Gate 13, the arrivals are just coming in. I see her. There she is. Just as poignant, the arrivals fold into the mix of people as if they have been gone.

I think of other departures and arrivals. I recall seeing my daughter, I am now going to visit, coming down that narrow, portable corridor with her haversack slung on one shoulder, overstuffed carrion bag cradled in her arms, her headphones making her oblivious to the stream of people flowing along with her. She was in her first year at university coming home for holiday in November — the first time since August. I wrapped myself around her as if she had been lost to me.

Today, my flight is two hours late. The book I am reading is not as interesting as the people leaving and coming. A little boy of five is meeting his grandfather for the first time. He looks up and up at the face of a man who is not that tall, except to a child, joy shines and I am wondering how one would capture this moment in words or on film.

When my flight is finally called, I gather my books and carry one bag. Since there is no one to see me off, I do not look back to see where I have come from. Instead, I think of my husband at work wondering if he has left yet, and my daughter at the other end wondering the same thing.

As I head towards the plane, I find myself remembering yet another arrival and departure. When I was newly wed, my 91-year-old grandfather died. We had been very close, and one evening, returning from his funeral, I arrived at the airport crying. My husband of only a year was waiting at the gate to take me in his arms. Because of my tears, everyone was looking at us, but I didn't care. Somehow the emotion I felt seemed not at all out of place for the airport.

Life needs to be this important all the time. I wish all the people who went on a journey could come back to find someone waiting for them. I also wish they could leave with someone to see them off. I think of my grandfather and realize that if dying is like this, a passage, then I am not afraid.

1.   What is the author doing while sitting at the airport?

(a) She is missing her husband and her daughter.

(b) She is wondering how one would capture child's the emotional gush in a story or on film.

(c) She is thinking about her grandfather who died at 91.

(d) She is reading an interesting book.

2.   The two ladies at the rail next to the grandmother and her grandson seem to be

(a) searching for someone who is lost.

(b) impassively talking to each other.

(c) looking around for the grandma's folks.

(d) in their own thoughts as they are unrelated to the grandmother.

3.   What point does the author possibly drive at through the passage?

(a) The author has long memories of airports.

(b) The author shows how caring people are.

(c) The author is lamenting over the loss of her grandfather.

(d) The author relates journeys with high emotions.

Passage – 8

A final year school student called Mathew stumbled into the science class, late for the seventh time. His teacher, Rebecca Sacra, wondered how such a bright boy could be so irresponsible. She then issued a reminder to her students. "Nine times late to class and you receive a failing grade regardless of your test scores." In the back of the room, Mathew seemed nonplussed.

Sacra decided to meet Mathew's father to explain the situation to him. She braced herself, though remembering the tough spots he'd bailed Mathew out of before — like the time Mathew was caught smoking in school or when he broke bounds.

But the father's reactions surprised Sacra. "I have been getting that boy out of trouble for years," he began. "May be it's time to demand more - not less - of Mathew. Go ahead and flunk him if that is what it takes to turn him around. What Mathew's dad dreaded even more was about the possibility that Mathew might go off to college before he learned to take responsibility for his own actions.

"You wouldn't really flunk me, would you?" incredulous Mathew asked his teacher the next morning. She assured him that she would. Mathew wasn't late ever again. The lesson Mathew's father discovered — that parents who want their kids to excel must choose the best parenting option, not the easiest — is something teachers wish all parents knew. Says Terry Lowe, an award-winning teacher, "Too many parents are quick to back off when kids object or complain. They bail them out of tough spots and make excuses or give in when the going gets tough. Kids are a long-term investment, and parents have to stop making short-term decisions about them."

1.   What is the central idea of the passage?

       (a) The Turning Around of Mathew

       (b) Lesson on Good Parenting

       (c) Lesson of Good Teaching

       (d) Essence of Being Didactic

2.   How does the author describe Mathew?

       (a) Mathew is essentially a burn.

       (b) Mathew has always tried his tricks in the class.

       (c) Mathew is a fluke who sometimes got good grades.

       (d) He is an intelligent kid acting in a weird manner.

3.   How did Mathew's father react on the earlier counts?

       (a) He was very strict and punished the kid rightly.

       (b) He was short-sighted and he bailed him out.

       (c) He was unconcerned as Mathew got good grades.

       (d) He tried to sit down and talk to Mathew.

4.   What essentially worked in Mathew's case?

       (a) The abilities of his father as a glib talker.

       (b) The fact that he continued getting high grades.

       (c) The fear that he would be reprimanded.

       (d) The over confidence that he could get away with anything.

5.   What was Mathew's father most afraid of when the teacher mentioned of his late-coming in class?

       (a) He thought his son would flunk.

       (b) He was afraid that his son would spoil his reputation.

       (c) He was afraid that this son would get into smoking.

       (d) He was afraid that his son would remain irresponsible and eventually go off to college.

Passage – 9

When Mrs. Gandhi was voted to power, it seemed that she would not be able to take on the formidable task of ruling a nation of 50 crore population with ease and comfort like her predecessors. But from the very beginning, Mrs. Gandhi proved herself to be a veritable member of the Parliament and a charismatic leader for the Congress. Following the footsteps of her father, Mrs. Gandhi stoically challenged the conventional and outdated theories of ruling the country. She spoke like a true politician. That apart, Mrs. Gandhi spoke as a national leader not as a Congress leader. The distinction is not easy to define, but it is there and in her Independence Day address Mrs. Gandhi preserved it. While, for example, she defended the record of her government and met the opposition criticism, she did so soberly without attacking the opposition and the press as she tends to do. She even went to the extent of saying that if she drew attention to activities of hostile external forces, she did not do so with a view to distracting attention from difficulties at home which she knew remained formidable. Similarly, while she emphasized the urgent need for preserving the country's unity and integrity, she did not blame opposition parties or other critics for the challenges facing the nation.

While the situation in Punjab continued to cause anxiety in view of the confrontationist policies of the Akali Dal and the SGPC, Tamils of Indian descent were are once again being massacred in Sri Lanka. Mrs. Gandhi spoke on both these issues with great care as befits a person in her position. But no careful listener could miss the point that her statement on recent developments in Sri Lanka reflected a deterioration in India's international position. The ruthless actions of the Sri Lanka armed force have been preceded by the induction of Israeli and British specialists in intelligence and anti-terrorist activities and the rejection, in fact, if not in name of India's mediatory services. Naturally, Mrs. Gandhi could not refer to this international consequence of the Akali and extremist activities in Punjab. But connection between Colombo's behaviour and the recent upheaval in Punjab is too obvious to have been missed by her. Sri Lankan authorities no longer regard it necessary to show any regard for this country's susceptibilities and interests and they feel free to butcher Tamils.

1.   Mrs. Gandhi

       (a) is more of a national leader than a Congress leader.

       (b) is only a national leader.

       (c) is both a national and Congress leader.

       (d) made no distinction between a national leader and a Congress leader.

2.   Which of the following is true?

       (a) Mrs. Gandhi blamed the opposition for the nation's plight.

       (b) Mrs. Gandhi was ruthless about the way she spoke about Sri Lanka.

       (c) Mrs. Gandhi felt that India's international position has deteriorated.

       (d) Mrs. Gandhi ignored the formidable difficulties at home.

3.   Punjab situation
   (a) caused Mrs. Gandhi to blame the Akali Dal and the SGPC.
   (b) is the result of a defiant posture adopted by Mrs. Gandhi's government.
   (c) was condemned by Mrs. Gandhi as the result of hostile opposition shown by the Akali Dal and the SGPC.
   (d) was spoken of by Mrs. Gandhi while exercising great care.

4.   The author views Mrs. Gandhi as
   (a) a connoisseur
   (b) a smart prime minister
   (c) an unequivocal speaker
   (d) a diplomatic politician

Passage – 10

When I am told by people that sports is just for fun and exercise, I really wonder whether they believe what they are saying . These very people who 'enjoy sports just for the sake of it', have also displayed belligerent emotions during a match played by their favourite sportsmen. A sportsground has been turned into a political issue. I am always amazed when I hear people saying that sport creates goodwill between nations, and that if only the common people of the world could meet one another at football or cricket, they would have no inclination to meet on the battlefield. Even if one didn't know from concrete examples (the 1936 Olympic Games, for instance) that international sporting contests lead to orgies of hatred, one could deduce it from general principles. Very often, the fiercest instinct of individuals raises its ugly head and thus ruins the show.

Nearly all the sports practised nowadays are competitive. You play to win, and the game has little meaning unless you do your utmost to win. On the village green, where you pick up sides and no feeling of local patriotism is involved, it is possible to play simply for the fun and exercise, but as soon as the question of prestige arises, as soon as you feel that you and some larger unit will be disgraced if you lose, the most savage combative instincts are aroused. Anyone who has played even in a school football match knows this. At the international level sport is frankly mimic warfare. But the significant thing is not the behaviour of the players but the attitude of the spectators; and behind the spectators, of the nations who work themselves into furies over these absurd contests, and seriously believe — at any rate for short periods — that running, jumping and kicking a ball are tests of national virtue.

Even a leisurely game like cricket, demanding grace rather than strength, can cause much ill-will, as we saw in the controversy over body-line bowling and rough tactics of the Australian team that visited England in 1921. Football, a game in which everyone gets hurt and every nation has its own style of play, which seems unfair to foreigners, is far worse. Worst of all is boxing. One of the most horrible sights in the world is a fight between white and coloured boxers before a mixed audience. But the boxing audience is always disgusting and the behaviour of the women, in particular, is such that the army, I believe, does not allow them to attend its contests. Two of three years ago, when Home Guards and regular troops were holding boxing tournaments, I was placed on guard at the door of the hall, with orders to keep the women out at any rate.

In England, the obsession with sport is bad enough, but even fiercer passions are aroused in young countries where games-playing and nationalism are both recent developments. In countries like India or Burma, it is necessary to have strong cordons of police to keep the crowd from invading the field in football matches. In Burma, I have seen the supporters of one side break through the police and disable the goalkeeper of the opposing side at a critical moment. The first big football match that was played in Spain about 15 years ago led to an uncontrollable riot. As soon as strong feelings of rivalry are aroused, the notion of playing the game according to the rules always vanishes.

1.   The author believes that
   (a) sport creates goodwill between the nations.
   (b) sportsmen will not be inclined to confront each other on the battle field.
   (c) international sporting contests lead to riotous outbursts of hatred.
   (d) the 1936 Olympic Games were the only instance of sporting contests leading to hatred.

2.   Which of the following is correct?
   (a) Sports are played for fun and exercise.
   (b) The feeling of being disgraced arouses the worst fighting animal instincts.
   (c) Sports have the quality of making better international relations.
   (d) The behaviour of players is significant.

3.   Which of the following is true?
   (a) Nations believe that display of sporting skills as a test of national virtue.
   (b) At the international level, sport is nothing more than a competitive game.
   (c) Spectator's attitude determines the tempo of the game.
   (d) A school football match is played with a feeling of local patriotism.

4. The author has suggested which of the following?

   (a) The game of cricket causes much ill-will.

   (b) Women spectators are the worst.

   (c) Because of their behaviour, women are kept out of the boxing audience of some matches.

   (d) The fight between a white and a black boxer is fascinating.

Passage – 11

In today's world matter as we know it, is made up of molecules, each of which is, on an average, roughly 1/125 millionth of an inch. These molecules are to be further broken down into atoms which are so minuscule in size, that almost 15-20 million of them could be placed in a row within the space of a millimetre and yet the full millimetre would not have been covered. The atom, until Rutherford's revelations in 1911, was relatively unheard of. Many scientists of the caliber of Moseley, Bohr, Compton, Urey and so on have also dwelt upon the complex problem relating to the mysterious architecture of the atom. It was, at the time, believed that voids, rather almost void spaces, actually consisted of particles revolving with a lightning velocity. These particles, whose existence had been proved by a series of ingenious laboratory experiments, were regarded to be so minute in size, that they were or as yet have not been seen or photographed. Thus evolved the concept of the atom, the ultimate and indivisible constituent of matter, as it has long since been regarded. It was believed that the atom was made up of two elements the proton or the positive element of an atomic nucleus and the electrons or the negative elements which revolve around the proton in an atom.

1. The primary purpose of the passage is to

   (a) honour the pioneering efforts of Rutherford and his followers.

   (b) refute the existence of submicroscopic particle.

   (c) illustrate how scientists measure molecular diameter.

   (d) summarize the then current findings on the composition of matter.

2. According to the passage, all of the following are true of the centre of the atom except that it

   (a) has not yet been seen by the naked eye.

   (b) contains elements that are positively charged.

   (c) is a little larger than a molecule.

   (d) follows experimentally determinable processes.

3. By referring to the space in a millimetre, the author intends to point up the atom's

   (a) density   (b) mystery

   (c) velocity   (d) minuteness

4. Which of the following relationships most closely parallels the relationship between the proton and the electrons described in the passage?

   (a) A hawk to its prey

   (b) A blueprint to a framework

   (c) A planet to its satellites

   (d) A compound to its elements

Passage – 12

As we have seen adaptive divergence is the scientific terminology used when organisms, which are alike in certain aspects, adopt entirely different characters while trying to adapt themselves to new and hostile environment. The opposite of adaptive divergence, that is adaptive convergence, is an interesting yet all too common occurrence in the process of evolution. It is when organisms which totally differ from one another take on similar modes of life or adjust themselves and become suited to survive in special sorts of environments. It is a fairly common phenomenon that invertebrate marine animals living firmly attached to the sea bottom or to some foreign object have tendency to develop a conical or sub-cylindrical form, examples of which are corals and sponges.

A more suited example being the streamlined fitness of most fishes for moving swiftly through water; they have no neck, the contour of the body is smoothly curved so as to give minimum resistance, and the chief propelling organ is a powerful tail fin. That some fossil reptiles (ichthyosaurs) and modern mammals (whales, dolphins) are completely fishlike in form, is illustrative of adaptive convergence, as these air-breathing reptiles and mammals, which are highly efficient swimmers, are in no way closely related to fishes. Unrelated or distantly related organisms that develop similarity of form to suit special environments are sometimes designated as homeomorphs (having the same form).

1. The author mentions ichthyosaurs and dolphins as examples of

   (a) modern mammalian life forms that are aquatic.

   (b) species with slightly greater mobility than other fish.

   (c) air-breathing reptiles closely related to fish.

   (d) organisms that have evolved into fishlike forms.

2. According to the passage, adaptive convergence and adaptive divergence are

   (a) manifestations of evolutionary patterns.

   (b) hypotheses unsupported by biological phenomena.

   (c) ways in which plants and animals adjust to a common environment.

   (d) demonstrated by reptiles and mammals.

3. It can be inferred that in the paragraph immediately preceding this passage the author discussed

    (a) marine intelligence

    (b) adaptive divergence

    (c) air-breathing reptiles

    (d) environmental impacts

4. The tone used by the author in the passage is one of

    (a) skepticism   (b) explanation

    (c) admiration   (d) disgust

5. According to the passage whales and dolphines may be classified as

    (a) mammals   (b) fossils

    (c) reptiles   (d) homeomorphs

Passage – 13

A piece of African artistry when first observed will appear to you as a single unitary object of immense artistic value. You do not tend to perceive it as a collection of myriad shapes and forms, which is essentially proof to the fact that these shapes and forms have been so skillfully moulded together that you, as the viewer, were so emotionally affected that you immediately saw what the artist was trying to convey by his sculpture.

It is quite common to address the reasons behind the achievement of this unique and unified picture, and the question of whether there are a set of fixed rules or plastic language which governs African sculpture so as to give it that powerful sense of communication. Another point of interest is that in the existence of this particular fixed code of operation, whether consciousness or instinct are the governing factors in the production of such high quality.

It is obvious from the study of art history that an intense and unified emotional experience, such as the Christian Credo of the Byzantine or 12th or 13th century Europe, when expressed in art forms, gave great unity, coherence and power to art. But such an integrated feeling was only the inspirational element for the artist, only the starting point of the creative act. The expression of this emotion and its realization in the work could be done only with discipline and thorough knowledge of the craft.

As a child, the African sculptor learns the use and significance of his tools and the various styles of sculpting associated with his tribe under the thorough guidance of his master, so when he grows up carving becomes second nature to him and he does not think of the rules but follows them automatically and instinctively. The fact that such rules have never been translated to words does not mean they do not exist, as such a common style or language of sculpting among all Africans can't be attributed to accident or pure co-incidence. The African carver may have often used these rules along with his individualistic skill and insight into art, but may have been totally oblivious to their existence for such is the consistency of African sculpture. Thus, there exists a great unfathomable mystery of such an art, tradition or talent which has been used by certain people, though they themselves are unconscious of this phenomenon, to follow a set style or rule which may later be analysed by someone only after the work of art has been created.

1. The author is primarily concerned with

    (a) discussing how African sculptors achieve their effects.

    (b) listing the rules followed in African art.

    (c) relating African art to the art of 12th or 13th century Europe.

    (d) integrating emotion and realization.

2. According to the passage, one of the outstanding features of African sculpture is

    (a) its esoteric subject matter

    (b) the emotional content of the work

    (c) the education of training of the artists

    (d) its 'foreignness' when compared to Western art

3. The author uses the phrase 'plastic language' to refer to African art's

    (a) mass reproduction

    (b) unrealistic qualities

    (c) modernistic orientation

    (d) sense of communication

4. The information in the passage suggests that an African carver might best be compared to

    (a) a chef following a recipe

    (b) a fluent speaker of English who is just beginning to study French

    (c) a batter who hits a home run in his or her first baseball game

    (d) a concert pianist performing a well-rehearsed concert

5. Which of the following titles best expresses the content of the passage?

    (a) *The Apprenticeship of the African Sculptor*

    (b) *The History of African Sculpture*

    (c) *How African Art Achieves Unity*

    (d) *The Unconscious Rules of African Art*

Passage – 14

Money changers have many modes or methods of making a profit from their enterprise. Out of these there are two irregular methods used unscrupulously by them to cheat the customers. If they state the correct price, then the customer may be assured of his being cheated as far as the weights are concerned and if the weights and measures used by these scoundrels are accurate then they will always understate the price of silver in the market. A surprising point to be noticed is that when dealing with Tartars these men, who thrive on cheating, will not only weigh the silver correctly but even allow a little more than the actual weight and even pay more than what is the current market price. You may be under the impression that they are losers in this transaction, and so it might be, if weight and price were the only two parameters. Their advantage is derived when they make their calculations of the net amount. The silver has to be reduced to specks and when it comes to this, these rascals really do reduce it by making the most flagrant miscalculations which the Tartars, who can count absolutely nothing beyond their own beards, are not only incapable of detecting but of which they are blissfully unaware. They are content with knowing that the full weight has been allowed and the correct price given and thus are of the opinion that their bullion was well sold.

1.   The primary purpose of this passage appears to be to

      (a) defend the economic practices of money-changers.

      (b) compare the character of the Tartars with that of the money-changers.

      (c) explain the relationship between price and weight.

      (d) describe the techniques the money-changers use to take advantage of their customers.

2.   Which of the following statements about Tartars is supported by the passage?

      (a) Tartars hide valuables in their beards.

      (b) Tartars are unaware of miscalculation's made by money changers.

      (c) Tartars sell specks of silver.

      (d) Tartars cheat their customers by employing fraudulent methods of weighing their goods.

3.   We can infer from this passage that the money-changers

      (a) are aware that Tartars are poor mathematicians.

      (b) have fixed prices for their transactions.

      (c) convert bullion into pure silver.

      (d) lose their transactions with the Tartars.

Passage – 15

There exist a few species of mice that demonstrate conditions which are neither complete hibernation nor aestivation. Contrary to hibernation, where they go into a long sleep under adverse conditions or the most unfavourable and serve season, these species become torpid for a couple of hours on a daily basis. The first time I came across this phenomenon was when I was working on the fat mice in Africa. The name is a very appropriate one for these mice, as they tend to resemble furry balls on account of their bodies being so full of fat. One of these mice was, for a period of almost five weeks, kept without food or water as a result of which it lost almost a third of its weight in fat but still appeared quite healthy. But fat storage as a way of surviving has rebounded or, in a certain manner been also to the disadvantage of the fat mice. Many African tribes regard the mice as a delicacy and hunt them with great tenacity. On being captured the mice are generally fried in their own fat, of which there is no scarcity. These mice spend the daytime hours of the dry season in such a deep state of torpor that they can even be manhandled without fear of being awakened. Their body temperature is a few degrees higher than laboratory room temperature and their respiration most irregular, several short pants and then a pause of up to 3 minutes. Just before sunset the mice would rise from their sleep and begin to respire as they normally do when awake. In the above case, the state of torpor was not as a result of shortage of food or abnormal temperatures. The forest dormouse of southern Asia and Europe exhibits periods of torpidity during the day time and has been on record for pausing up to 17 minutes between breaths. The leaf eared mouse of the Peruvian desert becomes torpid under severe or adverse conditions.

1.   The primary focus of the passage is to highlight

      (a) the inhumane treatment of laboratory specimens.

      (b) the irregularities of respiration in mammals.

      (c) the conditions that induce rodents to hibernate.

      (d) the species that exhibit brief periods of dormancy.

2.   It can be inferred from the passage that fat storage as a method of survival 'has rebounded' for fat mice for which of the following reasons?

      (a) It has enabled them to go without food and water for long periods of time.

      (b) It has made them particularly tempting to human predators.

      (c) It has made them so spherical that they cannot move easily.

      (d) It has caused them to adopt abnormal patterns of sleep.

3. This passage would most likely appear in which of the following types of publications?

   (a) A geographical atlas

   (b) A history of African exploration

   (c) A textbook on rodent biology

   (d) A guide to the care of laboratory animals

4. It can be inferred that in the paragraph preceding this passage the author most likely discussed

   (a) his initial journey to Africa

   (b) the problem caused by sleep deprivation

   (c) other types of dormant states

   (d) the physical appearance of rodents

Passage – 16

The father of the nation 'Mahatma Gandhi' was of the opinion that man has always been a social animal whose survival has been credited to his ingenuous ability to create the means by which groups of men remain united and retain their relationships with one another. Congregating under peaceful circumstances is one of the primary requisites of this form of sociability and the history of mankind has always been a movement through the time of human collectivities ranging from small nomadic tribal bands to a large and complex civilization.

The environment in which man strived to survive was never an easy one to adopt to and always posed a challenge to man with every step he took. This coupled with man's undying desire to survive was the driving force behind the introduction of an Orderly State which was governed by a set of rules, which came to be known as the law. Thus over the centuries, since the dawn of civilization, man has successfully spanned the eras of his evolution, and having done so, is now on the verge of exploring the vast and infinite expanse of his own galaxy.

Man may be deemed as the only living organism possessing within him the intellect to interpret his own evolution as a progressive step. The worth and the rights of every individual in complex groups, of which he was a member, increased simultaneously with every change in social life. Contrary to the belief that they would diminish, as civilizations evolved from small tribes, individual values now serve as a guide to the laws governing all men.

1. Which of the following is the best expression of the main idea of this article?

   (a) Oppression and Society.

   (b) The Evolution of Man.

   (c) Man's Animal Instincts.

   (d) The Basis for Social Order.

2. According to the article, unique to a man is the fact that he is

   (a) evolving from a simpler to a more complex being.

   (b) a social animal.

   (c) capable of noting his own progress.

   (d) capable of inflicting injury and causing violence.

3. A suitable title for this passage would be

   (a) The Evolution of Mankind

   (b) Mahatma Gandhi's View of Man as a Social Animal

   (c) Man the Superior Animal

   (d) The Evolution of Order and its Effect on Society

4. The word 'environment', in the passage is used in context with

   (a) the natural environment

   (b) the city life

   (c) man's relation with the wildlife around him

   (d) the factors surrounding man in his natural habitat which have a bearing on his behaviour

Passage – 17

Since the dawn of civilization mankind has always been plagued by some or the other form of disease. The number of lives accounted for by each disease has, through the decades, varied continually, though none of them can be singled out as the leading cause of death, collectively they are the leading cause of deaths. The origin or evolution of diseases has never been too clearcut a phenomenon, though some wishful dreamers even attribute it to Pandora's box of troubles.

A survey of the five leading causes of deaths during a period from the early 1900s to the mid 1900s shows a distinct and significant trend. In the early 1900s these causes in order of number of death's caused were:

i. Tuberculosis,

ii. Pneumonia,

iii. Intestinal diseases,

iv. Heart diseases,

v. and Cerebral haemorrhage and thrombosis.

A decade later the only change was that heart disease had moved from fourth to fifth place, tuberculosis now being second, and pneumonia third.

Toward the later part of this period, however, the list had changed profoundly. Heart diseases were far out in front; cancer, which had come up from eighth place, was second; and cerebral haemorrhage and thrombosis, third. Fatal accidents, which had been well down the list, were now fourth, and nephritis was fifth. All of these are, of course, composites rather than single diseases, and it is significant that, except for accidents, they are characteristic of the advanced rather than the early or middle years of life.

1. On the basis of the passage, which of the following statements is most tenable?

   (a) A cure for cancer will be found within this decade.

   (b) Many of the medical problems of today are problems of the gerontologist (specialist in medical problems of old age).

   (c) Older persons are more accident prone than are younger persons.

   (d) Tuberculosis has been all but eliminated.

2. Which one of the following trends is least indicated in the passage?

   (a) As one grows older, one is more subject to debilitating disease.

   (b) Pneumonia has become less common.

   (c) Relative to mortality rates for acute intestinal diseases, the mortality rate for cancer has increased.

   (d) The incidence of heart disease has increased.

3. Which one of the following statements is most nearly correct?

   (a) Such mortality trends (stated in the passage) are caused by decreased infant mortality.

   (b) The changes in the data reported are a function of improved diagnosis and reporting.

   (c) The mortality data are based on the records of physicians who practised continuously from 1900 to 1950.

   (d) There appears to be a greater change in the mortality patterns from 1910 to 1950 than in the decade ending in 1910.

4. It can be inferred from reading this passage that

   (a) longevity increased between 1900 and 1915.

   (b) longevity increased steadily between 1915 and 1950.

   (c) longevity increased significantly between 1900 and 1950.

   (d) longevity was not a factor in these findings.

5. A suitable title for this passage would be

   (a) The Cause of Diseases

   (b) Old age and its Vulnerability to Diseases

   (c) Longevity Through the First Half of the 19th Century

   (d) An Essay on the Hierarchy of Diseases as Causes of Death

Passage – 18

When we next saw Miss Charlotte, she had grown fat and her hair was turning grey. During the next few years it grew greyer and greyer until it attained an even pepper-and-salt iron-grey, and up to the day of her death, at 71, it was still that vigorous iron-grey, like the hair of an active man. From that time on, her front door remained closed, save for a period of six or seven years, when she was about forty, during which she gave lessons in China-painting. She fitted up a studio in one of the downstairs rooms, where the daughters and granddaughters of General Braxton's contemporaries were sent to her with the same regularity and in the same spirit that they were sent to church on Sundays with a twenty-five-cent piece for the collection plate. Meanwhile her taxes had been remitted.

Then the newer generation became the backbone and the spirit of the town, and the painting pupils grew up and fell away and did not send their children to her with boxes of colour and tedious brushes and pictures cut from the ladies' magazines. The front door closed on the last one and remained closed for good. When the town got free postal delivery, Miss Charlotte alone refused to let them fasten the metal numbers above her door and attach a mailbox to it. She would not listen to them and was adamant.

1. The major subject of the passage is

   (a) Miss Charlotte's attempt to earn a living

   (b) the mystery of Miss Charlotte's sudden aging

   (c) the indifference of the town folk

   (d) Miss Charlotte's changing relationship with the town

2. It can be inferred from the passage that General Braxton's contemporaries sent their daughters to Miss Charlotte because

   (a) they wanted them to learn China-painting.

   (b) they wished a tactful way of providing her with money.

   (c) their daughters lacked ladylike accomplishments.

   (d) they knew she was offering lessons for a limited time.

Passage – 19

As we have seen, generally the male insects are smaller than the female insects of the same species but, however, there are exceptions to this theory which can be understood. Size and strength would be of added advantage to the males as they generally engage in battle over the possession of a female and in the case of stag-beetles (Lucanus), the males are comparatively larger than the females. There are, however, other species of beetles which are known to fight together, where the males exceed the females in size though the relevance of this phenomenon is still unclear, but in some of these cases, as with the huge Dynastes and Megasoma, we can at least see no necessity for the males to be smaller than the females in order to mature faster as these beetles have a long life span and thus there would be sufficient time for the pairing of the sexes.

1. According to the author, the traits of the male Lucanus include which of the following?

I. Belligerence

II. Active intelligence

III. Superior bulk

(a) I only   (b) III only

(c) I and III only   (d) II and III only

2. It can be inferred from the name 'stag-beetles' that the members of this species most likely

(a) are warm-blooded mammals.

(b) are herbivorous by nature.

(c) have appendages that resemble horns.

(d) are as short-lived as their namesakes.

3. The paragraph preceding this one probably

(a) discusses a generalization about the size of insects.

(b) develops the concept that male insects do not live long after maturity.

(c) describes the distinguishing marks of female insects.

(d) discusses the role of intelligence in male insects.

4. This passage would be most likely to appear in

(a) a school textbook

(b) a magazine

(c) an essay on stag-beetles

(d) a book on insects

Passage – 20

Scattered on the surface of the earth, there are about 100 or more regions of isolated volcanic activity known to modern geologists as hot spots. Many of these so called hot spots are found lying deep in the interior of the tectonic plates which drift on the sea of molten rock and are unlike volcanos in the fact that volcanos are found on the boundaries of the great drifting plates. These hot spots move slowly and in certain cases, a trail of extinct volcanos is left as the plates move past them. Thus, they act as milestones along with their volcanic trails, depicting the movement of the tectonic plates.

The fact that the plates are constantly moving is way past any form of dispute. The complementary coastlines of Africa and South America and certain geological features that span the ocean are themselves proof that these two land masses were once joined and are how moving apart as new material is constantly introduced into the sea bed between them. The relative motion of the plates on which the continents lie has been constructed in detail, but this relative motion between the plates cannot be easily translated in to motion with respect to the earth's interior. It is not possible to determine whether both plates are moving in opposite directions or if one is stationary while the other floats away from it. Hot spots provide the instruments needed for measuring this movement and thus answering this question owing to the fact that they are deeply embedded in the earth's lower layers. It was from an examination of the hot spots that it has been deduced that the African plate has not moved, it has remained stationary for the past 30 million years while the other plates are moving away from it.

This is not the only important role that the hot spots have played, as it has now been revealed that they, to a certain extent, influence the geophysical processes that cause the plates to drift over the sea of molten rock that forms the earth's interior. When a tectonic plate rests over a hot spot the molten material coming up from the lower layers creates a broad dome, which as it grows and stretches tends to develop deep fissures, and in a few cases may cause the continent to rupture along the formation of these deep cracks thus forming a new ocean. Thus, as earlier theories provided explanations as to the continental mobility, the hot spots can explain their mutability.

1. According to the passage, which of the following statements indicate that Africa and South America once adjoined one another?

I. They share certain common topographic traits

II. Their shorelines are physical counterparts

III. The African plate has been stable for 30 million years

(a) I only   (b) II only

(c) I and II only   (d) II and III only

2. According to the passage, the hot spot theory eventually may prove useful in interpreting

(a) the boundaries of the plates.

(b) the depth of the ocean floor.

(c) the relative motion of the plates.

(d) major changes in continental shape.

3. The author regards the theory of plate movement as

(a) controversial   (b) irrefutable

(c) tangential   (d) dubious

Answer Keys

Passage – 1

   1. (a)   2. (c)   3. (b)   4. (d)   5. (d)   6. (a)

Passage – 2

   1. (d)   2. (c)   3. (d)   4. (a)   5. (c)   6. (b)

Passage – 3

   1. (c)   2. (c)   3. (c)   4. (a)   5. (d)   6. (a)

Passage – 4

   1. (a)   2. (c)   3. (a)   4. (b)

Passage – 5

   1. (c)   2. (c)   3. (d)   4. (b)   5. (d)

Passage – 6

   1. (d)   2. (a)   3. (d)   4. (b)   5. (b)   6. (a)

Passage – 7

   1. (b)   2. (c)   3. (d)

Passage – 8

   1. (b)   2. (d)   3. (b)   4. (c)   5. (d)

Passage – 9

   1. (a)   2. (c)   3. (d)   4. (d)

Passage – 10

   1. (c)   2. (b)   3. (a)   4. (c)

Passage – 11

   1. (d)   2. (c)   3. (d)   4. (c)

Passage – 12

   1. (d)   2. (a)   3. (b)   4. (b)   5. (d)

Passage – 13

   1. (a)   2. (b)   3. (d)   4. (d)   5. (d)

Passage – 14

   1. (d)   2. (b)   3. (a)

Passage – 15

   1. (d)   2. (b)   3. (c)   4. (c)

Passage – 16

   1. (d)   2. (c)   3. (d)   4. (d)

Passage – 17

   1. (b)   2. (a)   3. (d)   4. (c)   5. (d)

Passage – 18

   1. (d)   2. (a)

Passage – 19

   1. (c)   2. (c)   3. (a)   4. (d)

Passage – 20

   1. (c)   2. (d)   3. (b)

Solutions

Passage – 1

1. a   Refer to the line "Born on March 12, 1922 ......
typically all American childhood", given in second
paragraph of the passage. Hence, option (a) is
the correct answer.

2. c   Refer to the line "Kerouac first landed in the San....
on a merchant marine ship", given in the third
paragraph of the passage. Hence, option (c) is
the correct answer.

3. b   Refer to the line "Kerouac first landed in the San
Francisco Bay area...he soon met his kindred
spirit, Neal Cassady", given in the third paragraph.
Thus, option (b) is the correct answer.

4. d   The passage clearly states that *On the Road* was
written as a personal testament which means
autobiography. Hence, option (d) is the correct
answer.

5. d   Refer to lines "He split from the ranks of his ....
America's was effort in Vietnam.", "Born on March
12, 1922, in Lowell, Massachusetts ...... typically
all American childhood" and "Before becoming the
father ...... Lower East and Lower West sides"
given in paragraphs 5, 2 and 3 respectively. Hence,
option (d) is the correct choice.

6. a   The most suitable title for the passage is Post-war
Literature and a New Beginning.

Passage – 2

1. d   The whole passage resolves around Rock and roll
music and how it came into existence. Hence,
option (d) is the correct answer.

2. c   Refer to the line "African-American performers like
..... and blues, and jazz", given in the first
paragraph of the passage. All the musicians except
Elvis Presley have been stated as African -
American performers. Hence, option (c) is the
correct choice.

3. d   The first paragraph states that true rock-and-rock
is a combination of various elements from country,
western, gospel, rhythm and blues and jazz. So,
option (d) is the correct answer.

4. a   The first line clearly states that rock-and-roll was
invented in the United States in the 1950s.

5. c   The third paragraph states that many performers
copied songs from original artists.

6. b   All the options, correct (b) can be inferred from the
passage. Hence, option (b) is the correct answer.

Passage – 3

1. c   The passage mostly talks about the monotremes's
relation with both reptiles and mammals (refer to
the first three paragraphs). Hence, option (c) is
the correct answer.

2. c   The first paragraph clearly states that monotremes,
like other mammals, have hair, large brains and
mammary glands. Hence, option (c) is the correct
answer.

3. c   Refer to lines "They share some qualities ....
produce milk to nourish their offspring" given in
paragraph 1 of the passage. Hence, option (c) in
the correct choice.

4. a   The third paragraph states that monotreme babies
are born in early stage of development and depend
upon their parents. Hence, option (a) is the correct
answer.

5. d   The fourth passage states that the duck-billed
platypus is one of the three types of monotremes
in existence. Hence, option (d) is the correct
answer.

6. a   Refer to line "The female echidna lays one egg at a
time into a pouch that she develops in her abdomen",
given in fourth paragraph of the passage. Hence, option
(a) is the correct choice.

Passage – 4

1. a   The first paragraph clearly states that millions of
asteroids are the size of boulders. Hence option
(a) is the correct answer.

2. c   Refer to the line "An asteroid that hits .... a
bright flash of light" given in the first paragraph of
the passage. Hence, option (c) is the correct
answer.

3. a   Refer to the line - "smaller meteors such as the
one that caused the Metro's Crater in Arizona..."
Thus, option (a) is the correct answer.

4. b   The second paragraph states that there has not
been any historical record of a person being killed
by a meteorite. The only reported injury occurred
to an Alabama based woman. So, option (b) is the
correct answer.

Passage – 5

1. c   The passage states that within few weeks of the
movies release, a surprisingly similar incident
occurred at Three Mile Island. So we can say that
the nuclear accident in the movie was a
foreshadowing of actual events.

2. c   The second paragraph states that nuclear power
industry leaders have showed reluctance in
cooperating with the investigators of the accident.

3. d   Refer to lines "Perhaps we will .... the facts
remain unknown", given in the second paragraph
of the passage. Hence, option (d) is the correct
answer.

4. b Refer to the line "We do know that, despite .... the facts remain unknown", given in the second paragraph of the passage. Hence, option (b) is the correct answer.

5. d The passage clearly states that a real life nuclear power based accident occurred within few weeks of the movie's release. Hence, option (d) is not true as per the passage.

Passage – 6

1. d The second paragraph states that Aristole grew overnight trying to rescue and save what was left of his family. Hence, option (d) is the correct answer.

2. a Refer to the line "Not the least in horror .... being useful to the Turks", given in the first paragraph of the passage. Hence, option (b) is the correct answer.

3. d 'Catechism' in Roman Catholic use means a summary of religious instruction or doctrine. Hence, option (d) is the correct answer.

4. b The passage clearly states that Socrates Onassis was in a Turkish prison for trial as a political offender. Hence, option (b) is the correct answer.

5. b The first paragraph states that the Turks were taking horrible revenge for the Greek atrocities on Turkish population. Hence, option (b) is the correct answer.

6. a The third paragraph states that in order to save his father, Aristole needed a great deal of money. Hence, option (a) is the correct answer.

Passage – 7

1. b The sixth paragraph states that while sitting at the airport and waiting for his flight, the author observes a five year old child and his grandfather and wonders how someone would capture the moment share between them.

2. c Refer to the lines "A grandmother and grandson ... to help the grandmother", given in the third paragraph of the passage. Hence, option (c) is the correct choice.

3. d Refer to the line "I am sitting at an airport ... emotion is intense", given in the first paragraph of the passage. This aspect is also mentioned intermittently in other segments of the passage. Hence, option (d) is the correct answer.

Passage – 8

1. b The central idea of the passage is especially evident from the lines "The lesson Mathew's father ... short-term decisions about them", given in the third paragraph of the passage. It is quite clear that the central idea of the passage pertains to 'Good Parenting'. Hence, option (b) is the correct answer.

2. d Refer to the line "His teacher, Rebecca Sacra wondered how such a bright boy could be so irresponsible", given in the first paragraph of the passage. Hence, option (d) is the correct answer.

3. b Refer to the line "She braced herself, though ... or when he broke bounds", given in the second paragraph of the passage. Hence, option (b) is the correct answer.

4. c Refer to the line "You wouldn't really flunk ... wasn't late ever again" given in the third paragraph of the passage. This shows only one possibility, that Mathew feared being reprimanded and thus, started turning up on time. Hence, option (c) is the correct answer.

5. d Refer to the line "What Mathew's dad dreaded ... responsibility for his own actions", given in the second paragraph of the passage. Hence, option (d) is the correct answer.

Passage – 9

1. a Refer to the line "That apart Mrs. Gandhi spoke as a national leader not as a congress leader", given in the first paragraph of the passage. Hence, option (a) is the correct answer.

2. c The second passage states that Mrs. Gandhi's statement on recent developments in Sri Lanka reflected a deterioration in India's international position. Thus, option (c) is the correct answer.

3. d Refer to lines "While the situation in Punjab...as befits a person in her position", given in the second paragraph of the passage. Hence option (d) is the correct answer.

4. d The passage gives instances where Mrs. Gandhi exercised tact and sensitivity in dealing with individuals and issues. She never attacked the opposition or press and spoke on the Punjab and Sri Lankan issues with great care. Hence, she can rightfully be labelled a diplomatic politician.

Passage – 10

1. c Throughout the passage, the author states instances which show how international sports lead to orgies of hatred. When played at international scales, they mimic warfare and arouse strong feelings of rivalry. Hence, option (c) is the correct answer.

2. b Refer to the second paragraph line 4 - "as soon as the question of prestige arises...the most savage instincts are aroused". Hence, option (b) is the correct answer.

3. a The passage states that nations seriously believe that running, jumping and kicking a ball are a test of national virtue. Thus, option (a) is the correct answer.

4. c In the third paragraph, the author states that women are kept out of the boxing matches held in the army due to their behavior. Hence, option (c) is the correct answer.

Passage – 11

1. d Option (d) the correct answer. The other options strike themselves out as the passage does not deal with Rutherford's efforts or refute the existence of a particle, neither does it illustrate the method of measurement or analyse any one theory.

2. c The size of the nucleus (centre) of an atom, though smaller than the molecule of which it is a part, has not been discussed with relation to the molecule itself, i.e. if it is smaller or larger than the molecule. Hence, option (c) is the correct answer.

3. d The author wishes to impress upon the reader the 'minuteness' of the size of an atom.

4. c Just as the electrons revolve around a proton, satellites revolve around their planet. Hence, option (c) is the correct answer.

Passage – 12

1. d Refer to lines "That some fossil reptiles (ichthyosaurs) and ...... are fish like in form, given in the second paragraph of the passage. Hence, option (d) in the correct choice.

2. a The first paragraph states that adaptive convergence and divergence are part of the process of evolution. Hence option (a) is the correct answer.

3. b The passage starts with the line "As we have seen adaptive divergence..." This shows that the preceeding passage dealt with divergence.

4. b The author is trying to provide explanations with suitable examples to illustrate the theories of adaptive divergence of convergence. Hence, option (b) is the correct answer.

5. d The last few lines state that whales and dolphins adopt fishlike forms to suit special environments. Such organisms are called 'homeomorphs'.

Passage – 13

1. a Throughout the passage, the author discusses how African sculptors achieve the effects they desire. He talks of how they practice discipline and have thorough knowledge of their craft. Hence, option (a) is the correct answer.

2. b The third passage talks solely about the emotional experience of some African sculptures and how emotions are expressed by them. So option (b) is the answer.

3. d Refer to the line "It is quite common ... powerful sense of communication", given in the second paragraph of the passage. Hence, option (d) is the correct answer.

4. d At the time of the performance the Pianist does not refer to any rulebook but there are certain unwritten rules that are followed by him. Similarly, an African artist does the carving as a "second nature". Hence, option (d) is the correct choice.

5. d The passage concerns itself with the plastic language or unconscious rules governing African art and thus, option (d) is most suitable.

Passage – 14

1. d From the beginning lines of the passage one can easily infer that the primary purpose of the passage is to describe the techniques, modes and methods employed by the money changers to take advantage of their customers.

2. b Refer to the line - "these rascals really also reduce it... they are blissfully unaware." Thus, we can say that option (b) is correct.

3. a The money changers are able to cheat the Tartars only because they are aware that Tartars are incapable of detecting the miscalculations of these money changers. Hence, option (a) is the correct answer.

Passage – 15

1. d The primary purpose of this passage is to focus on the species of mice or rodents that exhibit or undergo brief periods of dormancy. Hence, option (d) is the answer.

2. b Refer to the line – "these rascals also it...they are blissfully unaware." These, we can say that option (b) is correct.

3. c The fact that the passage begins with the line "There exist a few species of mice ..." and then goes on to describe the species which display the tendency to remain torpid for certain periods, is in itself indicative that it may be an excerpt from a book on rodent biology.

4. c The passage starts by saying that there are some species which are neither the hibernating kind nor the aestivating kind, which are both periods during which the mice remain dormant hence we may assume that the previous paragraph dealt with the other types of dormant states.

Passage – 16

1. d Options (a) and (c) automatically disqualify themselves as there is no mention of violence or animal instincts in the passage. Option (b) sounds vague as we are not dealing with the evolution of man but rather the evolution of social order and orderly state. Hence, option (d) is the correct answer.

2. c   Options (b) and (d) are disqualified as they have no bearing to the passage. Option (a) deals with the evolution of man and deals with only the first paragraph of the passage. Option (c) has been clearly stated in the third paragraph.

3. d   Option (d) is most suitable as it concerns itself with the essence of the passage, i.e. social order.

4. d   The environment in the passage is, in totality, everything which is present in the natural habitat of a man and effects his behaviour be it in the city or in the wild.

Passage – 17

1. b   Towards the end of the passage it is clearly mentioned that with exception to accidents, the other diseases are more prone to advanced years or old age.

2. a   Options (b), (c) and (d) can all be clearly deduced from the passage which leaves only option (a) which has not been indicated at all.

3. d   As per the passage, during the decade after 1900s (upto 1910 or so) there were 5 main diseases which merely changed in order of importance. However, towards the latter part of the period from 1900 to 1950, the list of main diseases underwent profound change. Hence, option (d) is the correct answer.

4. c   The last few lines of the passage state that diseases that lead to death were predominant amongst elderly people (during the latter part of 1900 - 1950). Thus we can say longevity increased during this period.

5. d   Option (d) is a suitable title because the author wishes to depict the changing trend in the order and importance of various diseases as the leading causes of death.

Passage – 18

1. d   This passage is mainly concerned with how, as time progressed and generations changed, Miss Charlotte's relationship with the town changed.

2. a   The passage clearly states that General Braxton's contemporaries send their daughters to Miss Charlotte to learn China-painting.

Passage – 19

1. c   The passage states that male Lucanus engage in a battle over the possession of a female and are comparatively larger than the females. Hence, option (c) is the correct answer. The word 'belligerence' means warlike attitude.

2. c   The other options do not in any way fit as a beetle is an insect. Also stags have antlers (horns), which are probably similar to the appendages of these animals.

3. a   The opening line states that "As we have seen, *generally* the male insects are smaller than female insects..." The leads us to believe that the preceding paragraph discussed a generalization about insect size. Thus, option (a) is the correct answer.

4. d   The other options are not suitable as (a) and (b) are too vague and (c) concentrates only on the stag beetles. Thus, the correct option is (d).

Passage – 20

1. c   The author has stated that the similarity between the coastlines and certain geological features that span across the ocean are proof that South America and Africa were once joined.

2. d   Towards the end of the passage it has been explained by the author as to how the continental plates may rupture along the fissures created by hot spots and thus result in major changes in the shape of the continents.

3. b   The author has clearly stated in the passage that the theory of plate movement is way past any form of dispute hence irrefutable.

Paragraph Jumbles and Sentence Jumbles

Parajumbles are an important part of most competitive exams. In most entrance examinations three basic types of parajumbles can be seen:

- 4 sentence type
- 5 sentence type
- 6 sentence type : Usually when there are sixth sentences given, the first sentence and the sixth sentence are given in the correct position i.e. the start and the end and the four sentences between these are jumbled up.

To begin with we will look at the 4 sentence type questions. The other types will be discussed by way of exercises.

Parajumbles are not necessarily a test of your language skills. The good thing about parajumbles is that even if you are otherwise weak in English, that is if you find RC, vocabulary or grammar a challenge, you can still score extremely well in parajumbles. This is because you need to be as mechanical as possible in your approach.

Most people lose focus by reading the statements given in the parajumble over and over again. Sometimes, it is next to impossible to make out which sentence follows which one and all the options look equally correct. The greatest mistake is to try and read the parajumble in the sequence given in each option. Solving all options completely will only confuse you and waste a lot of time. An inexperienced person is bound to make the above mentioned mistakes and these questions are designed to catch such a person unaware.

The best way to solve a parajumble is to try and identify **mandatory pairs**. A mandatory pair is a sequence that you know cannot exist in any other order. There are many types of mandatory pairs. But there is only one basic tool to identify mandatory pairs – read mechanically and look only for keywords that will help you form a sequence or connection.

1. Names, proper nouns and pronouns:

Sometimes we can identify mandatory pairs or a longer sequence by the help of the names, proper nouns and pronouns used.

For instance:

A. **Both** were very angry.
B. **Singh** accused **Jogi** of corruption.
C. **Raman Singh** ordered an enquiry against his predecessor **Ajit Jogi**.

It is clear from the above example that statement C, which has the full form of both names, should precede the other two statements. Statement B uses only the second names of the concerned people. And statement A substitutes the names with the pronoun "both". Thus, A should follow B, and B should follow C. Therefore, the correct order is CBA.

2. Cause-effect:

There are instances where a clear cause-effect relationship can be identified. Such a relationship may exist in the form of a mandatory pair or may run through the entire parajumble.

For example:

A. While **Sachin** is a great batsman, **Kambli's** name is often associated with scams.
B. **Sachin Tendulkar** and **Vinod Kambli** are good friends.
C. **As a result**, their relationship has become strained.

Here it is easy to see that the use of "as a result" in statement C, establishes a cause and effect relationship. The correct sequence therefore, is BAC.

3. Chronology:

At times you can see a logical chain of events in the parajumble. It could also be in the form of a set of instructions to be followed in a certain order. If you look for keywords associated with the sequence, you can easily figure out the right order.

For instance:

A. In order to take full advantage of the ongoing city sale you must possess a good credit card.

B. It would **also** be nice to have friends to accompany you.

C. **Secondly**, you should have a vehicle of your own.

As you can see in the above example, statement C follows statement A. A gives the first and C gives the second condition. The use of "also" in B tells you that it should follow C. Therefore, ACB is the correct order.

4. Time reference

Some questions have a statement that refers to a point in time. The reference maybe in the past, present or future. Accordingly, you can decide its place in the sequence.

For example:

A. In the **future** perhaps, we may live on Mars.

B. During the **Stone Age**, man lived in caves.

C. **Presently**, man lives in concrete jungles.

The use of "Stone Age" in statement B, "presently" in C and "future" in A make it easy for us to identify the sequence. The past will always come first, followed by the present and then the future. The correct sequence then is, BCA..

5. Obvious openers

You may sometimes come across statements that are obvious openers, i.e. it is obvious that the parajumble will begin with those statements. These statements can be definitions, universal truths or philosophical statements.

For instance:

A. **Stratosphere** is one of the layers of the atmosphere.

B. **It** is the upper portion of the atmosphere, a nearly isothermal layer (layer of constant temperature) that is located above the troposphere.

C. **It extends** from its lower boundary of about 6 to 17 km (4 to 11 miles) altitude to its upper boundary (the stratopause) at about 50 km (30 miles).

It is clear to see that "it" in B and C refers to the "stratosphere" in statement. A. Statement A is thus an obvious opener and the correct order is ABC.

6. Obvious conclusions

Sometimes, you can easily figure out the conclusion in the parajumble. The conclusion helps to eliminate choices or to identify a mandatory pair.

For example:

A. On the mantelpiece were two clocks, some dogs, brass candlesticks and a tinted photograph of Annie.

B. You looked at the weed-grown vegetable garden through a stuffed fox's legs, over a partridge's head, along the red-paint-stained breast of a stiff wild duck.

C. **The best room** smelt of moth-balls and fur and damp and dead plants and stale, sour air. Two glass cases on wooden coffin-boxes lined the window wall.

D. **It was obvious that the room was rarely used.**

You can see that C introduces the room, A and B further describe it and D concludes the paragraph.

7. Keywords

Words like — so, therefore, however, hence, thus, moreover, but, because, nevertheless, yet, etc. — also help identify mandatory pairs.

For instance:

A. **Yet**, the cable guys control two-thirds of the market.

B. **Telephone firms** are now **cutting down their prices** to compete and grab their share of the internet market.

C. **Cable** net connections are **expensive**.

D. This is **because** there is a growing **demand for high speed** internet access.

It is clear from the above example that CA is a mandatory pair. C puts across a point that cable net connections are expensive. The use of "yet" in A, shows that despite being expensive, they hold a major share in the market. The use of "because" in D gives a reason for this phenomenon. Thus, C, A and D are connected to each other in that order. Statement B gives the effect of the phenomenon on the telephone firms. Hence, CADB is the correct sequence.

8. General to specific

Sometimes one gets confused about whether to move from general to specific or from specific to general.

For instance:

A. He made an interesting comment about our store's price policy.

B. He said that we could offer discounts and incentives to encourage people to buy in fewer quantities but to buy more frequently.

C. Discounts could vary from 10 to 15 per cent on every purchase.

D. The lesser the quantity, the more frequently customers will have to visit the store. The more frequent the visits, the more incentives they can earn.

In this case the confusion could be between BCD and BDC. Here, we will move from general to specific. C is a specific example for D and not vice versa. Therefore, the correct sequence is ABDC.

In order to master parajumbles it is important to get under their skin. Let's slowly build up on the concept of 'parajumbles'. Go through the following **solved examples** and follow the instructions given.

1.   Questions can become easy to solve if you pay more attention to only the first few words of every statement.

For instance:

A.   **Although, like the Talapadas, the Pardeshis also claim to be Rajputs** and Kshatriyas, most of them have not yet adopted traditional Rajput names for their lineages.

B.   **Only recently a few lineages** have begun to patronize the Vahivancha Barots, who have recorded their remembered shallow genealogies and grafted them on to mythical genealogies.

C.   **Each Pardeshi lineage** is known after its village of origin.

D.   **The latter provide them with Rajput clan names**, but they rarely use them in normal life.

In the above case, by reading only the highlighted words, you can clearly see a relationship between AC. A talks about Pardeshis and C continues as it starts with 'Each Pardeshi lineage..' Thus, only by reading the first few words of every statement you can establish at least one mandatory pair and usually eliminate at least 2 choices.

2.   Let's now learn to associate keywords and ideas and form sequences. Look at the following examples:

A.   Many **Western observers**, and under their influence many **Indian scholars** and **social critics** also, **have written** that India was almost completely a stagnant country, without true history, till she came into life-giving contact with Western civilisation in the eighteenth century.

B.   The so-called **joint family is one such notable institution.**

C.   There is a well-established **viewpoint** which alleges that **Hindu social institutions** have had a **blighting effect** on India's social and economic **development**.

D.   **They contend** that the economy and society in this country, and indeed the Indian mind, had remained frozen for about two thousand years till the British conquest of India introduced a vital element of dynamism into the 'native' society.

In the above example it can be seen clearly that CB is a mandatory pair. C talks of the blighting effect Hindu social institutions have had on the Indian economy and society;

and B continues by saying that the joint family is one such institution. The 'they' in D, refers to the observers, scholars and critics in A. Therefore AD is also a mandatory pair. Thus, the correct sequence is CBAD.

3.   Now let's learn to build up from small sequences to bigger ones.

I.   **A.** **Such is the difficulty** a carp faces in becoming a dragon.

      B. **Some are swept away** by the by the strong currents, **some fall prey** to eagles, hawks, kites and owls, and others are netted, scooped up or even **shot with arrows** by fishermen who line both banks of the falls.

      In the above case, B describes the different difficulties and A obviously sums up the explanation as it starts with 'such is the difficulty'. BA is then the mandatory sequence.

II.   **A.** Minamoto and Taira were like **two faithful watchdogs** at the gates of the imperial palace.

      B. They marvelled at the elegant parties of the court nobles and their ladies, just as monkeys in the trees are enraptured by the sight of the moon and the stars glittering in the sky.

      C. **They were eager to guard** the emperor as humble mountain folk are to admire the full moon on the fifteenth night of the eighth month as it rises from behind the mountains.

      Here, the 'they' in C clearly refers to the 'two faithful watchdogs' in A. Therefore AC is a mandatory pair. The correct sequence is ACB.

III.   **A.** The most **important ones** are the **family** and the **school**.

      B. Much of the **anger** that is publicly expressed **against the hierarchy of caste**—in the newspapers, on television, in conferences—is purposeless if not insincere.

      C. **Those** who are **serious about** carrying the **advance of equality** further, particularly in the domain that I have discussed, must **direct** their **attention to** the **institutions** that are the **real obstacles** in the path of that advance.

      D. **Equality**, at least at the higher levels of society, can no longer be significantly advanced by **attacking caste**.

      In the above case D introduces the fact that equality can no longer be established by attacking caste. B continues the point about anger against hierarchy of caste. The mandatory pair is DB and not BD because D is more general than B. C then goes on to identify the real obstacles and A names the most important ones. CA is therefore another mandatory sequence. Thus the correct sequence is DBCA.

IV. (i) The mighty warrior **General Li Kuang**, whose mother had been devoured by a tiger, **shot an arrow at the stone** he believed was the tiger.

A. Later **he** came to be **known** as **General Stone Tiger**.

B. But once **he realized it was only a stone**, he was **unable to pierce it again**.

C. The **arrow penetrated the stone** all the way up to its feathers.

D. **This story applies to you**. Though enemies lurk in the wait for you, your resolute faith has forestalled great dangers before they could begin.

(ii) **Realizing this, you** must strengthen your faith more than ever.

I clearly introduces a story and A sums up that story. C and B figure in between. D talks about the relevance of the story and finds continuation in II. The correct sequence then is I-CBAD-II.

V. A. **She had cherished hope-filed visions of America** as a land of freedom and democracy.

B. **Also, being a foreigner**, she could not make herself understood well in English, and they treated her coldly. At the same time, her husband had become physically abusive, and a rift had grown between them.

C. **Sadly**, however, **this woman's dream had been shattered**. Life with her in-laws was by no means easy financially.

D. **She was not alone**; many people in those days turned their eyes admiringly to **America**, imagining it as some sort of **dream land**.

E. **Her sense of regret grew** with each passing day. As her feelings of isolation and despair deepened, she would often stand crying on the beach, watching the crimson sun set into the sea beyond the horizon.

F. **The tears that streamed down her cheeks** flooded her already wounded heart with an aching, empty coldness, thus intensifying her sorrow.

A is an obvious opener. It talks about her hopes and dreams about America. D continues the point and talks further about other women who had dreamt of America. C then mentions that her dreams were sadly shattered. B adds more points about how her dreams were shattered. E talks about her sense of regret and F starts by talking of her consequent tears and sorrow. The correct sequence therefore is ADCBEF.

In para jumbles, you must read fast to link the end of a sentence to the beginning of another. Do not read all the sentences to form a link.

Let's take an example to understand this.

A. Miss Brazil walked like a panther.

B. The Japanese are very punctual. If you are late, they simply leave without you.

C. We were informed that rehearsals would be in an hour's time. In Japan, 8 a.m. means 8 a.m. and not 8.01 a.m.

D. I arrived at the hotel lobby and the guide introduced me to the other contestants. They were amazingly lithe and graceful.

(a) DACB

(b) CDAB

(c) BADC

(d) ABCD

Here we read it from the beginning, it is unlikely that the paragraph will start with A, a catwalk. Maybe it starts with B, we don't know. It's unlikely that it will start with C as 'we' is not defined in a preceding sentence. D could be a beginner as it talks about an arrival.

There is an option to begin with D — (a). It goes as DA. Does it fit? Yes, 'lithe and graceful . . . panther'. This will do! We can wind up immediately, but let's fit all the sentences together. DA — then? 'We were' will follow, with 'we' implying all the beauty contestants. And the last sentence of the paragraph is, of course, B, as '8 and not 8.01 . . . very punctual'.

Now that you know the real tricks needed to crack parajumbles, attempt exercises on your own.

Exercise

4-Sentence Type Paragraph Jumbles

Exercise – 1

Directions for questions 1 to 15: Arrange the letters A, B, C and D to make a sensible and coherent paragraph.

1.   A.   She was French, dressed exquisitely, spoke five languages and to my mind was astonishingly sophisticated.

   B.   As a 21-year-old journalist in Mexico, I met a most fascinating woman.

   C.   Christian Amanpour became my guide, my teacher, my inspiration for everything to do with journalism.

   D.   She was a journalist and had logged in over 20 years covering guerrilla warfare, the Tiananmen Square massacre, and various military conflicts around the world.

   (a) DBCA   (b) CDAB

   (c) BADC   (d) ABCD

2.   A.   So Ramkrishna Movement is not the history of a particular person or persons.

   B.   Despite completing a 100 years, the movement has still a youthful image, a contemporaneous trend.

   C.   Further ahead is a long road to traverse 'at least 15 more centuries' as prophesied by Swami Vivekananda before it can rest on its laurels.

   D.   The pageant of Ramkrishna Movement reflects not only the modes and manners of contemporary times but also a saga of a bygone era.

   (a) DBCA   (b) CBDA

   (c) BCAD   (d) DACB

3.   A.   The liver is your body's very own powerhouse.

   B.   It provides your entire body with energy to function normally.

   C.   The single biggest cause for liver damage is alcohol.

   D.   Therefore, any damage to the liver can short-circuit your body functions.

   (a) ABCD   (b) BCDA

   (c) CABD   (d) DACB

4.   A.   Especially when we feel there's a gap between how we are spending our time and what we feel is deeply important in our lives.

   B.   We're also living with the consequences of those choices.

   C.   We're constantly making choices about the way we spend our time from the major seasons to the individual moments in our lives.

   D.   And many of us don't like those consequences.

   (a) DABC   (b) ACDB

   (c) CBDA   (d) BDCA

5.   A.   Just three decades ago, there were fewer than a dozen significant books on the subject.

   B.   It reflects something of a 'popcorn phenomenon' with increasing heat and pressure of the culture creating a rapidly exploding body of literature and tools.

   C.   Our most recent survey led us through well over a hundred books, and a wide variety of calendar, planners, software and other time management tools.

   D.   In our effort to close the gap between the clock and the compass in our lives, many of us turn to the field of 'time management'.

   (a) ABCD   (b) BACD

   (c) CADB   (d) DACB

6.   A.   The mess that you've created is entirely your own doing.

   B.   And I don't blame the media or Nagma or anyone else other than you for that.

   C.   Because I don't think that there's much left about your personal life that's still a secret.

   D.   Why an open letter?

   (a) CADB   (b) DCBA

   (c) ACBD   (d) BACD

7.   A.   If these basic needs aren't met, we feel empty, incomplete.

   B.   We may try to fill the void through urgency addiction.

   C.   As a result, we may become complacent, temporarily satisfied with partial fulfilment.

   D.   There are certain things that are fundamental to human fulfilment.

   (a) DABC   (b) BCAD

   (c) CADB   (d) BDAC

8.   A.   Farmers are suddenly hot politically. So hot that our current Parliament session began with Sonia Gandhi and Mulayam Singh Yadav fighting over who should speak first for India's farmers.

   B.   Yadav claimed first right on grounds of his peasant origins but if he had anything more worthwhile to say than Sonia nobody knows.

C. It was the polemics that became the floor show.

D. And if this was not cabaret enough, we then had Parliament's most famous windbag, Renuka Chowdhury, driving to Parliament House on a tractor and effectively trivializing the issue.

(a) DABC   (b) ABCD

(c) BDCA   (d) CDBA

9. A. In some situations it may be desirable to divest the business before decline, or in the maturity phase.

B. Once decline is clear, buyers for the assets inside and outside the industry will be in a stronger bargaining position.

C. Selling the business early usually maximizes the value of the firm that can be realized from the sale of the business because, the earlier the business is sold the greater is the uncertainty.

D. On the other hand, selling early also entails the risk that the firm forecast of the future will prove incorrect.

(a) CABD   (b) ADBC

(c) BCDA   (d) DBAC

10. A. He hounded his former wife until she gave back $6,000 in cash he had given her as a wedding gift, then gave $4,000 of it to Li.

B. Now seven years later, the tables are turned.

C. "What are your conditions?" was the first thing he asked her.

D. She demanded a small house, money and jewellery.

(a) DABC   (b) CBAD

(c) ABCD   (d) CDAB

11. A. They are active, hard-working, competent, caring people dedicated to making a difference.

B. The fact that you picked up these sentences indicates that you can probably identify with what they're feeling.

C. Yet these people consistently tell us of the tremendous struggles they face daily while trying to put first things first in their lives.

D. Through our work at the Leadership centre, we've come in contact with many people from around the world, and we're constantly impressed by what they represent.

(a) DACB   (b) ADCB

(c) ABCD   (d) BDAC

12. A. Thus, we're not in control of our lives: PRINCIPLES are.

B. Universal laws or Principles do.

C. Basing our happiness on our ability to control everything is futile.

D. While we do control our choice of action, we cannot control the consequence of our choices.

(a) ADCB   (b) CDBA

(c) ACBD   (d) DBAC

13. A. There is no shortcut in life but there is a path.

B. The path is based on principles reversed throughout history.

C. If there is one message to glean, it is that a meaningful life is not a matter of speed or efficiency.

D. It's much more a matter of what you do and why you do it, than how fast you get it done.

(a) ABCD   (b) BCDA

(c) CDBA   (d) DBAC

14. A. All states except Maharashtra were in favour of the move.

B. When the matter came up at the meeting, the representative of Maharashtra vehemently opposed it, saying it would not be in the interest of students and people.

C. Evening law colleges all over the nation will be closed within six months, as per a decision taken by the Bar Council of India.

D. He argued that it would not be possible for working students to attend day colleges.

(a) CBDA   (b) CABD

(c) CDBA   (d) CADB

15. A. To at least the dozen authors who have been shortlisted, six in each category, that's probably exciting news.

B. In the same week, Jet Bookstores owner was interviewed for a TV show.

C. Last week, Ace Bookstore announced their 2nd Annual Function Award.

D. This time, they've upped the prize money from Rs. 2 lakh to Rs. 3 lakh.

(a) DACB

(b) CDAB

(c) DCAB

(d) CBDA

Exercise – 2

Directions for questions 1 to 15: Arrange the letters A, B, C and D to make a sensible and coherent paragraph.

1. A. The MTNL in a circular had made it mandatory for all operators to charge only Re 1 for every local call made to Mumbai.
   B. New Bombay residents are being forced to pay an extra rupee from every call made to Mumbai from local telephone booths despite orders to the contrary issued by MTNL.
   C. It had also warned that failure to comply would entail legal action.
   D. "We have in fact sent notices to around 100 call operators," said a senior officer of MTNL's vigilance section.

   (a) BDCA   (b) BCDA
   (c) ABDC   (d) BACD

2. A. He was accosted by a down-and-out fan, who appealed for assistance one day.
   B. Lester seemed not to hear, and continued on his way.
   C. "Please," said the old man feebly, "just a couple of pounds for a life-long fan."
   D. The brilliant jockey Lester PIggott was known to put his hardness of hearing to good effect.

   (a) DCBA   (b) DACB
   (c) DBAC   (d) CBAD

3. A. Helpful advice is given on matching the right speech and structuring, timing and delivering.
   B. For most of us, speech-making is an event to be dreaded.
   C. Also included are speeches for the sportsman, the sales force and special occasions.
   D. This book is designed to prevent those embarrassing nerves and blushes, providing all the essentials for a successful comic speech.

   (a) DBAC   (b) BDCA
   (c) BDAC   (d) DBCA

4. A. And if they're going to remember a single thing you said, it's likely to be the final line so make sure that it's worth remembering.
   B. Sir Thomas Beecham once said of his orchestra that the important thing was to 'begin and end together, what happens in-between doesn't matter very much'.
   C. If you can capture the attention of the audience with your first line, you're likely to have their attention for the rest of the speech.
   D. Pretty much the same can be said of making a comic speech.

   (a) BDCA   (b) CBAD
   (c) ABDC   (d) BCDA

5. A. As baseball's all-time home run king, he played 23 years as an outfielder for the Milwaukee Braves.
   B. After retiring as a player, he moved into the Atlanta Braves front office as executive vice president.
   C. Aaron Hank was a baseball player and executive born in Alabama.
   D. He holds many of baseball's most distinguished records.

   (a) CBDA   (b) CADB
   (c) CDBA   (d) CABD

6. A. But the real story behind the filming of *The Beach* looks like concluding in ecological disaster and court cases.
   B. Witnesses say it is now a 'forlorn scene of ugly bamboo fences and dead native plants'.
   C. It was the ultimate Hollywood dream, the most handsome man in the world on the most idyllic beach in the Orient.
   D. The location of the film *The Beach* has repeatedly been wrecked after several months of filming.

   (a) DCAB   (b) DBAC
   (c) CADB   (d) CABD

7. A. K. Gilt has given investors an annualised return of 10.58%.
   B. But we're not resting on our laurels.
   C. Nine months ago, we launched our first two schemes K. Gilt and K 30.
   D. And K 30, the equity scheme, has yielded an absolute return of 102.20%.

   (a) CDAB   (b) ABCD
   (c) CABD   (d) CADB

8. A. Interested candidates should send their detailed bio datas to the following address within seven days.
   B. Axel, the readymade garment division of Silky Silk Mills Ltd., is a leading player in the fashion industry.
   C. Marketing executive — whose job will include interacting with corporate clients and procuring orders.
   D. In our march towards the future, we are looking for a dynamic person for the following position.

   (a) BDCA   (b) BCDA
   (c) BADC   (d) DBAC

9. A. Bill Austin belongs to a profession as rare as those objects he delicately deals with, clocks.
    B. The world of a collector is romantic, rarefied, revolving around priceless antiques.
    C. His life could fill a book with enough more for many a sequel.
    D. It is always a pleasure meeting Austin.
    (a) BADC   (b) BCDA
    (c) DBAC   (d) ABCD

10. A. This enables member countries to work together in an atmosphere of greater trust and understanding than generally prevails among nations.
    B. It is also a 'family' of nations, originally linked together in the British Empire.
    C. It now concentrates on building the common heritage in language, culture, law and education.
    D. The Commonwealth is an association of governments set up so that member countries can support each other.
    (a) DBCA   (b) DBAC
    (c) DABC   (d) ABCD

11. A. There is a danger of a bomb wiping out a whole continent.
    B. The threat from the Taliban is great.
    C. India must start a world campaign against terrorism.
    D. Hence, disarmament is a must.
    (a) CBDA   (b) ABCD
    (c) CDAB   (d) CBAD

12. A. These delays will only worsen unless remedial measures are soon adopted.
    B. Legal delays have become a topic of routine discussion.
    C. But no one has taken concrete steps to tackle them.
    D. Although the Chief Justice of India has repeatedly urged the government to appoint more judges, there has been no response.
    (a) ABCD   (b) BCDA
    (c) DCBA   (d) CBDA

13. A. It also empowers us to visualize ourselves living our mission statement even in the most challenging circumstances, and to apply principles in effective ways in new situations.
    B. It's the endowment that enables us to see ourselves and others differently and better than we are now.
    C. It enables us to write a personal mission statement, set a goal, or plan a meeting.
    D. Creative imagination is the power to envision a future state, to create something in our mind, and to solve problems synergistically.
    (a) DACB   (b) BCDA
    (c) DBCA   (d) ADBC

14. A. We may be alone or we may choose to be with friends or family.
    B. But our most significant life is our deep inner life.
    C. We have our private life, where we're away from the public.
    D. In a sense, we each live three lives, we have our public life, where we interact with other people at work, in the community, at social events.
    (a) ADBC   (b) BCDA
    (c) ADCB   (d) DCAB

15. A. Thus, everyone's task is unique as his specific opportunity to implement it.
    B. Everyone has his own specific vocation in life.
    C. Everyone must carry out a concrete assignment that demands fulfilment.
    D. Therein he cannot be replaced, nor can his life be repeated.
    (a) ACDB   (b) BCDA
    (c) ABCD   (d) DCBA

Exercise – 3

Directions for questions 1 to 15: Arrange the letters A, B, C and D to make a sensible and coherent paragraph.

1. A. For this reason, no week's experience would be complete without some kind of evaluation that enables us to process it.
    B. It takes us back to the beginning of the process again, but with greater capacity.
    C. Evaluation is the first and final step in a living and learning cycle that creates an upward spiral of growth.
    D. The value of any week is not limited to what we do in it; it's also in what we learn from it and become as a result of it.
    (a) ABCD
    (b) DACB
    (c) CDAB
    (d) BCDA

2. A. The communist regime in Russia has collapsed, and alongwith it, the communist government in East European nations has also collapsed.
    B. The powerful communist lobby is no more, the tension of cold war has ended.
    C. Yet, tension still exists in many parts of the world.
    D. If these tensions lead to another world war, the whole world would be destroyed.
    (a) ADBC   (b) CBDA
    (c) BCDA   (d) ABCD

3. A. However, within nine years of the defeat of the Sikhs, the English regime was shaken by the widspread revolt of 1857 against the rule of East India Company.
    B. Since then, they resorted to the policy of expansion and eventually established rule almost over the whole of India.
    C. The English defeated the Sikhs in 1848 and apparently they had no opponent.
    D. The victory of the English in the Battle of Plassey in 1757 laid the foundation of the political rule of the English who had come to India for trade.
    (a) ABCD   (b) DBCA
    (c) CBDA   (d) DCBA

4. A. After the British left India, the French started negotiations with the Indian Government.
    B. All French colonies decided to merge with India, putting an end to French rule in India.
    C. It was decided that the decision about territories under the French should be made on the basis of plebiscite.
    D. The French had witnessed the plight of the British imperialism due to the thrust of the Indian National Movement.
    (a) CADB   (b) CDBA
    (c) DACB   (d) DBCA

5. A. The Indian Tricolour replaced the Union Jack.
    B. At midnight of August 14, 1947, that is on August 15, Independence was celebrated throughout India.
    C. Pt. Nehru stepped into the office as the first Prime Minister of Independent India.
    D. Transfer of power and Independence Day celebrations were held in Delhi.
    (a) DBAC   (b) BDAC
    (c) CBAD   (d) ABCD

6. A. Hitler became the dictator of Germany.
    B. In 1934, Hitler assumed the Presidentship of Germany along with Chancellorship.
    C. He abolished the Federal System of Government and established centralized government.
    D. On becoming the Chancellor, Hitler concentrated all power in his hands.
    (a) DBCA   (b) ABCD
    (c) CBDA   (d) DCBA

7. A. The number of the unemployed increased enormously.
    B. Trade suffered, banks collapsed and industries were closed.
    C. The national income of the United States started declining.
    D. In 1929, the United States was hit by economic depression.
    (a) DCBA   (b) BCDA
    (c) ABCD   (d) DCAB

8. A. It became necessary for the industrial nations of Europe to search for markets outside their own countries.
    B. England was the birthplace of the industrial revolution.
    C. Soon after England, industries and factories grew in France and Germany as well.
    D. 19th-century Europe experienced a fast growth of industries.
    (a) BDAC   (b) DBCA
    (c) ABCD   (d) DBAC

9. A. If your tour has been arranged by Rajasthan Tourism Development Corp., you can travel by jeep through a special route.
    B. Ranthambore is best known for its wildlife sanctuary.
    C. Here you can spot tigers and lions.
    D. The other attraction is the Ranthamba Fort, which involves a steep climb.
    (a) ADBC   (b) ABCD
    (c) BCAD   (d) BCDA

10. A. Don't forget that, ever.
    B. Your footwear are being noticed just as much as your smile.
    C. You can go in for a fourth elegant pair, which you can keep at the office.
    D. Ideally, you should have at least three pairs of shoes, one for rigorous daily wear, another for special occasions and a third for sport or leisure activity.

(a) BADC   (b) DCBA

(c) BDCA   (d) DCAB

11.   A. But in the secret war being waged on German morale in the 1940's, it was a deadly serious device.

      B. The reviled rodents have always been a hazard to health, but rarely as lethal a threat as this.

      C. It is hard to imagine Q, the gadgetry mastermind from the James Bond films, producing anything so crude.

      D. The exploding rat, designed to wreak havoc in the enemy workplace, emerged for the first time last week from the dusty files of the public record office at Kier.

(a) CADB   (b) BCDA

(c) CDBA   (d) CBDA

12.   A. Humans hardly look at every move in a position.

      B. If a position contains 30 moves, a human would consider about five or six.

      C. This is a highly efficient method, since it is likely that other moves are inferior.

      D. However, this efficiency comes at a price.

(a) ABCD   (b) BACD

(c) DBAC   (d) ACDB

13.   A. Personally I am very fond of strawberries and cream, but I have found that for some strange reason, fish prefer worms.

      B. I thought about what they wanted.

      C. I often went fishing up in Maine during summer.

      D. So when I went fishing, I didn't think about what I wanted.

(a) DBAC   (b) CADB

(c) DABC   (d) ABCD

14.   A. Why did Carnegie pay a million dollars to Schwab?

      B. One of the first people to be paid a salary of over a million dollars a year was Charles Schwab.

      C. Schwab later left to take over the then troubled BCS and rebuild it into one of the most successful companies in the US.

      D. He had been picked by Andrew Carnegie to become the first president of the USSC in 1921.

(a) BADC   (b) BDCA

(c) ABDC   (d) BACD

15.   A. They worked from morning till late at night.

      B. The women's work was very hard.

      C. During the war there were no men in the village, so the women had to do everything.

      D. They were anaemic, exhausted and had stiff shoulders.

(a) ABCD   (b) CBAD

(c) DCAB   (d) ABDC

Exercise – 4

Directions for questions 1 to 15: Arrange the letters A, B, C and D to make a sensible and coherent paragraph.

1.   A. A digital delivery system in digital cameras will allow theatres to switch films with a phone call, saving millions per movie on negative costs.

      B. These digital images will be so interactive that they will allow a moviemaker to download a bit character or the Roman Colosseum for negligible cost.

      C. Moreover, within five years, digital images of actors and backgrounds will be interactive.

      D. Soon the technology of digital cameras that can shoot in natural light will remove the film for filmmaking.

(a) CDBA   (b) CDAB

(c) DACB   (d) ADCB

2.   A. Many people believe that calcium-rich foods will make their nails stronger.

      B. But actually, Calcium plays little or no part in strengthening them.

      C. This is because nails are made of a protein called keratin.

      D. The small white flecks that appear on nails are thought to be the result of a lack of keratin.

(a) ACBD   (b) ADBC

(c) ABCD   (d) CABD

3.   A. His first task for that day was to change an air-vent pipe on top of the tank.

      B. On stepping on its roof, he felt heat of the radiation through the soles of his thick work boots despite the tank's layer of insulation.

      C. Puzzled he swung around and saw steam hissing from a breather pipe in the centre of the tank, a sign that pressure was mounting inside.

      D. Suddenly, he heard a roaring sound.

(a) CDBA   (b) ACDB

(c) ABCD   (d) CADB

4.   A. The government gave them food — huge pots of rice, vegetables and fruits.

      B. I started the first feeding centre for children in a converted motorshed.

      C. All I had to do was organise the children.

      D. Children were running wild.

(a) ABDC   (b) DABC

(c) DCAB   (d) ABCD

5.   A. Author, socialist and a mother of four, Locke is a historian of the social history of her country for the past half century.
   B. From advocating rights for the unemployed to the legalization of family planning, Locke's commitment to social justice is continuous.
   C. Her interest in Maori culture led her to study and become fluent in the Maori language.
   D. This enabled her to contribute to a better understanding of Maori culture and history.
   (a) ABCD   (b) CADB
   (c) CABD   (d) ABDC

6.   A. Public officials are often criticized for not being accessible to their constituents.
   B. Carl Lanford had for many years frequently admonished his staff to allow people to come and see him.
   C. Yet the citizens of his community were blocked by his secretaries when they called.
   D. The fault sometimes lies in overprotective assistants who don't want to overburden their bosses with too many visitors.
   (a) ABCD   (b) ADBC
   (c) CABD   (d) CDBA

7.   A. My father was a farmer initially.
   B. Eventually he started a pharmacy with his younger brother.
   C. He invested all the money from the sale of his farming land in it.
   D. He was a far-sighted person and wanted to do something else.
   (a) ACDB   (b) ADBC
   (c) ACBD   (d) DACB

8.   A. Philosophers have been speculating on the rules of human relationships for thousands of years.
   B. It is not new, it is as old as history.
   C. Zoaraster taught it to his followers in Persia 2,500 years ago.
   D. Out of all that speculation, there has evolved only one precept.
   (a) ACBD   (b) BDAC
   (c) ABDC   (d) ADBC

9.   A. We sometimes find ourselves changing our minds without any resistance or heavy emotion.
   B. If we are told however that we are wrong, we resent the imputation and harden our hearts.
   C. We not only resent the imputation that our watch is wrong but that our conception of the canals of Mars is subject to revision.

   D. It is obviously not the ideas themselves that are dealt to us but our self-esteem that is threatened.
   (a) ABCD   (b) ACBD
   (c) ABDC   (d) BDAC

10. A. I have found it of enormous value when I can permit myself to understand the other person.
   B. Our first reaction to most of the statements is an evaluation or a judgement rather than an understanding to it.
   C. Why should I do this? Is it necessary to permit oneself to understand another?
   D. I think it is.
   (a) BADC   (b) BACD
   (c) ACDB   (d) ABCD

11. A. Part of our responsibility deals with setting up and maintaining incentive systems and standards for our operators so they can make more money by producing more yarn.
   B. Recently we have expanded our capabilities to enable us to run more than 12 different varieties.
   C. Now, our operations manager had worked out a new system that would enable us to pay the operator by the class of yarn she was running at any particular time.
   D. The system we were using worked fine when we had only two or three different types of yarn.
   (a) ADBC   (b) CADB
   (c) DBCA   (d) DBAC

12. A. Has Jasmine gone nuts?
   B. No, she hasn't, say psychologists.
   C. Hers is a classic case of pre-results stress.
   D. Most students her age go through this phase of uncertainty.
   (a) ADBC   (b) CADB
   (c) DBCA   (d) ABCD

13. A. Most people feel that if you complete your studies, you will get some decent job.
   B. Why is after all sports considered a waste of time?
   C. But if you spend your initial years in sports, there is no guarantee of any financial security.
   D. The answer lies in the fear of livelihood.
   (a) ADBC   (b) CADB
   (c) BDAC   (d) DBAC

14. A. I personally feel that it can be a disadvantage for others and persons like me.
     B. But studying Hindi as a subject in class XII does not seem quite right.
     C. I do like to read Hindi novels at times.
     D. I was always weak in Hindi.
     (a) ADBC   (b) CBDA
     (c) DBCA   (d) DBAC

15. A. I would say there are four pillars of learning in the 21st century.
     B. Learning to know, learning to do, learning to live together and learning to be.
     C. These are the inputs required to create a competent, confident and committed citizen.
     D. And if we can achieve these three Cs through education, I would say we have all the character inputs in a person.
     (a) ABCD   (b) CADB
     (c) DBCA   (d) DBAC

Exercise – 5

Directions for questions 1 to 10: Arrange the letters A, B, C and D to make a sensible and coherent sentence.

1.   A. to win the trophy three times
     B. the Fifa Ballon d'Or prize for the best player of 2011,
     C. Lionel Messi has won
     D. becoming only the fourth player in history
     (a) BCAD   (b) CDAB
     (c) CBDA   (d) DBCA

2.   A. of repeated attacks by the secessionist United Liberation Front of Assam (Ulfa), but
     B. for the people of Guwahati, bomb blasts
     C. a leopard straying into a town is rare, particularly during the day
     D. and other terror attacks were not uncommon till recently, because
     (a) BDAC   (b) CBDA
     (c) ABCD   (d) DCAB

3.   A. the director dreamed
     B. he came close to realizing that goal
     C. and in this extraordinarily beautiful existentialist anti-epic
     D. of telling stories entirely through images,
     (a) BCAD   (b) BDCA
     (c) ADBC   (d) ADCB

4.   A. to create his own genre of martial-arts comedies.
     B. and his early screen days as "the next Bruce Lee"
     C. Jackie Chan survived a boyhood in a punishing Peking Opera school,
     D. the most important and entertaining star of east Asian cinema,
     (a) ACDB   (b) DCBA
     (c) CABD   (d) BDAC

5.   A. a well organized, pre-dawn heist
     B. thieves have carried out
     C. taking two oil paintings by 20th century masters Pablo Picasso and Piet Mondrian
     D. at Greece's biggest state art museum,
     (a) DACB   (b) CDBA
     (c) BDCA   (d) BADC

6.   A. but as has been the case for the past decade,
     B. known as CES kicks off next Tuesday in Vegas,
     C. the annual gadget bacchanalia
     D. the most important new product in consumer electronics won't be there
     (a) CBAD   (b) ADBC
     (c) BCDA   (d) DACB

7.   A. Alexis Weissenberg, whose love of music from the age of 3 saved him and his mother from a World War II concentration camp
     B. Bulgarian-born French pianist
     C. has died
     D. and carried him to the heights of performances with Herbert von Karajan and Leonard Bernstein,
     (a) ACBD   (b) ABCD
     (c) BADC   (d) BCDA

8.   A. makes Iran's leaders indifferent, at best, to Washington's condemnation of his conviction.
     B. the 28-year-old American sentenced to death in Tehran on Monday for allegedly spying for the CIA,
     C. the bad news for Amir Mirzai,
     D. is that the current state of relations between Iran and the U.S.
     (a) CBDA
     (b) CABD
     (c) CBAD
     (d) CDBA

9.   A. terrorist attacks by the Kurdish rebels,

     B. a PKK insurgency in 1984, has so far claimed around 40,000 lives, victims of armed battles,

     C. the conflict in the southeast, which began with

     D. and often savage reprisals by the Turkish army and security forces

     (a) DACB   (b) CBAD
     (c) ADBC   (d) BDCA

10. A. when a suicide bomber hit a funeral of

     B. the last major bombing was

     C. in September close to the Swat Valley,

     D. a tribal elder opposed to the Taliban, killing 31 people

     (a) DCAB   (b) ADCB
     (c) CBDA   (d) BCAD

6-Sentence Type Paragraph Jumbles

Exercise – 6

Directions for questions 1 to 10: Arrange the letters A, B, C and D to make a logically coherent paragraph between 1 and 6.

1.   1. Another way to reduce or eliminate X-ray exposure of the gonads is to use special lead shields over the reproductive organs during X-rays of the abdomen or lower back.

     A. This is easy to do for male patients, but sometimes impossible for females.

     B. The location of the ovaries in the abdomen means that the shield sometimes would obscure needed parts of the X-ray picture.

     C. Why are they made?

     D. The best way to reduce exposure, obviously, would be to eliminate unnecessary X-ray examinations.

     6. Sometimes the patient pressures the doctor into ordering an X-ray because he feels that an examination is incomplete without one.

     (a) DABC   (b) ABDC
     (c) BACD   (d) CBAD

2.   1. Pystech International, a UK-based company, has devised a wide range of psychometric tests that assess attributes like personality, values, aptitudes and abilities.

     A. The system provides a printed report of the candidate's performance on a particular test or a battery of tests.

     B. Genesys has assessment batteries for clerical, technical, sales, graduate trainees and managerial selection.

     C. The tests are available in an integrated form as Genesys, a software package.

     D. The design of these tests is based upon norms and standards as fixed by the British Psychological Society.

     6. The system is being used by international establishments like AT&T, ANZ Bank, Ford UK and South African Airways among others.

     (a) ACBD   (b) ADBC
     (c) DCAB   (d) ABDC

3.   1. My big problem with buzzwords is that they willfully ignore the human element in most management situations.

     A. Coining a new phrase to describe what managers do is just clever repackaging.

     B. There will always be another 'new and improved' package that will capture their fancy.

     C. The new package may attract people but packaging alone won't hold their attention.

     D. The concepts that last don't rely on a nifty turn of phrase.

     6. They rely on an understanding of people.

     (a) BADC   (b) DACB
     (c) ACBD   (d) CBAD

4.   1. In 1984, when I wrote my first book, *What They Don't Teach You at Harvard Business School,* IMG had 500 employees in 19 offices around the world generating several hundred million dollars in revenue.

     A. Today, we have 2,000 employees and 67 offices in 26 countries, and revenues have surged well beyond the billion-dollar mark.

     B. As a result, the managing examples you'll read here are personal.

     C. In the interval, I feel I have faced many of the same situations that challenge (if not befuddle) every other manager.

     D. They have all involved me or our company in some way.

     6. In other words, they are real.

     (a) BADC   (b) DACB
     (c) ACBD   (d) CBAD

5.   1. A lot of expertise is involved in building a house.

     A. In effect, you are 'subcontracting' out the assignment.

     B. Unless you are a master at carpentry, masonry, electricity, plumbing and other building trades, you don't build a house by yourself.

C. Instead, you hire a contractor who, in turn, hires subcontractors skilled at carpentry, masonry, plumbing, etc.

D. You hire the contractor, in large part, on the basis of the quality of the subcontractors he deals with and on his ability to get them to do quality work on budget and on time.

6. There's some risk involved, because you have to trust the contractor's choice of subcontractors.

(a) BADC (b) BDCA

(c) ABCD (d) BCAD

6. 1. Money may be the universal unit of measurement for keeping score in business, but some employees try to conceal their feelings about it.

A. I actually prefer dealing with such type of people, because they are so direct.

B. However, an employee's true feelings about money are inevitably revealed at salary review time.

C. Their effort on the job is in direct proportion to their monetary reward.

D. That's when a normally agreeable or docile individual can turn into a rapacious dynamo who has itemized the dollar value of every contribution he has made at work during the previous year.

6. It's commerce in its simplest form: quid pro quo.

(a) ABDC (b) BDAC

(c) BADC (d) ABCD

7. 1. In the 1960s and '70s, we built our company by hiring a lot of smart MBAs from the best of schools.

A. Our company was writing the rules as we went along.

B. But we also knew that 'experience' was meaningless in our business.

C. Part of this was practicality (we could afford them).

D. Sports marketing was so unique that there weren't many, if any people with legitimate expertise.

6. So we hired the best young people we could find, with no experience, and taught them how we wanted things done.

(a) ABCD (b) CBDA

(c) CDAB (d) ACDB

8. 1. Our definition of the influence that learning has on drives is more easily understandable in other areas of human behaviour in which drive and instinct are factors.

A. The same applies to the sex drive or to the instinct for danger and protection.

B. We can put a hold on it for some time till it vanishes.

C. Applied to the drive to eat, it means, for example, that we do not have to eat the very moment we are hungry.

D. We do not have to give in to an aggressive impulse: we can direct it, suppress it, or divert (transform) it to other impulses.

6. Again applied to the drive toward sleep, this means that among humans, sleep is instinctual behaviour that can be guided by a learning process.

(a) ABCD (b) CBDA

(c) CDAB (d) DCBA

9. 1. Portmann has attempted the most convincing explanation of this phenomenon.

A. If the term of pregnancy for the human embryo were comparably as long as among other mammals, pregnancy would have to last two years.

B. He would as the saying goes, be ready to flee the nest (Portmann).

C. His formulation refer to man's 'physiologically premature birth' as the reason that man in terms of instinct, is the weakest living creature on earth.

D. If humans were carried to such a term, all sense organs would be fully developed, and the newborn would be able to sit, stand and walk, would already have bladder control, and would even be somewhat able to speak.

6. Since this is not the case, however, maturation among humans must take place outside the uterus.

(a) CADB (b) DABC

(c) BADC (d) ABCD

10. 1 Quotas are imposed on imported steels.

A. Lots of small mills will crop up.

B. This will not help big Indian mills.

C. They will take business away from the big steel mills.

D. The situation would remain the same.

6. The policy-makers will have to devise another scheme.

(a) CADB (b) ABCD

(c) DABC (d) BACD

5-Sentence Type Paragraph Jumbles

Exercise – 7

Directions for questions 1 to 10: Arrange the letters A, B, C, D and E to make a logically coherent paragraph.

1. A. Extremely subjective attitudes and values are usually used in judging one's own sleep.

    B. If one spends New Year's Eve among friends, one may go home at 3 in the morning in an animated and good mood, have a relaxed sleep, and be slightly fatigued the next day without attaching too much importance to the matter.

    C. But if one falls asleep shortly after 3 a.m. under normal circumstances, the consiousness of having slept little makes one tossing back and forth with increasing disquiet, and getting more and more nervous, one is exhausted and desperate rather than animated and in a good mood as on New Year's Eve.

    D. But in both instances the amount of amount of sleep is the same, in fact, the hour of falling asleep is exactly the same.

    E. The only difference is in the evaluation, the initial psychic state, the expectation concerning sleep, and the subjective judgment about the lack of sleep.

    (a) BADCE   (b) DACBE

    (c) ABCDE   (d) CBADE

2. A. Some years ago I had to regularly deal with an executive who was notorious for being an emotional powder keg.

    B. Obviously, if I wanted something from him, it was important to catch him when he was on a roll.

    C. This rampant emotionalism often served him well.

    D. When things were going his way, he could be incredibly clever, dynamic and unyielding.

    E. When things turned sour, he tended to be incredibly argumentative and unyielding.

    (a) BCDAE   (b) ABCDE

    (c) DCBAE   (d) ACDEB

3. A. The normal impulse in forming a committee is to stack it with senior people, to form a 'blue ribbon' committee that is the be-all and end-all of decision-making bodies.

    B. There are several things wrong with this approach.

    C. Your most senior people are probably your busiest people.

    D. First, from a practical standpoint, an elite committee is harder to convene on a regular basis.

    E. They have the most crowded calendars, and they have the most projects demanding their attention.

    (a) BADCE   (b) DACBE

    (c) ABDCE   (d) CBADE

4. A. They were away, and he had promised to keep an eye on the place, he crossed the street to check.

    B. She found an extension cord plugged into a kitchen outlet and leading down the basement stairs.

    C. By 5 p.m., Norman E. Toothman was worrying about his neighbours' basement.

    D. An hour later, when he had failed to come home, his wife went to the neighbours' looking for him.

    E. Rain flooded the streets of Cherry Hill, NJ, one day in August.

    (a) ECADB   (b) DABCE

    (c) BADCE   (d) ABCDE

5. A. The amount that goes through you depends on how much of a contact you make.

    B. When you plug an appliance in and turn it on, the current flows in and out of the appliance over two wires, one 'hot', the other 'grounded' or neutral.

    C. If you touch the hot wire, or if it is in contact with the metal frame of the appliance, electricity will try to leak off through you to the ground.

    D. It may be only a slight shock if you're dry-handed or standing on a dry rug for dry skin has high electrical resistance.

    E. How do Ground Fault Circuits work?

    (a) EBACD   (b) ABCDE

    (c) DABCE   (d) EBCAD

6. A. But when Susie was only 21 months old, her mother left her in the kitchen "for just a minute" to hang up washing outdoors.

    B. Before she was born, her mother pored over booklets about baby care.

    C. Later, her mother conscientiously brought her to my office for inoculations and followed my feeding instructions regularly.

    D. During the 'minute', the little tyke climbed on a chair and put a handkerchief through the electric wringer.

    E. The case of Susie G. is typical.

    (a) BACDE   (b) EABCD

    (c) DABCE   (d) EBCAD

7. A. Familiar practice among young people is the tendency to shift the day-night rhythm towards the direction of late night hours or even towards the early morning hours.

    B. Interestingly enough, this can especially be observed among vivid dreamers.

    C. The assertion of greater mental efficiency during the evening and night hours so often made by students after having shifted day into night (advancing) can at best be supported by the observation that there is less distraction and disturbance at night than during the day.

    D. Thinking really requires a rested brain.

    E. The habit conceals dangers, however, which mainly consists in diminished mental productivity and an impaired ability to concentrate.

    (a) BACDE   (b) ABCDE
    (c) EBDCA   (d) ABECD

8. A. In addition to its welcome characteristic of inducing sleep, it has the problematic side effect of lowering the blood pressure and consequently of supplying areas in which circulation is already weak with even less blood and oxygen.

    B. In this context, we wish to recall a phenomenon already mentioned in an earlier passage — namely that during the night the functioning of organs periodically changes.

    C. For example, the pulse frequency changes, and so does perspiration, depth and frequency of breathing and the blood pressure becomes lower.

    D. With these changes in mind, it then becomes understandable why a sleeping pill containing barbiturate acid can have an absolutely disastrous effect on an older person.

    E. One of the essential components of sleep inducing medications in the market is barbituric acid.

    (a) ACDBE   (b) EABCD
    (c) EBDCA   (d) ADCBE

9. A. Their sleep behaviour was then observed and recorded.

    B. Test subject A, to be quoted later, was impeded from dreaming for seven nights.

    C. The occurrence of dreaming was then impeded for five nights.

    D. Special attention was given to the synchronic sleep phases.

    E. Some volunteer test subjects were permitted first to spend several nights in the sleep laboratory in order to become accustomed to being there.

    (a) EBACD   (b) ABECD
    (c) BACDE   (d) EADCB

10. A. Of this, most is infrared light, so called because it vibrates more slowly than the colour red at one end of the visible spectrum.

    B. We cannot see infrared radiation, but we feel it as heat.

    C. Ultraviolet is more energetic than visible or infrared light.

    D. The rest of the unseen light is ultraviolet, so named because it vibrates faster than the colour violet at the other end of the spectrum.

    E. More than half of the sun's radiance is invisible to human eyes.

    (a) EABDC   (b) AEBCD
    (c) BACDE   (d) DAECB

Exercise – 8

Directions for questions 1 to 10: Arrange the letters A, B, C, D and E to make a logically coherent paragraph.

1. A. This causes an electrochemical change by splitting off unpaired neutrons called free radicals from cell molecules.

    B. These highly reactive agents produce toxin products that poison or irritate surrounding tissues and apparently contribute to the swelling and leakage of tiny blood vessels in the skin — a process we know as sunburn.

    C. Thus, free radicals can impair cellular renewal in our bodies hastening the aging process.

    D. They may also damage the genetic blueprints cells used in reproducing.

    E. Both visible and invisible solar radiation penetrate our skin's surface, smashing into living cells.

    (a) EABDC   (b) ABCDE
    (c) BACED   (d) DACEB

2. A. This happens because the governments have used the pension schemes to redistribute income from young workers to retired people.

    B. As population growth slows down, the number of old people grows, and the burden of supporting them falls on a diminishing number of young people.

    C. It's because the old people have formed strong lobbies which can topple governments.

D. The pension schemes go bankrupt, and governments have to prop them up with subsidies funded out of taxes in the general population. Why do they do this?

E. Pension schemes are poison pills: all through the western world, pension schemes have brought governments close to bankruptcy.

(a) EABDC   (b) ADECB

(c) CABDE   (d) EDACB

3. A. After the cleaning and rinsing job is done, the hair should comb easily when wet, free of tangles, and be in a manageable condition for combing when dry.

B. Therefore, it should spread easily and disperse quickly into the hair and on the scalp.

C. Finally, the shampoo should rinse out fast and without leaving the air tacky and sticky.

D. A shampoo should be viscous enough to stay on the palm before application over the head.

E. Physical properties of a shampoo too are very important.

(a) ADBEC   (b) EDBCA

(c) BEDAC   (d) EDBAC

4. A. It's considered the equivalent of prostitution.

B. I didn't look beautiful.

C. I was very malnourished and my teeth were in a bad way.

D. Also, Bosnians are wary of the western modelling world.

E. I was very suspicious when she first approached me.

(a) BDACE   (b) EBCDA

(c) BACDE   (d) DABEC

5. A. The main reason for this is very low literacy among women and very low availability of contraceptives.

B. Television can be a powerful medium of spreading awareness, but it has decided to opt for entertainment.

C. Nothing wrong with that but what about lessons in-between all those soaps about extra-marital affairs.

D. No rural couple is going to opt for birth control if it means travelling several kilometres, usually on foot, to buy a packet of contraceptives.

E. Statistics indicate that within UP, Bihar, Rajasthan and MP, the problem of population control is more acute in certain districts than others.

(a) CADEB   (b) BEADC

(c) EADBC   (d) DABCE

6. A. When Zeenat Aman cried on my show, people thought I was instrumental.

B. This time too, a star and his mother almost cried during the shoot.

C. But once bitten, twice shy, I switched off the cameras as soon as I saw the tears welling in their eyes.

D. What they did not know was that I tried my best to shift the subject from Mazhar Khan, but she wouldn't let me.

E. And requested them to get a hold on themselves.

(a) CBDAE   (b) CBEAD

(c) ACDEB   (d) ADBCE

7. A. With all these defences, why do we get sunburned at all?

B. After the first burning doses of ultraviolet rays have begun unleashing free radicals, cells in the top layers of skin begin reproducing rapidly.

C. The skin thickens and hardens making it more difficult for ultraviolet rays to penetrate.

D. If even this fails and the skin flushes with sunburn, it will speed up its normal but usually unnoticed shedding — or 'peeling' — of damaged and old cells.

E. The skin has other defence mechanisms.

(a) AEDCB   (b) EBCDA

(c) BACED   (d) AEBDC

8. A. But research in the United States and England suggests that some of PABA's chemical byproducts are phototoxins; they become poisons when struck by sunlight.

B. The use of such preparations is generally wise, say doctors.

C. But now scientists are worried that some sunscreen products may in some cases do as much harm as good.

D. For example, para-aminobenzoic (PABA) has been praised as an excellent defence against ultraviolet ray: it is used in dozens of today's most effective suntan preparations.

E. To compensate for this foolishness, we smear our skins with more than $200 million worth of suntan creams and lotions each year.

(a) EADCB   (b) EBCDA

(c) BAECD   (d) AEBDC

9.   A. Infrared and ultraviolet light are not being blocked to the same degree.

   B. You squint and the pupils of your eyes contract to protect the delicate visual receptors inside.

   C. But when you walk into sunshine while wearing improperly filtered sunglasses, your eyes feel protected — and your pupils remain wide open — even though they may be in danger.

   D. For, in fact, many sunglasses screen out only visible light.

   E. To understand why the scientists are worried reflect on what happens when you walk into bright sunlight without sunglasses.

   (a) ADCBE   (b) EBCDA
   (c) EBACD   (d) EBADC

10. A. At 11.23 a.m. lifeguard Lec Anderson had spotted a young boy in trouble and dashed into the surf expecting that chief guard Gary Guertin would follow with a lifeline.

   B. Guertin, however, was already preoccupied with saving an elderly couple he had seen flailing helplessly in the waves.

   C. "The water was pouring away from the beach." Guertin later told a reporter.

   D. Soon the water was swarming with 50 or 60 victims — shrieking people suddenly being swept out to sea by a violent current.

   E. On the morning of August 21, 1973, several dozen people nearly lost their lives off Nauset Beach on Cape Cod, Massachusetts.

   (a) ADCBE   (b) EBCDA
   (c) EBACD   (d) EABDC

Answer Keys

Exercise – 1

1. (c)	2. (a)	3. (a)	4. (c)	5. (d)	6. (b)	7. (a)	8. (b)	9. (a)	10. (d)
11. (a)	12. (b)	13. (a)	14. (b)	15. (b)					

Exercise – 2

1. (d)	2. (b)	3. (c)	4. (a)	5. (b)	6. (c)	7. (d)	8. (a)	9. (a)	10. (a)
11. (d)	12. (b)	13. (c)	14. (d)	15. (b)					

Exercise – 3

1. (b)	2. (d)	3. (d)	4. (c)	5. (b)	6. (a)	7. (a)	8. (b)	9. (d)	10. (a)
11. (a)	12. (a)	13. (b)	14. (b)	15. (b)					

Exercise – 4

1. (c)	2. (a)	3. (c)	4. (b)	5. (a)	6. (b)	7. (b)	8. (d)	9. (a)	10. (c)
11. (a)	12. (d)	13. (c)	14. (b)	15. (a)					

Exercise – 5

1. (b)	2. (a)	3. (c)	4. (d)	5. (d)	6. (a)	7. (d)	8. (c)	9. (a)	10. (d)

Exercise – 6

1. (b)	2. (c)	3. (c)	4. (c)	5. (d)	6. (b)	7. (b)	8. (d)	9. (a)	10. (d)

Exercise – 7

1. (c)	2. (d)	3. (c)	4. (a)	5. (d)	6. (d)	7. (d)	8. (b)	9. (d)	10. (a)

Exercise – 8

1. (a)	2. (a)	3. (b)	4. (b)	5. (c)	6. (d)	7. (b)	8. (b)	9. (b)	10. (d)

Solutions

Exercise – 1

1. c   B introduces the lady who is being talked about. A follows B as it describes her. D talks about what she does and C tells what effect that has on the author. Hence, the correct sequence is 'BADC'.

2. a   D introduces the topic. B talks about the years the mission has seen till now. C continues further by talking about the future of the movement. A concludes the paragraph by giving an opinion about the mission.

3. c   AB forms a mandatory pair as the pronoun 'it' in sentence B refers to the liver mentioned in A. Sentence D follows B as it states a consequence of any damage to the liver. The mandatory sequence 'ABD' is present only in option (c), hence it is the correct answer.

4. c   The beginnings of A and D clearly suggest that, none of them can be the beginning of the paragraph. B cannot be the starting of the paragraph due to 'also' in the sentence. Thus, the best choice to begin the passage with is 'C'. The rest of the options fit in accordingly. B talks about consequences and D states that many of us don't like these consequences. So, D must follow B. Hence, 'CBDA' is the correct sequence.

5. d   D introduces the 'time management' concept. A takes us back three decades ago when there were not enough books on the subject. C talks about the current scenario when there are plenty of books. Hence, 'DAC' form a mandatory sequence and is present only in option (d).

6. b   B and C cannot be the openings of the paragraph as they start with 'and' and 'because' respectively. 'DC' forms the opening mandatory pair wherein D asks a question and C answers it. 'BA' forms the trailing mandatory pair wherein the author says that he does not blame anyone else (media or Nagma) but the person in question himself. 'DCBA' is the correct sequence.

7. a   D opens the sentence by talking about the basic human needs. A follows by telling what will happen if these needs are not fulfilled. Thus, DA is mandatory. B follows A as it tells up what happens as a result of the emptiness we feel. Hence, 'DAB' is a mandatory sequence which is present only in option (a).

8. b   'AB' is a mandatory pair. A introduces Mulayam Singh Yadav and Sonia Gandhi. B further elaborates A. C follows B as it refers to polemics between the two politicians. D concludes the paragraph.

9. a   'CA' is a mandatory pair and introduces the topic of selling business. 'Decline' in A connects with B. Thus B follows A. 'D' states the alternate view as it starts with 'on the other hand'. Hence, 'CABD' is the correct sequence.

10. c   'AB' forms a mandatory pair as the 'now' in B refers to the previous incident. And that incident is clearly mentioned in A. C and D go on to give the results of the 'tables...turned' in B. Thus, option (c) is the correct answer.

11. a   The author talks about knowing people from around the world at the leadership centre in D. In A he describes these people while in C we get to know the people's viewpoint of the life they lead. B is the last sentence as it appeals to the readers. Hence, 'DACB' is the correct sequence.

12. b   A and D start with 'thus' and 'while', thus making them inappropriate to be at the beginning of the paragraph. B is incomplete in itself. Thus, the option which can fit best in the beginning is C. Only option (b) begins with sentence C. So, 'CDBA' is the correct sequence.

13. a   'AB' is a mandatory pair as A talks about a path and B describes the path. This pair is present only in option (a). Hence, 'ABCD' is the correct sequence.

14. b   C talks about a decision to close evening law colleges. A tells that except Maharashtra all other states agreed. 'BD' presents Maharashtra's point of view as to why it was against the rule. Hence 'CABD' is the correct sequence.

15. b   C introduces the topic with the announcement of the award. D follows by telling about the increased prize money this time. Hence, 'CD' forms a mandatory pair. A follows D as it refers to the increase in prize money as 'exciting news'. Hence 'CDAB' is the correct sequence.

Exercise – 2

1. d   'BA' is a mandatory pair where B refers to the MTNL' orders and A states what the orders are. C follows A as the pronoun 'it' in sentence C refers to MTNL (sentence A). Hence, 'BAC' is a mandatory sequence. This is present only in option (d). Thus, option (d) i.e. 'BACD' is the correct answer.

2. b   D introduces the hard of hearing jockey Lester Piggott. 'AC' describes an event when he was followed by an old fan, pleading for financial help in C. B gives the reaction of Lester. Hence, 'DACB' is the correct sequence.

3. c B introduces the topic of speech making. D talks about a book on this topic meant to improve speech making. 'AC' provides a look at the contents of the book. Hence, 'BDCA' is the correct sequence.

4. a B introduces the topic mentioning orchestra in the sentence. D compares an orchestra performance to a public speech. C mentions the most important and necessary thing for both orchestra and speech making. A follows C as the pronoun 'they' in A refers to the audience mentioned in C.

5. b C introduces Aaron Hank a baseball player. A talks about his performance and D about his records. B talks about what he did after he retired as a player.

6. c C introduces the passage by talking about dreams to make a wonderful movie with a big star and wonderful location (The Beach). The mandatory pair 'AD' follows C by stating the consequences of filming the movie. B is the trailing sentence, which provides witness accounts. Hence, 'CADB' is the correct sequence.

7. d C introduces and talks about two investment schemes. A and D tell about the results of both the schemes, where D follows A because of the 'And' in the beginning of the sentence in D. Hence, 'CAD' forms a mandatory sequence which can be found only in option (d).

8. a The paragraph is an advertisement given for a particular job. It starts with B introducing the company in which the post is available. D tells about the type of people they require, while C specifies the particular post and his job profile. A asks the interested candidates to apply to a given address. Hence, 'BDCA' is the correct sequence.

9. a B introduces the topic, talking about antique collectors in general. Then A takes the case of a particular clock collector Bill Austin. D describes him as a nice person to meet. And C talks more about Bill's life. Hence, 'BADC' is the correct sequence.

10. a D introduces Commonwealth with its purpose. It is followed by B as the pronoun 'it' in B refers to 'Commonwealth' in D. C further elaborates the organization's function.

11. d C states the author's viewpoint as to what India should do to combat terrorism. B states the reason and A states what can happen if action is not taken. D concludes the passage.

12. b B discusses the problem of legal delays and C tells that nothing has been done to tackle them. D presents the Chief Justice's point of view and A talks about the delays. Hence, 'BCDA' is the correct sequence.

13. c D will be the opening sentence because in the rest of the sentences 'creative imagination' is referred to as 'It'. A has to be the last statement as 'also' is mentioned in it.

14. d The paragraph has to start with D as it generally talks about the types of life people lead. The rest of the sentences then deal with individual life in each sentence. B has to be the last sentence as it starts with 'But'. Hence, 'DCAB' is the correct sequence.

15. b The paragraph cannot start with A or D because they begin with 'Thus' and 'Therein' respectively, which points out that these sentences are in continuation and not starters. Thus, the only valid option left is (b) which starts with sentence B that introduces the main theme of the paragraph.

Exercise – 3

1. b 'DA' is a mandatory pair as A cites the reason for the statement expressed in D. 'CB' is the trailing mandatory pair as the word 'IT' in B refers to 'Evaluation' in C.

2. d A mentions the collapse of the communist regime in Russia and East European countries. B mentions that due to this cold war has also ended. In contrast to this C mentions that despite all this, tension still exists and states that these tensions could lead to another world war.

3. d The paragraph progresses in a chronological order. In D it mentions the Battle of Plassey in 1757 and moves further on to 1848 in C and later to 1857 Revolt in A.

4. c D introduces the topic stating that the French had seen what had happened to the British. A mentions the French negotiating with India once the Britishers left. C states the conditions for negotiations and B states the result. Hence, 'DACB' is the correct sequence.

5. b The passage talks about the Indian independence. B mentions the exact moment when India attained independence. D talks about the celebrations and A mentions the change of flags. Hence, 'BDA' forms a mandatory sequence. This sequence can only be seen in option B. Hence, 'BDAC' is the correct sequence.

6. a   D starts with telling about Hitler becoming the chancellor of Germany. B will follow because it talks about Hitler becoming the President. C follows B as it talks about Hitler's establishing a centralised government, thus becoming a dictator (mentiond in A).

7. a   D talks about the economic depression hitting USA. 'CB' talks about its effects on the national income as well as trade, finance and industry. A mentions that due to 'CB' unemployment increased. Hence, 'DCBA' is the correct sequence.

8. b   D introduces the topic of industrial growth in the 19th- century Europe. B mentions England to be the place of origin for this. C follows, mentioning other countries which followed England's example.

9. d   B introduces the city of Ranthambore and that it is famous for its wildlife sanctuary. C will follow as it goes into a little detail mentioning the special attractions of the sanctuary. Then D has to follow as it starts with 'The other' and mentions other attractions of the city. At last A provides a way to reach the city.

10. a   'BA' is the opening mandatory pair which states that one should not forget the fact that the look of his/her footwear is noticed just as much as his/her smile. 'DC' is the trailing mandatory pair as D talks about having three pairs of shoes while C talks about an extra fourth pair. Hence, 'BADC' is the correct sequence.

11. c   C talks about a character Q in the James Bond movies. The 'exploding rat' mentioned in D refers to the 'so crude' in C, making 'CD' a mandatory pair. B takes the argument further and A follows B. Hence, 'CDBA' is the correct sequence.

12. a   A presents a statement and B elaborates the point. So 'AB' is mandatory. C talks about efficiency followed by D which states that this efficiency comes at a price.

13. b   C starts with stating that the author went fishing during summer. In A he expresses his preferences in eating at the same time mentioning what fishes prefer to eat. 'DB' is mandatory as its states that the author did not think about his own wants but about the fish's wants. Hence 'CADB' is the correct sequence.

14. b   B introduces Schwab and the mandatory pair 'DC' follows it by showing his journey from being the first president of USSC to joining BCS. A is the last sentence as it poses a question that would perhaps be answered in by the author in a subsequent passage. Hence, 'BDCA' is the correct sequence.

15. b   The passage starts with C describing the time of war when women had to do everything as there were no men in the villages. B tells that they had to work very hard. A mentions that they had to work all day and thus became weak and exhausted as mentioned in D. Hence, 'CBAD' is the correct sequence.

Exercise – 4

1. c   D introduces a new technology for digital cameras. 'AC' elaborates on what the new digital cameras would be able to do. Interactive in 'B' connects B to C. Hence, 'DACB' is the correct sequence.

2. c   A starts by stating a myth about calcium making the nails strong. B breaks the myth by saying its false. C takes the argument forward and introduces another protein called Keratin. D follows by stating the result of a lack of Keratin. Hence, 'ABCD' is the correct sequence.

3. c   A is the opening sentence as it introduces the subject of the passage i.e. changing of an air-vent pipe on a tank. B follows as the word 'its' used in it refers to 'the tank' mentioned in sentence A. Sentence C follows B as it states what the man did once he felt heat through his work boots (stated in B). D concludes the passage. Hence, 'ABCD' is the correct sequence.

4. b   D states the condition of the children. A tells what the government has done for the children. In 'BC' the author states what he is doing for the children.

5. a   The paragraph cannot start with C as the subject is addressed as 'her'. Thus, the paragraph has to start with A as it introduces the subject. D will follow C because 'this' in sentence D refers to 'her interest' stated in C. Hence, 'ABCD' is the correct sequence.

6. b   A states a criticism of public officials. D states the probable reason. B cites an example. C follows B as the pronoun 'his' refers to Carl (in B). Thus, 'ADBC' is the correct sequence.

7. b   The subject is mentioned as 'he' in B, C and D. Thus, the paragraph will start with A mentioning the father's occupation. D mentions his qualities and his plans to do something else. B talks about his starting a new business. C mentions that he invested all the money he had in his new business.

8. d   'AD' is mandatory as it talks about speculation on rules of human relationships. B follows claiming this speculation to be quite old with C giving the time of its origin. Hence, 'ADBC' is the correct sequence.

9. a   A presents a phenomenon and B further elaborates it. C follows B as it further talks about the 'resent' mentioned in sentence B. This mandatory sequence can be found only in option (a).

10. c   'AC' is mandatory a pair. A talks about permitting oneself to understand the other person and C questions this. D provides the answer to the question in C. Hence, 'ACDB' is the correct sequence.

11. a   A talks about setting up a new system to produce more yarn. D tells us about the system being used earlier which worked for two or three types of yarn. B talks about the latest system which can run more types of yarn.

12. d   A asks a question and B answers it. So 'AB' is mandatory. 'CD' then discuss 'AB'.

13. c   B starts the paragraph with a question about the usefulness of sports. D answers the question. Thus, the paragraph has to start with 'BD'. This mandatory pair exists only in option (c).

14. b   C starts the paragraph by mentioning the author's liking for Hindi novels. But B mentions that he was not good at studying Hindi as a subject. In D he further states that he was actually weak in Hindi as a school subject and thus it is a disadvantage for him and others like him (mentioned in A).

15. a   A talks about four main points or pillars of learning in today's time. B mentions all four. Thus, 'AB' is mandatory. C mentions that these pillars are required to make a committed, competent and confident citizen. In D these qualities are referred to as the 3 Cs.

Exercise – 5

1. c   Lionel Messi is the subject of the sentence and B describes what Messi has won; hence 'CB' forms a mandatory pair. D and A follow B. Therefore, the correct answer is option (c).

2. a   'BD' forms a mandatory pair because the bomb blasts mentioned will obviously follow other terror activities. A takes the argument forward as it explains the fact stated in B and D. Therefore, the correct answer is option (a).

3. d   'AD' forms a mandatory pair as D describes what the director dreams about in A. B is a continuation of C. Hence, the correct answer is ADCB.

4. b   The sentence cannot possibly start with A and B and so options (a) and (d) can be eliminated. C will follow D as D describes Jackie Chan. Therefore the correct sequence is 'DCBA'.

5. d   'BA' forms a mandatory pair as A describes what the thieves in B have carried out. So, the correct answer is option (d).

6. a   'CB' forms the opening mandatory pair as B states the name of the annual gadget bacchanalia i.e. 'CES'. This can be found only in option (a). Therefore the correct answer is option (a).

7. c   'AD' forms a mandatory pair as D continues the argument stated in A. This pair can be found only in option (c). Hence, the correct option is (c).

8. a   B has to follow C as it describes the proper noun mentioned in C. 'AD' is a mandatory pair as it shows a clear cause and effect relationship. Therefore, option (a) is the correct answer.

9. b   C introduces the subject i.e. conflict in the south east. B, A and D form a sequence and so the correct answer is option (b).

10. d   AD form a mandatory pair as the 31 people killed in D is because of the suicide bomber mentioned in A. Therefore, option (a) is eliminated. However, the sentence cannot begin with 'AD' and so, we can eliminate option (b) too. Therefore, the correct answer will be option (d).

Exercise – 6

1. b   1 mentions an alternative method to reduce the effects of X-rays. A states that this is easy for males but not for females. B mentions the reason why and D provides ways through which even females can be saved from the harmful effect of the X-rays. Hence, the correct sequence is 'ABDC'.

2. c   1 talks about psychometric tests to measure personality and other such values. D talks about how these tests were developed and designed. C mentions the package in which the tests are available. A talks about what the tests provide and about their results. B mentions for which all positions the tests are available.

3. c   1 talks about the author not really liking buzzwords while A states exactly what buzzwords do which according to the author is just packing the old stuff in a new material. C then tells what the new packing does. It just attracts people but doesn't hold attention for long. According to the author, better and better packaging will keep on capturing people's attention as mentioned in B. Hence, 'ACBD' is the correct sequence.

4. c   1 is followed by A which compares the scenario of 1984 to the present day. C follows as it refers to the interval between 1984 and today. This opening pair (AC) is only stated in option (c).

5. d   1 talks about the varied knowledge being involved in building a house. B talks about the different people who help build a house, as B mentions that a person cannot build a house by himself and

needs people who are masters in their own fields. C follows talking about hiring a contractor who brings these people together. A summarises the whole process. Hence, 'BCA' forms a mandatory sequence which can be found only in option (d).

6. b   1 talks about employees concealing their feelings about money. B will follow as first of all it starts with however which implies 'in contrast' and the sentence talks about employees revealing their feelings at salary time. D mentions that people change altogether at such a time. And A states that this is the type of people the author deals with.

7. b   The author talks about how he started his company by hiring fresh MBAs. C provides a probable reason for such a move - affordability. B provides the second reason and that is that the company did not require experienced people and thus hired fresh MBAs. D talks about their marketing strategies.

8. d   Let us take the steps — first, the theory of D is applied to C (the method in B), then to A (sex drive) then finally to sleep in 6. Hence, 'DCBA' is the correct sequence.

9. a   1 talks about a phenomenon explained by Portmann but does not clearly mention it. Thus, C follows 1 as it specifies what the phenomenon is (human birth). A compares birth in humans to other animals in terms of pregnancy or gestation time. D elaborates by stating the functions a human being's newborn could perform if its gestation was as long as that of other mammals. B follows D as it also refers to a newborn. Hence, 'CADB' is the correct sequence.

10. d   1 talks about quotas being imposed on imported steel. B talks about its effect and A further mentions the result of all this. The word 'They' in C refers to small mills in A, thus connecting 'AC'.

Exercise – 7

1. c   A presents a statement followed by an example to prove it in B. C presents another example with the conditions slightly changed. D compares both examples and analyses them. E presents the result or the outcome of the analysis.

2. d   B, C, D or E cannot start the paragraph as the subject is referred to as 'him' or 'his'. Thus, A would be the opening sentence. A talks about the behaviour of an executive and C tells how such a behaviour helped him. 'DE' presents situations when things were going his way.

3. c   The passage is about forming committees and appointing people in it. Thus, the paragraph starts with A which starts with forming a committee and

appointing senior people in it. B objects this approach. D provides a reason for this objection (elaborates this point).

4. a   E starts the paragraph by describing a rainy day in August. The paragraph carries on in a story format. C mentions Toothman worrying about his neighbour's basement as rain had flooded the streets. A states that the neighbours were away and had asked Toothman to look after their place, (so he goes to check). D mentions Toothman's wife going to look for him when he does not return even an hour later and B tells what she finds there.

5. d   The paragraph starts with a question in E. B follows by explaining the mechanism of a current flow. C states the consequences of touching a live wire. Hence, 'EBCAD' is the apt sequence.

6. d   E introduces the character Susie. G. The paragraph moves in a chronological order. 'BC' talks about what happened before she was born. A then talks about an incident when Susie was 21 months old and D tells exactly what Susie did.

7. d   'AB' is the opening pair as A gives us the subject of the discussion and the word 'this' used in B refers to 'Familiar practice' mentioned in A. E further elaborates on 'familiar practice'. Hence, 'ABE' forms a mandatory sequence. However, this sequence can only be found in option (d). So option (d), 'ABECD' is the correct answer.

8. b   E talks about the sleep inducing medicine barbituric acid. A talks about its characteristics while 'BC' provides an example to prove it.

9. d   The paragraph talks about an experiment on sleep behaviour. E starts with talking about volunteers getting ready for the experiment. A talks about the initial observations that were made during the experiment. 'DCB' states the step taken during it.

10. a   E introduces the topic of sunlight. A then talks about one of the components of sunlight — infrared light. B provides more information on this. D talks about the second component ultraviolet light followed by C, which provides more information on it.

Exercise – 8

1. a   E introduces the topic and talks about the process of solar radiations penetrating the human skin. 'AB' discusses the effects of this process. C would be the last option because it starts with 'Thus' which implies it is the concluding statement.

2. a   E introduces the topic of pension schemes and their effects. A states the reason why this happens. BDC further elaborates the cause why pension schemes fail.

3. b E introduces the topic of physical properties of a shampoo. D talks about the properties of a good shampoo. It tells how it should be before being applied on the scalp. B talks about the stage when it is applied on the hair. C talks about the rinsing stage followed by A which talks about drying the hair.

4. b In E the author talks about being suspicious on being offered a modelling offer. In B she reveals the reason for her suspicion - that she was not beautiful. In C she goes one step ahead and describes herself. 'DA' describes the outlook of Bosnians towards modelling.

5. c E introduces the topic of the discussion i.e. population control being a big problem. A provides reasons for this. D further goes into detail probing why a rural couple would not opt for birth control. 'BC' elaborates on how television also does not do its bit to spread awareness.

6. d The host of a talk show discusses an episode when Zeenat Aman appeared as a guest and what people thought about it in 'A'. D brings out the real picture. B then shifts to the present time when again a certain guest cried. C presents the hosts reaction.

7. b The paragraph discusses defence mechanisms of the skin, introducing the topic in E. B starts from the beginning explaining what happens when ultraviolet rays penetrate the skin. 'CD' provides the result of all this.

8. b E introduces the topic of the usage of suntan creams and lotions. B presents the view of doctors regarding this. C presents the contradictory view held by scientists today. 'DA' provides an example to prove the scientists viewpoint.

9. b E introduces the topic and the topic being talked about here is the effect of sunlight on the eyes. B presents the effect of direct sunlight on the eyes. 'CD' discusses effect of sunlight on eyes when we wear improper sunglasses. A states the conclusion that improper sunglasses don't block harmful sun rays.

10. d E starts off with stating what happened on a particular day in August 1973. A further goes into detail describing what happened 'BD' continues with the chain of events in this particular order.

PART – II : VOCABULARY

Common Confusables

- **accede, exceed**

  Accede means to agree, to allow; exceed means to go beyond, to surpass.

- **accept, except**

  Accept means to give approval or to receive willingly. Except means to exclude or leave out.

- **adapt, adept, adopt**

  Adapt means to adjust, adept means skilled and adopt means to take as your own.

- **adverse, averse**

  Adverse means inauspicious, hostile; averse means disinclined, repelled.

- **advice, advise**

  Advice is the noun and advise the verb.

- **affect, effect**

  Affect is a verb; effect is more usually a noun. When used as a verb it means to achieve, fulfil, realise. Effect means a result or a consequence.

- **aloud, allowed**

  Aloud means out loud, speaking so that someone else can hear you; allowed means permitted.

- **already, all ready**

  Already means by this time; all ready means prepared.

- **altogether, all together**

  Altogether means wholly; all together means everybody in a group.

- **all right, alright**

  All right is the correct form; alright is grammatically incorrect.

- **allude, elude**

  Allude means to refer to; elude means to dodge or escape.

- **allusion, illusion**

  Allusion is an indirect reference or hint; illusion means deception or mirage.

- **all ways, always**

  All ways means by every way or method; always means all the time, forever.

- **annual, annul**

  Annual means yearly; annul means to make void or invalid.

- **anyone, any one**

  Anyone means anybody, any person at all; any one means any one person and is followed by "of".

- **appraise, apprise**

  Appraise is to assess or estimate. Apprise is to inform or notify.

- **ascent, assent**

  Ascent is an upward movement; assent means agreement.

- **assistance, assistants**

  Assistance means help or aid; Assistants is the plural of assistant, one who gives help.

- **assure, ensure, insure**

  Assure means to guarantee; ensure means to make sure; insure means to protect against loss or damage.

- **auger, augur**

  Auger is a tool; augur means to predict.

- **baited, bated**

  Baited usually refers to traps or snares. When the reference is to someone who is hardly daring to breathe, the correct word is always bated.

- **bare, bear**

  Bare means naked; bear (apart from being a large animal) means to carry.

- **bazaar, bizarre**

  Bazaar is an exhibition or fair; bizarre means weird, grotesque, alien.

- **beside, besides**

  Beside means by the side of; besides means in addition to.

- **biannual, biennial**

  These two are really tricky! Biannual means happening twice a year; biennial means every two years.

- **blonde, blond**

  Because these are borrowed from French there is a feminine and masculine form. Blonde is feminine and blond is masculine.

- **bore, boar, boor**

  Bore as a noun is a boring or tiresome person, or something that you don't like doing; boar is a male pig; boor is a rude or insensitive person.

- **board, bored**

  Board is a long sheet of wood, also a group of people as in "Board of Directors", and as a verb means to go onto a ship, plane or other form of public transport; bored means not interested.

- **born, borne**

  Born is always the beginning of life, borne means carried.

- **bought, brought**

  Bought is the past tense of buy, brought is the past tense of bring.

- **braise, braze**

  Braise means to cook slowly in liquid (usually meat); braze most commonly means to solder with an alloy of copper and zinc.

- **brake, break**

  Brake means to stop; break means to smash.

- **bridal, bridle**

  Bridal has to do with brides and weddings; bridle as a noun means a halter or restraint; as a verb it means to restrain or to draw oneself up in anger.

- **by, buy, bye**

  By is a preposition meaning next to; buy means purchase; bye means farewell or good-bye.

- **canvas, canvass**

  Canvas is cloth or fabric; canvass means to seek votes, to survey, to sell door-to-door.

- **capital, capitol**

  Capital means the seat of government; money invested; excellent. Capitol is the building where government meets.

- **censor, sensor**

  Censor as a verb means to officially inspect and make deletions or changes (in books, letters, movies, etc.) usually because the deleted or changed material is regarded as offensive or harmful in some way, though movies these days are more likely to be given a rating instead; as a noun it refers to the official who does the censoring. Sensor is something that senses (for instance a burglar alarm has many sensors: for movement, body heat, etc.)

- **collaborate, corroborate**

  Collaborate means to work with someone; corroborate means to establish the truth of something.

- **compliment, complement**

  Compliment means praise or congratulate. You always pay someone a compliment, not a complement. Complement means to supplement, round out.

- **continual, continuous**

  Continual means something that happens frequently, with breaks between the occurrences. Continuous means something that happens without stopping!

- **co-operation, corporation**

  Co-operation (usually spelt without the hyphen in US English) means working together; corporation is a business organisation.

- **correspondence, correspondents**

  Correspondence is written communication; correspondents are those who write it.

- **creak, creek**

  Creak is both a noun and a verb and means squeak or groan (for instance, rusty hinges and loose floorboards creak); creek is a noun and means a waterway or stream.

- **credible, creditable**

  Credible means believable; creditable means praiseworthy or deserving credit.

- **criteria, criterion**

  Criterion is singular; criteria is plural.

- **curb, kerb**

  Curb means to control, as in "curb your temper", while kerb is the edge of a footpath or sidewalk.

- **desert, dessert**

  Desert means to abandon (and can also be a noun, meaning a wasteland); dessert is the sweet course of a meal.

- **device, devise**

  Device is a noun, meaning a gadget or (particularly in writing terms) an invention; devise is a verb, meaning to invent or plot.

- **discreet, discrete**

  Discreet means respectful, prudent; discrete means separate or detached from others.

- **draft, draught**

  Draft refers to the first writing of your novel or story (or any other document). You can also be drafted (enlisted or recruited) into the army, navy, etc.

  Draught is an air movement, a drink (as in "draught of ale") or refers to a horse (or other animal) used for pulling ploughs, etc (e.g., "draught horse").

- **elicit, illicit**

  Elicit means to extract or draw out; illicit means not legal.

- **eminent, imminent**

  Eminent means distinguished, famous; imminent means near, close at hand.

- **everyday, every day**

  Everyday means commonplace, ordinary; every day is used for something that happens daily.

- **everyone, every one**

  Everyone means every person in a group; every one means each person and is always followed by "of".

- **fair, fare**

  Fair means average, good-looking, pale, and unbiased. Fare is the money you pay to go somewhere by bus, train, plane, taxi, etc. It can also refer to a passenger.

- **farther, further**

  Farther is used for physical distance; further for non-physical.

- **faze, phase**

  The most common error is the use of phase when the writer means faze. To faze someone is to fluster or confuse them, whereas phase is mostly used in reference to a stage in someone's life—though it can be a stage in almost anything else.

- **flare, flair**

  Flare means to flash or blaze and (as a noun) is a pyrotechnic device; flair means ability or skill.

- **forbear, forebear**

  Forbear means to refrain from; forebear is an ancestor or forefather.

- **foreword, forward**

  Foreword is the preface in a book, usually written by someone who is not the author; forward means ahead, near the front.

- **forth, fourth**

  Forth means forward; fourth is after "third".

- **foul, fowl**

  Foul can mean dishonourable (by foul means), disgusting (a foul smell), entangle (rubbish dumped in the river can foul fishing lines); fowl is a bird.

- **found, founded**

  Found is the past tense of find; founded means started.

- **gibe, jibe**

  Gibe means to taunt; jibe means to agree, correspond or tally; in boating it means to shift the sails.

- **gorilla, guerrilla**

  Gorilla is a large ape; guerrilla is a particular kind of soldier.

- **hail, hale**

  Hail means to greet or to come from (as in "She hails from Mangalore") and as a noun it is frozen raindrops; hale means healthy or (as a verb) to haul.

- **hanged, hung**

  A criminal is always hanged; a picture is hung.

- **herd, heard**

  Herd is a group of animals; heard is the past tense of hear.

- **here, hear**

  Here refers to a location (as in "over here"). Hear is always what your ears do.

- **hoard, horde**

  Hoard means to stockpile and as a noun it is a cache of stockpiled stuff; horde is a large group.

- **hole, whole**

  Hole is an opening; whole means complete.

- **home, hone**

  Home is where one lives (or where the heart is!); hone means to sharpen.

- **immemorial, immortal**

  Immemorial means ancient beyond memory (as in the cliché "since time immemorial"); immortal means deathless, eternal.

- **intolerable, intolerant**

  Intolerable; means tiring, onerous crushing; intolerant means biased, prejudiced. Someone cannot be intolerable of another's beliefs.

- **irregardless, regardless**

  There is no such word as irregardless; the correct word is regardless

- **its, it's**

  It's is short for 'it is' and its is possessive—always.

- **later, latter**

  Later means afterwards; latter is the second of two things.

- **lay, laid**

  "Our hens lay every day."

  "The hens laid ten eggs yesterday."

- **lay, lie**

  "I lay down because I didn't feel well" and "I lie on my bed and read".

- **lead, led**

  Lead (pronounced led) is a heavy metal or (pronounced 'leed') the present tense of led.

- **lend, loan**

  Lend is a verb meaning to give something temporarily to someone; loan is a noun, meaning the temporary transfer of something to someone else.

- **lessen, lesson**

  Lessen means to make less; lesson is something you learn.

- **liable, libel**

  Liable means subject to, answerable for or likely; libel is written (as opposed to spoken) untruths about someone, which are injurious to that person's reputation, and for which you may be taken to court – though this distinction in defamation is applicable in English law, not Indian law.

- **licence, license**

  In British usage, licence is always the noun and license the verb.

- **lightening, lightning**

  Lightening means making lighter or brighter; lightning (which is always a noun) is what comes out of the sky, usually followed by a crack of thunder.

- **lose, loose**

  Lose always means mislaying or dropping something and not being able to find it, while loose means slack or free.

- **manner, manor**

  Manner means method, appearance, class, character; manor is strictly a large, stately house.

- **mantel, mantle**

  Mantel is the shelf above a fireplace, or the fireplace surrounding; mantle is a cloak or blanket.

- **marshal, marshall**

  Marshal is a military officer or a sheriff; marshall is a verb.

- **meet, mete, meat**

  Meet means to encounter (and can also mean fit or suitable); mete means to allot, apportion or distribute; meat refers to flesh as food.

- **mute, moot**

  Mute as a verb means to silence or quieten down, as a noun it's a little gadget used by string players (particularly violinists) to soften the sound from their instruments. As an adjective it means dumb or making no sound, as in "He looked at me in mute appeal." Moot means debatable.

- **no, know**

  Sounds silly that someone might mix these up, but it happens! No is always the opposite of yes; know is to be certain (that you know the difference!)

- **overdo, overdue**

  It baffles me that people get these mixed up, but they do. Overdo means to exaggerate or carry something too far; overdue is what your bills are when you forget to pay them!

- **passed, past**

  Passed is the past tense of pass. Past means a time that has gone.

- **peace, piece**

  Peace means the absence of war (or even noise); piece is a portion of something.

- **peer, pier**

  Peer as a noun means a person who is your equal and as a verb it means to squint or look obliquely at something; pier is a type of wharf or dock. pear (a fruit) and pare (to peel).

- **plain, plane**

  Plain means obvious, also unadorned or lacking in good looks; plane is a carpenter's tool or an abbreviation of aeroplane.

- **patience, patients**

  Patience means forbearance; patients are people under medical care.

- **peek, pique, peak**

  Pique means to excite or irritate; peek means to peep or snoop; peak as a noun means the summit or tip, and as a verb means to climax.

- **pour, pore**

  You pour sauces, gravies, etc, over your dinner, while pore means to study something—so, "pore over the book", not "pour over the book", which reads as though you might be damaging the book with an unnamed liquid substance!

- **practice, practise**

  In British usage, practice is always the noun and practise the verb.

- **premise, premises**

  Premise usually means assumption, supposition, while premises means an apartment, house or building and its grounds.

- **presence, presents**

  Presence means being near at hand; presents are gifts.

- **principal, principle**

  Principal means chief or main, also the amount borrowed in a loan; principle means regulations or ideals.

- **profit, prophet**

  Profit means gain, earnings, advantage, and is usually associated with business. A prophet is a seer, a diviner.

- **quiet, quite**

  Quiet means without noise; quite when used in fiction usually means moderately, but can also mean totally or entirely.

- **rain, reign, rein**

  Rain is the water that comes down from clouds; reign means to rule; rein is a strap, usually leather, for controlling an animal, especially a horse.

- **raise, raze**

  These two are exact opposites. Raise means to lift or build up and raze means to pull down.

- **reality, realty**

  Reality is real life; realty is real estate.

- **reference, reverence**

  Reference is something referred to, reverence means respect.

- **regimen, regiment**

  Regimen is a noun and is mostly used to refer to a prescribed way of life, or diet or exercise. It is also the action of governing. Regiment as a verb means to direct, command; as a noun it refers to a military unit.

- **residence, residents**

  Residence is a house; residents are the people who live there.

- **respectfully, respectively**

  Respectfully means politely; respectively means in the order stated.

- **retch, wretch**

  Retch means to gag or try to vomit; wretch is a grovelling person, a creep.

- **rifle, riffle**

  Rifle (apart from being a firearm) means to steal; riffle means to leaf through or browse.

- **right, rite, write**

  Right means correct; rite is a ceremony, usually religious; write means to make words.

- **road, rode**

  Road is a long surface for cars and other vehicles; rode is the past tense of ride.

- **role, roll**

  Role is a part in a play or film; roll as a noun is a document or something that is cylindrical in shape and as a verb it means to make something into a cylindrical shape, to turn or spin.

- **sale, sail**

  Sale is either offering something for purchase ("for sale") or offering it at a special price ("on sale"); sail is part of a ship or boat.

- **scene, seen**

  Scene is the place where something happens; seen is the past participle of see.

- **seam, seem**

  Seam is most often used to refer to the joining of two pieces of fabric with thread, but it can refer to other types of joins; seem means appear.

- **sell, cell**

  Sell is to exchange for money; cell is a small room (invariably lacking in comfort); also an organism (as in "stem cells"); the small divisions in something large such as a container or a table in a web page or word-processed document.

- **sever, severe**

  Sever means to separate, detach; severe means grim, stern.

- **serf, surf**

  Serf means slave or servant; surf is a wave and as a verb is also the action of riding the waves on a board or using a computer to find something on the Internet.

- **shear, sheer**

  Shear means to cut or clip; sheer means transparent (as in "sheer nylon hosiery"); steep (as in "a sheer drop"); total or absolute (as in "sheer stupidity").

- **shore, sure**

  Shore as verb means to brace or support; as a noun it is usually a beach but can also be a support or a brace; sure means certain, confident. So you do not sure up a company by borrowing more capital; you shore it up.

- **singly, singularly**

  Singly means individually, one-by-one; singularly means strangely.

- **site, sight, cite**

  Site always refers to location or place: building site; archaeology site. Sight always refers to vision, as in the cliché "a sight for sore eyes".

  Cite means to summon, or to refer to a source,

- **some time, sometime**

  Some time is a period of time and sometime means at some time not specified.

- **sole, soul**

  Sole as an adjective means single, as in "the sole cause of the problem"; as a noun it is a type of fish and the under part of a foot or a shoe. Soul generally refers to the invisible part of you that lives on after you die; also heart or mind; a human being (as in "no living soul").

- **stationary, stationery**

  Stationary means standing still.

  Stationery refers to writing paper.

- **statue, statute, stature**

  Statue is a carved or moulded likeness; statute is law; stature means height or status.

- **straight, strait**

  Straight means without bends; strait is a passage of water.

- **taut, taught, taunt**

  Taut means tight or firm; taught is the past tense of teach; taunt equals jeer, insult.

- **tenant, tenet**

  Tenant is one who rents a property; tenet is a principle or belief.

- **there, their, they're**

  There is a location: "Put it over there."

  Their is the possessive of they: "Their coats."

  They're is short for "They are ."

- **to, too, two**

  To is a preposition meaning towards; too means also or extremely (as in "You are walking too fast for me"); two is the number after one.

- **throes, throws**

  Throes are violent spasms or painful struggles, though not always physical. Throws means hurls or tosses. As a noun it means blankets or other types of covering.

- **vane, vain, vein**

  Vane is something that shows from which direction the wind is blowing;

  vain means too concerned about how one looks (though one can be vain about other things, of course!) and also means useless, as in "a vain attempt"; vein is a blood vessel, a channel.

- **venal, venial**

  Venal means dishonest, dishonourable; venial means forgivable, unimportant (as in "venial sins").

- **verses, versus**

  Verses is the plural of verse, something a poet writes; versus means against, in comparison with.

- **verse, worse**

  Verse is rhythmic writing, worse means of a poorer quality or lesser standard.

- **vicious, viscous**

  Vicious means savage, cruel; viscous means thick, gummy.

- **waist, waste**

  Waist is the part of your body around which you fasten your belt; waste as a noun mostly refers to stuff that's thrown away. As a verb it usually means to squander.

- **wary, weary**

  Wary means careful; weary means tired.

- **wave, waive**

  Wave means to flap your hand in farewell and as a noun is also a breaker on the beach; waive means to give up one's rights or claim.

- **waver, waiver**

  Waver means to be undecided; waiver means the giving up of rights or claims.

- **weak, week**

  Weak is the opposite of strong; week is seven days, Sunday to Saturday.

- **wet, whet**

  Wet as a verb means strictly to pour liquid on something. Whet means to sharpen or stimulate.

- **which, witch**

  Which is one of a group; witch is a sorcerer.

- **whose, who's**

  Whose is possessive, and who's is short for "who is".

- **wont, won't**

  Wont means accustomed; won't is short for "will not".

- **yoke, yolk**

  Yoke as a verb means to bind or confine. Yolk is the yellow part of an egg.

- **your, you're**

  Your is possessive and you're is short for "you are".

CHAPTER 4

Idioms

Use of Idioms

Idioms are expressions that convey a meaning that cannot be derived from the conjoined meanings of its elements.

Example:

The meaning of "to break ice" in the literal and idiomatic senses is:

Literal meaning: Before the bartender made the drink, he _broke the ice_ with a spoon and dropped it into the glass.

Idiomatic meaning: Before the conference began, the speaker _broke the ice_ with a joke.

The meaning of the idiom _to break the ice_ is:

1. to make a beginning and / or
2. to get through the first difficulties in starting a conversation or discussion.

Taking another example, the idiom **'jaundiced eye'** does not refer to a person afflicted with jaundice but that the person views something with a prejudice or bias. In a sentence, it would be used as: Since the terrorist attacks, all members of a certain community have been viewed with the jaundiced eye.

In this section, you are provided with a short conversation between **A** and **B**. A makes a statement or asks a question, to which B responds with an idiom. You are required to choose from the three options given as to what it is that B means to say.

Let us work out an example:

A: The situation in this company is deteriorating drastically.

B: It is bound to happen when you have the tail wagging the dog.

The obvious clue is that B has referred to something that is bad for business. The idiom "the tail wagging the dog" reverses the subject and the object - in normal circumstances a dog would wag the tail. So we need to look for something that is contrary to the normal and good business practices.

The options for what B means to say are:

(a)   The economy is run down

(b)   The Board of Directors is inefficient

(c)   The CEO's secretary is playing a dominating role

What would you choose?

Not (a) as it is bad for business but does not show a reversal of doer and deed.

Not (b) for the same reason.

(c) is the correct answer as it refers to the secretary being dominating when actually he/she is in a subordinate role.

There are no hard and fast rules to attempting this section. The more fiction and literary pieces you read, the greater the chances that you will understand meanings of idioms. You should also study these in grammar books and practise using them in your conversations. There are some websites that provide lists of idioms and their meanings. You could also get online practice. Finally, if you have to rely on guessing, common sense and logical thinking could help you through. To carry the day, you need to have more than two strings in your bow. (Can you decipher the meaning of this sentence?)

Now, try to solve the questions given below.

You have to select, from the three options, which one explains what **B** means, in response to **A**.

1.   A: Manohar deserved to be promoted; it is a pity he was not.

       B: That's what happens if you rub your boss the wrong way.

       What does B mean:

       (a) Manohar did not get along with his boss.

       (b) The boss favoured someone else.

       (c) Something Manohar had done or said had upset the boss.

2.   A: These are difficult times my family is going through.

       B: I know, but remember, every cloud has a silver lining!

What does B mean?

(a) The family will soon come into money and wealth.

(b) Every bad situation has something good coming out of it.

(c) Things are not what they seem.

3.   A: Nehru's 'Tryst with Destiny' speech is a sample of great oratory.

     B: It makes my hair stand on end, each time I hear or read it.

What does B mean?

(a) B is scared with what the speech conveys.

(b) B is emotionally moved by the speech.

(c) B thinks Nehru was a great orator.

4.   A: Are you all set for the entrance exam tomorrow?

     B: I know most topics like the back of my hand.

What does B mean?

(a) I am not well prepared in some areas.

(b) I am putting most topics to memory.

(c) I know most topics very well.

5.   A: I am finding it rather difficult to negotiate a higher salary with my boss.

     B: I suggest you spell out your demands in black and white.

What does B mean?

(a) Be clear and specific about what you want.

(b) Give your demands in writing.

(c) Take care of the presentation of your letter.

Important Idioms and Phrases

S.No.	Idioms & Phrases	Meaning
1	A ballpark figure	A general financial figure
2	A big gun	An important person
3	A bird in the hand is worth two in the bush	What you have is worth more than what you might have later
4	A bird's eye view	A view from a very high place that allows you to see a very large area
5	A blessing in disguise	a good thing that seemed bad at first
6	A blue Stocking	A learned/educated or intellectual woman
7	A Bolt from the Blue	Something completely unexpected that surprises you
8	A bone of contention	A source of quarrel
9	A bosom friend	A very close friend
10	A brown study	Dreaming
11	A burnt child dreads the fire	One who has had previous unpleasant experience is always scared of situations where such experiences are likely to be repeated
12	A cash cow	A product or service that makes a lot of money for a company
13	A close shave	Narrow escape
14	A cock and bull story	A foolishly incredible story
15	A dime a dozen	Something common
16	A Fidus Achates	A faithful friend or a devoted follower
17	A fish out of water	Anyone in an awkward
18	A hard nut to crack	A difficult problem
19	A house of cards	A poor plan
20	A litmus Test	A method that helps to know if something is correct
21	A little learning is a dangerous	People who don't understand something fully are dangerous
22	A man of straw	A man of no substance
23	A miss is as good as a mile	Comes nowhere near it. If someone narrowly misses the target it still is treated as a missed one or failure.
24	A nine days' wonder	An event which relates a sensation for a time but is soon forgotten
25	A penny for your thoughts	Tell me what you're thinking

26	A penny saved is a penny	Money you save today you can spend later
27	A perfect storm	the worst possible situation
28	A picture is worth 1000 words	Better to show than tell
29	A snowball effect	Events have momentum and build upon each other
30	A snowball's chance in hell	No chance at all
31	A stitch in time saves nine	Fix the problem now because it will get worse later
32	A storm in a teacup	A big fuss about a small problem
33	A thorn in the flesh	A constant source of annoyance
34	A wee bit	A little
35	A Wet Blanket	A person who discourages enjoyment or enthusiasm
36	A white elephant	A useless possession which is extremely expensive to keep
37	Above all	Chiefly, Mainly
38	Above board	Honest and open
39	Actions speak louder than words	Believe what people do and not what they say
40	Add fuel to the fire	To aggravate the situation
41	Add insult to injury	To make a bad situation worse
42	Afraid of one's own shadow	To become easily frightened
43	All that glitters are not gold	Things are not always as attractive as they appear
44	Alpha and omega	The beginning and the end
45	An acid test	A critical test
46	An Adonis	A very handsome man
47	An Ananias	A Liar
48	An Apollo	A Man with Perfect Physique
49	An apple a day keeps the doctor	Apples are good for you
50	An axe to grind	A personal interest in the matter
51	An ounce of prevention is worth a pound of cure	You can prevent a problem with little effort. Fixing it later is harder.
52	Apple of one's eye	Being cherished
53	Apple Pie Order	In perfect order
54	Arcadian Life	A blissful, happy, rural and simple life
55	As right as rain	Perfect
56	At a snail's pace	Very slowly
57	At arm's length	To keep at a distance
58	At daggers drawn	Bitterly hostile
59	At First Blush	At first sight
60	At home	Comfortable
61	At one's beck and call	Under his control
62	At one's wit's end	In a state where one does not know what to do
63	At sea	Confused and lost
64	At sixes and sevens	In a disordered/disorganized manner, chaotic
65	At the drop of a hat	Willingness to do something instantly
66	At the eleventh hour	At the last moment
67	Back out	To withdraw from a promise or contract
68	Back Upon	To be relevant
69	Back-Up	To support and sustain
70	Bag and Baggage	With all one's belongings

71	Bark up the wrong tree	Accuse or denounce the wrong person
72	Barking up the wrong tree	To be mistaken, to be looking for solutions in the wrong place
73	Barmecide feast	Imaginary Benefits
74	Be in a tight corner	In a very difficult situation
75	Be on cloud nine	Be very happy
76	Beat around the bush	Avoid saying what you mean, usually because it is uncomfortable
77	Beating around the bush	Avoiding the main topic
78	Bee-line	The shortest distance between two places
79	Behind one's back	Without one's Knowledge
80	Behind the scenes	In Private
81	Better late than never	Better to arrive late than not to come at all
82	Between the devil and the deep	Between two dangers
83	Birds of a feather flock together	People who are alike are often friends (usually used negatively)
84	Bite off more than you can chew	Not able to complete a task due to lack of ability
85	Bite off more than you can chew	Take on a project that you cannot finish
86	Bite the bullet	To get something over with because it is inevitable
87	Black and blue	Full of Bruises
88	Blessing in disguise	Something good and useful that did not initially seem that way
89	Blow up	To explode
90	Bolt from the blue	Something that happened without warning
91	Break a leg	Good luck
92	Break Down	Failure in something
93	Break off	To end or discontinue
94	Break the ice	To initiate a social conversation or interaction
95	Break Up	To disperse/dissolve
96	Bring to light	Disclose
97	Bring up	To rear
98	Burn bridges	Destroy relationships
99	Burn one's fingers	Get into trouble by interfering in other's affairs
100	Burn the midnight oil	Work or study hard
101	Bury the hatchet	End the quarrel and make peace
102	By fits and starts	In short periods, not regularly
103	By hook or by crook	By fair or foul means
104	By leaps and bounds	Rapidly
105	By the skin of your teeth	Just barely
106	Call a spade a spade	Speak frankly and directly
107	Call forth	To provoke
108	Call it a day	Stop working on something
109	Call out	To shout
110	Call upon	To order
111	Calm before the storm	Something bad is coming, but right now it's calm
112	Can't judge a book by its cover	Cannot judge something primarily on appearance
113	Care killed the cat	Don't fret and worry yourself to death
114	Carry on	To continue
115	Castaway	To throw aside
116	Cat and dog life	Life full of quarrels
117	Catch up with	To overtake
118	Catch up with	To overtake

119	Chew the cud	Ponder over something
120	Chip on your shoulder	When someone is upset about something that happened a while ago
121	Close fisted	Mean
122	Cock and bull story	Made up story that one should not believe
123	Come hell or high water	Possible obstacles in your path
124	Come off	To take place
125	Come off with flying colors	Be highly successful
126	Come rain or shine	No matter what
127	Comparing apples to oranges	Comparing two things that cannot be compared
128	Cost an arm and a leg	Be very expensive
129	Crocodile tears	Hypocritical Tears
130	Cross one's t's and dot	Be precise, careful and one's i's exact
131	Cry Down	To make little of
132	Cry for the moon	Ask for the impossible
133	Cry out against	To complain loudly against
134	Cry over spilled milk	Complaining about a loss or failure from the past
135	Curiosity killed the cat	Stop asking questions
136	Cut and dried	Readymade
137	Cut out	Designed for
138	Cut somebody some slack	Don't be so critical
139	Cut the mustard	Do a good job
140	Cut your cloth according to your cloth	Live within your income
141	Cutting corners	Doing something poorly in order to save time or money
142	Devil's Advocate	To present a counter-argument
143	Devil's bones	Dice
144	Devil's Playthings	Playing Cards
145	Die in harness	Die while in service
146	Do something at the drop of a hat	Do something without having planned beforehand
147	Do unto others as you would have them do unto you	Treat people fairly. Also known as "The Golden Rule"
148	Don't give up the day job	You are not very good at something. You could not do it professionally
149	Don't put all your eggs in one	Do not put all your resources in one basket (in one place or thing)
150	Don't beat a dead horse	Move on, this subject is over
151	Don't count your chickens before they hatch	Don't count on something good happening until it's happened.
152	Don't cry over spilt milk	There's no reason to complain about something that can't be fixed
153	Don't put all your eggs in one basket	What you're doing is too risky
154	Drop out	To fall
155	Drop-in	To Visit Casually
156	Easy does it	Slow down
157	Every cloud has a silver lining	Adverse conditions do not last forever
158	Every dog has his day	Sooner or later, everyone has his share of good fortune
159	Every dog has his day	Everyone gets a chance at least once
160	Evil days	A period of misfortune
161	Fall back	To Recede; To Retreat
162	Fall down	From a higher position to a lower one
163	Fall off	To Withdraw; To Drop Off

164	Fall under	To come under
165	Familiarity breeds contempt	The better you know someone the less you like him
166	Feather one's own nest	Make money unfairly
167	Feeling a bit under the weather	Feeling slightly ill
168	Fit as a fiddle	In good health
169	Fool's paradise	False sense of happiness
170	Fortune favours the bold	Take risks
171	Foul play	Cheating
172	Gain ground	Become Popular
173	Get a raw deal	To not be treated as well as other people
174	Get a second wind	Have more energy after having been tired
175	Get a taste of your own medicine	Get treated the way you've been treating others (negative)
176	Get along	To Prosper; To Progress; To Proceed
177	Get into	To be involved in
178	Get on with	To Live Pleasantly Together; To Progress
179	Get out of hand	Get out of control
180	Get something out of your	Do the thing you've been wanting to do so you can move on
181	Get wind of something	Hear news of something secret
182	Get your act together	Work better or leave
183	Give a dog a bad name and	Once a person loses his reputation
184	Give cold shoulder	To ignore
185	Give in	To Surrender; To Yield
186	Give over	Not to do any longer
187	Give someone the benefit of the doubt	Trust what someone says
188	Go after	To Follow; To Pursue
189	Go back to the drawing board	Start over
190	Go by	To follow
191	Go Down	To be accepted
192	Go down in flames	Fail spectacularly
193	Go on a wild goose chase	To do something pointless
194	Go to the devil	Be off
195	Go without	To remain without
196	Golden handshake	A big sum of money given to a person when he/she leaves a company or retires
197	Good things come to those who	Be patient
198	Good wine needs no bush	There is no need to advertise something good
199	Halcyon Days	A time when there are peace and happiness in the land
200	Hand to mouth	Live on only basic necessities
201	Hang about	To Loiter near a place
202	Hang in there	Don't give up
203	Hang upon	To depend upon
204	Hard and fast rules	Strict rules
205	Harp on the same string	Dwell on the same subject
206	Haste makes waste	You'll make mistakes if you rush through something
207	Have a card up one's sleeve	Have a secret plan in reserve
208	Have your head in the clouds	Not be concentrating

209	He has bigger fish to fry	He has bigger things to take care of than what we are talking about now
210	He has no backbone	He has no will of his own
211	He who laughs last laughs	I'll get you back for what you did
212	Hear it on grapevine	To hear rumors about something or someone
213	Hear something straight from the horse's mouth	Hear something from the person involved
214	He's a chip off the old block	The son is like the father
215	He's not playing with a full deck	He's dumb
216	He's off his rocker	He's crazy
217	Hold out	To Endure; To Refuse to yield; To continue; To offer
218	Hold to	Abide By
219	If the cap fits, wear it	If you think the remarks refer to you, then accept the criticism
220	If wishes were horses, beggars might ride	If wishing could make things happen, then even the most destitute people would have everything they wanted
221	In cold blood	Deliberately and without emotion
222	In hot water	In trouble
223	In the heat of the moment	Overwhelmed by what is happening at the moment
224	It is a poor workman who blames his tools	If you can't do the job, don't blame it on others
225	It is always darkest before the	Things are going to get better
226	It takes one to know one	You're just as bad as I am
227	It takes two to tango	Both people involved in a bad situation are responsible for it
228	It's Greek to me	Something that is not understandable
229	It's raining cats and dogs	It's raining hard
230	Jump the bandwagon	To join a popular activity or trend
231	Keep off	To ward off
232	Keep one's fingers crossed	The anxiety in which you hope that nothing will upset your plans
233	Keep up with	To keep pace with
234	Kill two birds with one stone	To solve two problems at a time with just one action
235	Know which way the wind is	Understand the situation (usually negative)
236	Last straw	The final problem in a series of problems
237	Leave no stone unturned	Use all available means
238	Let sleeping dogs lie	Leave something alone if it might cause trouble
239	Let the cat out of the bag	Reveal a secret
240	Like a cat on hot bricks	Very nervous
241	Like a fish out of water	In a strange situation
242	Like riding a bicycle	Something you never forget how to do
243	Like two peas in a pod	They're always together
244	Live and learn	I made a mistake
245	Lock, stock and barrel	The whole of everything
246	Look before you leap	Take only calculated risks
247	Make a clean breast of it	Confess – especially when a person has done a wrong thing
248	Make a face	To show dislike or disappointment through facial expressions
249	Make a long story short	Tell something briefly
250	Make hay while the sun shines	Take advantage of all opportunities
251	Make up one's mind	Decide
252	Mean business	Being Serious or Dedicated
253	Miss the boat	It's too late
254	Nip in the bud	Destroy in the early stage

255	No avail	Without any result
256	No pain, no gain	You have to work for what you want
257	Not a spark of decency	No Manners
258	Off-color	Not in the usual form
259	On Account of	Due to
260	On cloud nine	Very happy
261	On no account	Not for Any Reason
262	On tenterhooks	In a state of suspense and anxiety
263	On the ball	Doing a good job
264	On thin ice	On probation. If you make another mistake, there will be trouble.
265	Once bitten, twice shy	You're more cautious when you've been hurt before
266	Once in a blue moon	Something that happens very rarely
267	One swallow does not make a summer	It is unreliable to base one's conclusions on only a single test or incident
268	One's bread and butter	One's means of livelihood
269	Open the floodgates	Release something that was previously under control
270	Out of the blue	Happen unexpectedly
271	Out of the frying pan and into the	Things are going from bad to worse
272	Out of the question	Impossible
273	Out of the way	Strange
274	Out of the wood	Free from difficulties and dangers
275	Out on a limb	Do something risky
276	Over the Top	Totally excessive and not suitable for the occasion
277	Pay off old scores	Take revenge
278	Piece of cake	Something that is easy to understand or do
279	Play devil's advocate	To argue the opposite, just for the sake of argument
280	Play second fiddle	Take an unimportant part
281	Pull someone's leg	To joke with someone
282	Pull yourself together	Calm down
283	Push one's luck	Trying to obtain more than what one has
284	Put a spoke in one's wheel	To upset one's plans
285	Put something on ice	Put a projet on hold
286	Put the cart before the horse	Put or do things in the wrong order
287	Rain cats and dogs	Rain heavily
288	Rain on someone's parade	To spoil something
289	Rank and File	Ordinary People
290	Read between the lines	Understand the hidden meaning
291	Reap the harvest	Benefit or suffer as a direct result of past actions
292	Roll-up sleeves	To get yourself prepared
293	Run like the wind	Run fast
294	Saving for a rainy day	Saving money for later
295	See eye to eye	To be in agreement with
296	Shape up or ship out	Work better or leave
297	She is no chicken	She is older than she says
298	Shot in the dark	A complete guess
299	Show a clean pair of heals	Run away

300	Sink your teeth into	Do something with a lot of energy and enthusiasm
301	Sitting on the fence	Hesitate between two decisions
302	Skating on thin ice	Do or say something risky
303	Slow and steady wins the race	Reliability is more important than speed
304	Smell a rat	Suspect something foul
305	Snowed under	Busy
306	So far so good	Things are going well so far
307	Speak of the devil!	This expression is used when the person you have just been talking about arrives
308	Spill the beans	To disclose a secret
309	Spread like wild fire	Spread quickly
310	Stand in a good stead	To be useful or be of good service to someone
311	Stick to one's guns	Remain faithful to the cause
312	Strike while the iron is hot	To act at the right time
313	Take a back seat	Choose to be less important in a role
314	Take a leaf out of one's book	Imitate one
315	Take a rain check	Postpone a plan
316	Take it with a grain of salt	Don't take it too seriously
317	Take one to task	Rebuke
318	Take the plunge	Venture into something of one's interest despite the risks involved
319	Take to one's heels	Run away
320	Take with a grain/pinch of salt	To doubt the accuracy of information
321	That ship has sailed	It's too late
322	That's the last straw	My patience has run out
323	The ball is in your court	When it is up to you to make the next decision or step
324	The best of both worlds	The benefits of widely differing situations enjoyed at the same time
325	The best thing since sliced bread	A really good invention
326	The early bird gets the worm	The first people who arrive will get the best stuff
327	The elephant in the room	The big issue, the problem people are avoiding
328	The Heel of Achilles	A Weak Point
329	The pen is mightier than the	Words and communication have a greater effect than war
330	The pot calling the kettle black	Someone criticizing someone else he is just as bad
331	The whole nine yards	Everything, all the way.
332	There are clouds on the horizon	Trouble is coming
333	There are other fish in the sea	It's ok to miss this opportunity. Others will arise.
334	There's no such thing as a free	Nothing is entirely free
335	Think the world of	Admire someone very much
336	Those who live in glass houses shouldn't throw stones	People who are morally questionable shouldn't criticize others
337	Throw caution to the wind	Take a risk
338	Throw out of gear	Disturb the work
339	To all names	To abuse
340	To assume airs	To affect superiority
341	To backbite a person	To speak disguise about someone
342	To balance the books	To make certain that the amount of money spent is not more than the amount of money received.
343	To be in the doldrums	To be in low spirits

#	Idiom	Meaning
344	To be snowed under	To be very busy
345	To beat about the bush	Talk irrelevantly
346	To bell the cat	To face the risk
347	To bite the dust	To be Defeated in Battle
348	To blow one's own	To praise one's own trumpet achievement
349	To breadth one's last	To Die
350	To break the back of anything	To perform the most difficult part
351	To burn candle at both ends	To waste lavishly
352	To burn one's boats	Go back on a decision
353	To burn the candle at both ends	To expend energy in two directions at the same time
354	To cook the books	To modify financial statements
355	To die in harness	To continue at one's occupation until death
356	To eat humble pie	To apologize humbly and to yield under humiliating circumstances
357	To get bent out of shape	To get upset
358	To get the sack	To be dismissed from your job
359	To Grind	To have some selfish objective in view
360	To hit below the belt	To act unfairly in a contest
361	To jump from a frying pan into	To come out of one trouble and get into a worse
362	To keep the ball rolling	To keep things going
363	To kick the bucket	To die
364	To lead to the altar	To marry
365	To make bricks without straw	To attempt to do something without proper materials
366	To move heaven and earth	To make a supreme effort
367	To play ducks and drakes	To act foolishly or inconsistently
368	To pour oil on troubled waters	To make peace
369	To set the Thames on fire	To do something sensational or remarkable
370	To square the circle	To attempt something impossible
371	To stand aloof	To keep to oneself and not mix with others
372	To step into dead man's shoes	To come into an inheritance
373	To take the chair	To preside a meeting
374	To throw cold water upon	To discourage efforts
375	To throw dust in one's eyes	To try to deceive someone or mislead someone
376	To Upset the Apple Cart	To disturb the peace
377	To work your fingers to the bone or to sweat blood	To work really hard
378	Tooth and nail	With all one's power
379	Turn a deaf ear	Disregard / ignore what one says
380	Turn over a new leaf	Change for the better
381	Under his thumb	Under his control
382	Under the weather	Sick
383	Wash one's dirty linen	Discuss unpleasant in public-private matters before strangers
384	Wave a dead chicken	Do something useless
385	We see eye to eye	We agree
386	Weather the storm	Go through something difficult
387	We'll cross that bridge when we come to it	Let's not talk about that problem right now

388	When it rains it pours	Everything is going wrong at once
389	Whole nine yards	Everything. All of it
390	With a high hand	Oppressively
391	Wrap one's brain around	Concentrate on something to understand
392	Wrap your head around	Understand something complicated
393	You can catch more flies with honey than you can with vinegar	You'll get what you want by being nice
394	You can lead a horse to water, but you can't make him drink	You can't force someone to make the right decision
395	You can say that again	That's true, I agree
396	You can't have your cake and eat it too	You can't have everything
397	You can't judge a book by its	This person or thing may look bad, but it's good inside
398	You can't make an omelet without breaking some eggs	There's always a cost to doing something
399	Your guess is as good as mine	To have no idea about anything
400	Zero in on something	Focus all attention on one thing

CHAPTER 5

Phrasal Verbs

Use of Phrasal Verbs

You must be using phrasal verbs in your everyday language, without being aware of it. The passage below is a person's description of a typical morning. Read the paragraph and observe the underlined words. These are phrasal verbs uses that adds clarity to the writing.

The alarm goes off at 7:00. I wake up, lean over and turn off the alarm. I get up quickly and go downstairs. I put on the coffee. I go back upstairs and have a shower. I sing a song in the shower. I put on my clothes. When I come downstairs again, I have my first cup of coffee. Mmmmm! Then I have some toast and a second cup of coffee. I wash my cup and tidy up the kitchen. I take my bag and set off to work. It is 8:00 am. I lock up the house before I go. Sometimes I run to catch the bus. I get on the bus and go for three or four stops. Then I get off the bus. I go to work and say "GOOD MORNING!" to my first class. It is 8:45am.

It is best that you learn phrasal verbs through everyday reading and practice. Learning lists is a possibility but can be boring and not as effective. A list is provided for your reference. Remember this is not all-inclusive, but gives you a wide variety of phrasal verbs in everyday use.

The best way to become familiar with phrasal verbs (and you need to, as these are often set as "Complete the Sentence" exercises in your entrance exams. More than that, you need these in everyday conversation and in your written work.) is to be a regular reader of books. Fictional works are recommended, as are topical articles.

You will really help yourself if you read fiction and make a note of all the phrasal verbs you encounter. With phrasal verbs, nothing succeeds like practice!

You will see just how many phrasal verbs are used in everyday language when you set about making sentences with the many phrasal verbs with 'up' in them:

act up	blow up	break up	bring up	brush up
catch up	clean up	close up	get up	give up
grow up	hang up	keep up	line up	look up
open up	pass up	show up	sign up	take up
tear up	throw up	turn up	wrap up	

Note: Separable phrasal verbs can remain together when using an object that is a noun or noun phrase.

- I picked Tom up. (separable) OR I picked up Tom (inseparable).
- They put their friends up (separable). OR They put up their friends (inseparable).

Separable phrasal verbs MUST be separated when a pronoun is used:

- We picked him up at the station. **NOT** We picked up him at the station.
- They put them up. **NOT** They put up them.

Provided below is a list (by no means exhaustive) of phrasal verbs, with their meanings and how they should be used in sentences.

Verb	Meaning	Example
blow up	explode	The terrorists tried to blow up the railroad station.
bring up	mention a topic	My mother brought up that little matter of my prison record again.
bring up	raise children	It isn't easy to bring up children nowadays.
call off	cancel	They called off this afternoon's meeting.
do over	repeat a job	Do this homework over.
fill out	complete a form	Fill out this application form and mail it in.
fill up	fill to capacity	She filled up the grocery cart with free food.
find out	discover	My sister found out that her husband had been planning a surprise party for her.

give away	give something to someone else for free	The filling station was <u>giving away</u> free gas.
give back	return an object	My brother borrowed my car. I have a feeling he's not about to give it <u>back</u>.
hand in	submit something (assignment)	The students <u>handed in</u> their papers and left the room.
hang up	put something on hook or receiver	She <u>hung up</u> the phone before she hung up her clothes.
hold up	delay	I hate to <u>hold up</u> the meeting, but I have to go to the bathroom.
hold up (2)	rob	Three masked gunmen <u>held up</u> the Security Bank this afternoon.
leave out	omit	You <u>left out</u> the part about the police chase down Asylum Avenue.
look over	examine, check	The lawyers looked over the papers carefully before questioning the witness. (They <u>looked</u> them <u>over</u> carefully.)
look up	search in a list	You've misspelled this word again. You'd better <u>look</u> it <u>up</u>.
make up	invent a story or lie	She knew she was in trouble, so she made up a story about going to the movies with her friends.
make out	hear, understand	He was so far away, we really couldn't <u>make out</u> what he was saying.
pick out	choose	There were three men in the line-up. She picked out the guy she thought had stolen her purse.
pick up	lift something off something else	The crane <u>picked up</u> the entire house. (Watch them <u>pick</u> it <u>up</u>.)
point out	call attention to	As we drove through Paris, Fleur pointed out the major historical sites.
put away	save or store	We <u>put away</u> money for our retirement. She <u>put away</u> the cereal boxes.
put off	postpone	We asked the boss to <u>put off</u> the meeting until tomorrow. (Please <u>put</u> it <u>off</u> for another day.)
put on	put clothing on the body	I <u>put on</u> a sweater and a jacket. (I <u>put</u> them <u>on</u> quickly.)
put out	extinguish	The fire-fighters <u>put out</u> the house fire before it could spread. (They <u>put</u> it <u>out</u> quickly.)
read over	peruse	I <u>read over</u> the homework, but couldn't make any sense of it.
set up	To arrange, begin	My wife set up the living room exactly the way she wanted it. She set it up.
take down	make a written note	These are your instructions. <u>Take</u> them <u>down</u> before you forget.
take off	remove clothing	It was so hot that I had to <u>take off</u> my shirt.
talk over	discuss	We have serious problems here. Let's <u>talk</u> them <u>over</u> like adults.
throw away	discard	That's a lot of money! Don't just <u>throw</u> it <u>away</u>.
try on	put clothing on to see if it fits	She <u>tried on</u> fifteen dresses before she found one she liked.
try out	test	I <u>tried out</u> four cars before I could find one that pleased me.
turn down	lower the volume	Your radio is driving me crazy! Please <u>turn</u> it <u>down</u>.
turn down (2)	reject	He applied for a promotion twice this year, but he was <u>turned down</u> both times.
turn up	raise the volume	Grandpa couldn't hear, so he <u>turned up</u> his hearing aid.
turn off	switch off electricity	We <u>turned off</u> the lights before anyone could see us.
turn off (2)	Repulse	It was a disgusting movie. It really <u>turned</u> me <u>off</u>.
turn on	switch on the electricity	<u>Turn on</u> the CD player so we can dance.
use up	exhaust, use completely	The gang members <u>used up</u> all the money and went out to rob some more banks.

These phrasal verbs and their meanings are literal, and you should have no difficulty remembering them.

Practice: Make another sentence using each of the words given above. You may need to use the dictionary to get the meanings.

Inseparable phrasal verbs always remain together. It makes no difference if a noun or pronoun is used.

- We set off for the beach. / We set off for it.
- They are looking after the children. / They are looking after them.

Verb	Meaning	Example
call on	ask to recite in class	The teacher <u>called on</u> students in the back row.
call on (2)	visit	The old minister continued to <u>call on</u> his sick parishioners.
get over	recover from sickness or disappointment	I <u>got over</u> the flu, but I don't know if I'll ever <u>get over</u> my broken heart.
go over	review	The students <u>went over</u> the material before the exam. They should have *gone over* it twice.
go through	use up; consume	They country <u>went through</u> most of its coal reserves in one year. Did he <u>go through</u> all his money already?
look after	take care of	My mother promised to <u>look after</u> my dog while I was gone.
look into	Investigate	The police will <u>look into</u> the possibilities of embezzlement.
run across	find by chance	I <u>ran across</u> my old roommate at the college reunion.
run into	Meet	Carlos <u>ran into</u> his English professor in the hallway.
take after	Resemble	My second son seems to <u>take after</u> his mother.
wait on	Serve	It seemed strange to see my old boss <u>wait on</u> tables.
The meaning of these phrasal verbs is not literal and you will find it helps if you make your own sentences right away and *go over* them often.		

Practice: Make another sentence using each of the words given above. You may need to use the dictionary to get the meanings.

Three-word Phrasal Verbs

Some verbs are followed by two prepositions (or adverbs). These phrasal verbs are **ALWAYS** inseparable.

- I'm looking forward to meeting John. OR I'm looking forward to meeting him.
- They didn't get on with their mother. OR They didn't get on with her.

Verb	Meaning	Example
break in on	interrupt (a conversation)	I was talking to my mother on the phone when the operator <u>broke in on</u> our call.
catch up with	keep abreast	After our month-long trip, it was time to catch up with the neighbours and the news around town.
check up on	examine, investigate	The boys promised to <u>check up on</u> the condition of the computer from time to time.
come up with	to contribute (suggestion, money)	After years of giving nothing, the old parishioner was able to come up with a thousand-dollar donation.
cut down on	curtail (expenses)	We tried to <u>cut down on</u> the money we were spending on entertainment.
drop out of	leave school	I hope none of my students <u>drop out of</u> school this semester.

get along with	have a good relationship with	I found it very hard to get along with my brother when we were young.
get away with	escape blame	Janik cheated on the exam and then tried to get away with it.
get rid of	eliminate	The citizens tried to get rid of their corrupt mayor in the recent election.
get through with	finish	When will you ever get through with that program?
keep up with	maintain pace with	It's hard to keep up with the Joneses when you lose your job!
look forward to	anticipate with pleasure	I always look forward to the beginning of a new semester.
look down on	despise	It's typical of narrow-minded citizens to look down on their geographical neighbours.
look in on	visit (somebody)	We were going to look in on my brother-in-law, but he wasn't home.
look out for	be careful, anticipate	Good instructors will look out for early signs of failure in their students.
look up to	respect	First-graders really look up to their teachers.
make sure of	verify	Make sure of the student's identity before you let him into the classroom.
put up with	tolerate	The teacher had to put up with a great deal of nonsense from the new students.
run out of	exhaust supply	The runners ran out of energy before the end of the race.
take care of	be responsible for	My eldest sister took care of us younger children after Mom died.
talk back to	answer impolitely	The star player talked back to the coach and was thrown off the team.
think back on	recall	I often think back on my childhood with great pleasure.
walk out on	abandon	Her husband walked out on her and their three children.

Phrasal Verbs which Don't Take Objects

Some phrasal verbs do not take objects. These phrasal verbs are **ALWAYS** inseparable.

*   The thieves got away. The bus broke down on the way to work. She got up early.

Verb	Meaning	Example
Break down	stop functioning	That old Jeep had a tendency to break down just when I needed it the most.
catch on	become popular	Popular songs seem to catch on in Bangalore first and then spread around.
come back	return to a place	My father promised that we would never come back to this horrible place.
come in	enter	They tried to come in through the back door, but it was locked.
come to	regain consciousness	He was hit on the head very hard, but after several minutes, he started to come to again.
come over	to visit	The children promised to come over, but they never do.
drop by	visit without appointment	We used to just drop by, but they were never home, so we stopped doing that.
eat out	dine in a restaurant	When we visited Paris, we loved eating out in the sidewalk cafes.

get by	survive	Uncle Harish didn't have much money, but he always seemed to get by without borrowing money from relatives.
get up	arise	Grandmother tried to get up, but the couch was too low, and she couldn't make it on her own.
go back	return to a place	It's hard to imagine that we will ever go back to Pune.
go on	continue	He would finish one Dickens novel and then just go on to the next.
go on (2)	happen	The cops heard all the noise and stopped to see what was going on.
grow up	get older	Ramanuj grew up to be a lot like his father.
keep away	maintain distance	The judge warned the stalker to keep away from his victim's home.
keep on	continue with the same	He tried to keep on singing long after his voice was ruined.
pass out	lose consciousness,	He had drunk too much; he passed out on the sidewalk outside the bar.
show off	Show haughtily	Whenever he sat down at the piano, we knew he was going to show off.
show up	arrive	Day after day, Danesh showed up for class twenty minutes late.
wake up	arouse from sleep	I woke up when the rooster crowed.

Practice: Make a another sentence using each of the words given above. You may need to use the dictionary to get the meanings.

<u>TIP!</u>

<u>**If you are not sure whether a phrasal verb is separable or inseparable, ALWAYS use a noun or nouns phrase and DO NOT separate. In this manner, you will always be correct!**</u>

Rules of Spelling

Do you find yourself misspelling words often? Are you handicapped without the 'spell check' function on your computer? Are you fed up and irritated at losing marks for silly spelling errors? Don't be! Improving your spelling is really quite simple, and all you have to do is keep a few simple rules in mind. Use this spelling guide to make sure you don't lose marks for pointlessly silly mistakes!

SPELLING PLURAL NOUNS

1. Most words add **s** to the root forms without any change (barn - barns).

2. Words ending in sh, ch, ss, x, and z, usually add es to form the PLURAL (bush - bushes).

3. Words ending in a consonant and y change the y to I, and add es (party - parties).

4. Some words ending in f change the f to v and add es (calf - calves).

5. Some singular words have different words for their plural form (man - men; mouse - mice; goose-geese).

SUFFIXES

1. A letter or a syllable placed after a word to form a new word is called a 'suffix'. Some suffixes are: 's', 'es', 'ed', 'ing', 'er', 'est', 'ly', 'ful', 'able', 'ible', 'ment', 'ive', 'ance', 'ence', 'ion', 'tion', 'ition', 'ation', 'sion', 'ous', 'ious', 'less', and 'al'. Most often, these suffixes are used to derive the adjectival form of a noun. Sometimes a word may even have two suffixes. For example, 'respectfully' has the two suffixes 'ful' and 'ly' added to the root word 'respect'.

2. Many words are formed by adding 'ed' and 'ing' without any change (furnish - furnished - furnishing).

3. Words ending in a silent 'e' drop the 'e' before adding 'ed' and 'ing' (move - moved - moving).

4. Words ending in a consonant and 'y' change the 'y' to 'i' before adding 'ed', but do not make any change before adding 'ing' (deny - denied - denying).

5. Words ending in a vowel and 'y' add 'ed' and 'ing' without making any other change (delay - delayed - delaying).

PREFIXES

1. A syllable placed before a word to change its meaning is called a 'prefix'. Some prefixes are 'im', 'un', 'in', 'co', 'dis', 'inter'. Very often, you will find that a prefix has the effect of deriving the opposite of the word it is added on to.

DOUBLING THE FINAL CONSONANT

1. Words of one syllable ending in a single consonant preceded by a single vowel double the final consonant before adding 'ed' and 'ing' (trim - trimmed - trimming).

2. Words of two or more syllables double the final consonant before adding 'ed' and 'ing' when these conditions are met: the last syllable ends in a single consonant preceded by a single vowel, and the accent is on the last syllable (refer - referred - referring).

POSSESSIVE FORMS

1. Singular nouns form the possessive by adding an apostrophe and 's' (pilot - pilot's).

2. Plural nouns that end in 's' add only an apostrophe to form the possessive (aviators - aviators').

3. Plural nouns that do not end in s add the apostrophe and s to form the possessive (men - men's).

CONTRACTIONS

1. A word or phrase that has been shortened by leaving out some of the letters is called a 'contraction'.

2. An apostrophe is used to show that the letters have been omitted (won't - will not), (o'clock - of the clock).

CAPITALS

1. The beginning of a sentence is always capitalised (The day was bright and sunny.).

2. The names of holidays are capitalised (Christmas, Valentine's Day).

3. The names of the months of the year and the days of the week are capitalised (January, Monday).

4. The names of countries are capitalised (India, Great Britain).

5. When you write the name of a particular avenue or street, capitalise the words avenue and street (Fifth Avenue, Oak Street).

6. The abbreviations Mr., Mrs. and Ms. are always capitalised and followed by a period (Mr. Callahan, Mrs. Perry, Ms. Smith).

7. The names of deities are capitalised (God, Allah, Buddha, Saviour).

8. The word 'republican' is capitalised when it refers to the Republican party (The Republicans won the election.). That is, when a word that can be used as both a common noun and a proper noun is used in the latter sense, make sure you capitalise it.

9. When words like senator and general are used as titles with a person's name, they are capitalised (General Herkes distinguished herself in battle.).

10. We capitalise the words capitol, senate, building, supreme and court when referring to the Capitol Building, the Senate, the Supreme Court of Canada.

LETTERS AND SYLLABLES

1. The vowels are a, e, i, o, u, and sometimes y and w. The other letters are consonants.

2. Two vowels written together often have the sound of a single vowel. (In brain, the 'ai' has the sound of 'a'. In 'eagle' the 'ea' has the sound of a long 'e', but in 'bread' it has the sound of a short 'e'. This rule will help you with the 'ei' and 'ie' words: 'i' comes before 'e' except after 'c' or when sounded like 'a', as in 'neighbour' and 'weigh'.

3. A syllable is a word or part of a word, which has one vowel sound and is spoken as a unit. (boy is a one-syllable word; chil-dren is a two-syllable word; or-na-ment is a three syllable word. In every word of two or more syllables one syllable is given more emphasis than the other. This extra emphasis is called accent, and is shown in the dictionary by an accent mark (')

4. (In meet' ing the first syllable is accented.) Most words have only one accented syllable, but some have more than one (in' for ma' tion). The accent that is the heavier is called the primary accent. The other accent is called the secondary accent.

5. In your dictionary each word is re-spelled according to its pronunciation. The vowels are marked according to their sounds, and the accented syllables are shown. The marks for the vowel sounds are called diacritical marks. These marks vary from dictionary to dictionary. Please consult the beginning of your own dictionary for the explanation of diacritical marks used in that particular publication.

6. The two words at the top of each dictionary page are called guidewords. The guidewords are the first and last words on that particular page.

SPECIAL WORDS

1. Compound Words are made by writing two small words together to make one larger word. (newspaper, somebody)

2. A root word is the root, or beginning word, from which another word is made. 'Play' is the root word of 'plays', 'played' and 'playing'.

3. Derived words are words that come from other words. 'Suitable' is derived from 'suit'; 'advertisement' from 'advertise'. Sometimes the spelling of the root word is slightly changed in the derived word.

4. A synonym is a word having almost the same meaning as another word. (replied - answered; accurate - exact)

5. An antonym is a word that is opposite in meaning to another word. (private -public; good - bad)

6. Homonyms are words that are pronounced alike but which are spelled in different ways and have different meanings (knew - new; steel - steal; deer - dear)

Looks a little complicated, doesn't it? But don't worry – remember that you don't have to go about learning these rules – you must acquire the habit of following these rules over time. The more you read and write, the easier it will be for you to avoid spelling mistakes! Most important of all – use your dictionary well! It has a wealth of information on how to use words, in speech as well as in writing, and you would be giving up a wonderful opportunity to improve your English if you don't make full use of the lexicon!

CHAPTER 7

Cloze Test

Developing vocabulary skills will also enable one to solve Cloze test. A cloze test is a paragraph from which certain words have been replaced with a blank. There are four words given for every blank. One has to choose the most appropriate word from the given options. Strategies for solving the Cloze test:

1. Read the whole paragraph alongwith the missing blanks and try to find out the main idea.
2. Try to find out the connotation indicated by the author, such as whether the paragraph is positive, negative or neutral. This will give further clue in effectively selecting the words for each blank.
3. Try to trace various linking words such as conjunctions and prepositions which give further clue regarding the type of word required for the blank.

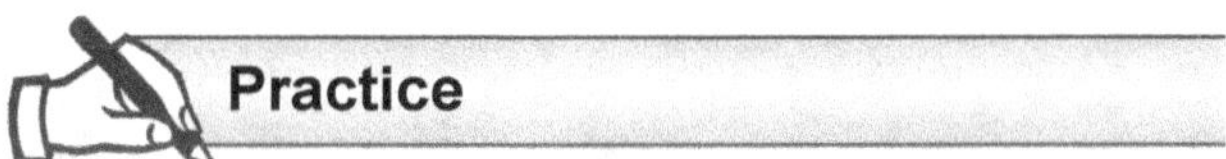

Practice

Directions: Read the following paragraph and choose the most appropriate word for each blank. The first one has been done for you. Look at the explanation for the first one on the next page.

Only public universities have the potential to be truly world class institutions. Institutions and programmes of national ___1___ have already been identified by the Government. But these institutions have not been ___2___ or consistently supported. The top institutions require sustained funding from public sources. Academic salaries must be high enough to attract excellent scientists and scholars. Fellowships and other grants should be available for bright students. An academic culture that is based on merit-based norms and competition for advancement and research funds is a necessary component, as is a ___3___mix of autonomy to do creative research and accountability to ___4___ productivity. World class universities require world class professors and students — and a culture to sustain and ___5___ them. A clearly

___6___academic system has not been created in India — a system where there are some clearly ___7___ institutions that receive significantly greater resources than other universities. One of the main reasons that the University of California at Berkeley is so good is that other California universities receive much less support. India's best universities require sustained state support — they require the ___8___ that they are indeed top institutions and deserve ___9___ support. But they also require effective management and an ___10___ of an academic meritocracy. At present, the structures are not in place to permit building and sustaining top-quality programmes even if resources are provided.

1.   (a) prominence   (b) level
   (c) standards   (d) prestige

2.   (a) primarily   (b) compulsarily
   (c) precisely   (d) adequately

3.   (a) fundamental   (b) judicious
   (c) relevance   (d) nominal

4.   (a) ensure   (b) enable
   (c) attain   (d) sustain

5.   (a) challenge   (b) stimulate
   (c) provoke   (d) promote

6.   (a) established   (b) explained
   (c) defined   (d) differentiated

7.   (a) identified   (b) justified
   (c) associated   (d) selective

8.   (a) preference   (b) recognition
   (c) status   (d) permission

9.   (a) immense   (b) sufficient
   (c) exceptional   (d) commensurate

10.	(a) ethos	(b) aestheticism
	(c) iota	(d) element

[Answers: 2.(d), 3.(b), 4.(a), 5.(b), 6.(d), 7.(a), 8.(b), 9.(d), 10.(d)]

First, read the whole paragraph in order to orient yourself with the given subject matter.

Explanation

Word Class: Prominence (noun), Level (noun), Standards (noun), Prestige (noun)

Function and Contextual Clues:: The word in the blank should reveal some quality that these institutions possess. This can be ascertained from the word 'national' which precedes the blank.

From the given choices - 'Prominence' means something that is particularly noticeable'. 'Level' pertains to an even surface, 'standard' refers to a benchmark or customs established by authority' and 'prestige' means reputation.

The choices for the first blank are quite close. However, it is the next sentence that provides another contextual clue. It explains that the chosen institutions have not been supported consistently. Also, the first sentence presents the condition that only public universities can become world class institutions. Therefore, the government has recognized some institutions that have the potential. So the meaning of the given sentence is that institutions that have this potential or whose potential is clearly identifiable; such institutions have already been spotted by the government. Thus, out of the four choices 'prominence' fits best. 'Level, prestige and standard' do not fit because the government is not setting a benchmark for the institutions. In fact the government is only identifying the institutions that have the potential of becoming world class institutions.

Now, using the same approach fill the other blanks and complete the paragraph.

Given below are passages that contain blanks that are supposed to be filled in with the appropriate word from the four given choices. You can scan through the passage in an instant to get the gist, and then read carefully and fill in the blanks. Remember that consistency in logic and context is the key to develop the overall paragraph.

Exercise

Passage – 1

Many young people have had no chance of going to the mountains. I earnestly hope that the chance may ... 1 ... especially to those who live in ... 2 ... cities. We have two bits ... 3 ... grand mountain country nearer than ... 4 ... Alps or Scotland, the Snowdon District ... 5 ... the Lake District. The sooner they ... 6 ... National Parks the better, places of ... 7 ... secured for us and future generations to ... 8 ... in, to climb in, or to ... 9 ... alone in. Let us see that they are ... 10 ... used; not as Hitler and Mussolini ... 11 ... the Alps to foster in young ... 12 ... the love of domination, and to ... 13 ... them for aggressive warfare. Let us ... 14 ... them as places where we may ... 15 ... adventure, and, refreshment for mind and ... 16 ... Mountaineering has this advantage over ... 17 ... other sports, entertainment depends very little ... 18 ... on natural ability or technical skill ... 19 ... nobody loses because somebody wins. By all ... 20 ... study the climbing technique if it interests you.

1.	(a) happen	(b) occur
	(c) come	(d) get

2.	(a) the	(b) a
	(c) your	(d) we

3.	(a) of	(b) in
	(c) at	(d) for

4.	(a) some	(b) those
	(c) the	(d) an

5.	(a) in	(b) of
	(c) and	(d) on

6.	(a) become	(b) approach
	(c) turn	(d) reach

7.	(a) beauty	(b) loveliness
	(c) prettiness	(d) cleanliness

8.	(a) stand	(b) run
	(c) walk	(d) dance

9.   (a) get   (b) be
       (c) feel   (d) stay

10.   (a) always   (b) well
       (c) accurately   (d) correctly

11.   (a) used   (b) abused
       (c) misused   (d) accused

12.   (a) population   (b) men
       (c) children   (d) world

13.   (a) instruct   (b) train
       (c) teach   (d) tutor

14.   (a) use   (b) desire
       (c) regard   (d) adjust

15.   (a) feet   (b) experience
       (c) find   (d) search

16.   (a) soul   (b) spirit
       (c) body   (d) conscious

17.   (a) most   (b) none
       (c) some   (d) all

18.   (a) indeed   (b) of course
       (c) certainly   (d) surely

19.   (a) for   (b) and
       (c) when   (d) while

20.   (a) accounts   (b) standards
       (c) means   (d) rights

2.   (a) feels   (b) offers
       (c) owes   (d) acknowledges

3.   (a) money   (b) gratefulness
       (c) thanks   (d) gratitude

4.   (a) labours   (b) discoveries
       (c) achievements   (d) successes

5.   (a) strange   (b) useful
       (c) advantageous   (d) profitable

6.   (a) decrease   (b) disappear
       (c) alleviate   (d) belittle

7.   (a) unrest   (b) discomfort
       (c) anxiety   (d) sacrifice

8.   (a) possible   (b) impossible
       (c) plausible   (d) impertinent

9.   (a) use   (b) relevance
       (c) cost   (d) value

10.   (a) peace   (b) rest
       (c) relief   (d) comfort

11.   (a) large   (b) big
       (c) wide   (d) broad

12.   (a) work   (b) labour
       (c) effort   (d) enterprise

13.   (a) easy   (b) resourceful
       (c) fortunate   (d) unlucky

14.   (a) subjected   (b) averse
       (c) inclined   (d) used

Passage – 2

Science has made an ... 1 ... contribution to the relief of human suffering and humanity ... 2 ... a deep debt of ... 3 ... to scientists whose ... 4 ... and sacrifices have led to the many ... 5 ... discoveries and inventions which have done so much to ... 6 ... human pain and ... 7... . It is indeed ... 8 ... to calculate the ... 9 ... of science in providing ... 10 ... to suffering mankind. In the first place, machines have to a ... 11 ... extent replaced human ... 12 ... . The men of today are more ... 13 ... than their brethren of two generations past who were ... 14 ... to severe physical strain.

1.   (a) excessive   (b) enormous
       (c) intensive   (d) active

Passage – 3

The country has made considerable progress in the ... 1 ... of health with which the common men, the poorer sections of society, are ... 2 ... concerned. The result of the progress can be ... 3 ... from the fact that the average expectancy of life has increased. The rate of mortality has ... 4 ... . The number of medical colleges has increased. About 800 public health centers have been ... 5 ... in development blocks. It is ... 6 ... that all the centers do not have doctors. It must, however, be ... 7 ... that constant efforts are being made to make up the leeway.

There is, however, a great demand for the opening of new hospitals. It is not possible to provide trained personnel everywhere.

1. (a) domain   (b) area
   (c) field   (d) region

2. (a) somewhat   (b) purely
   (c) vitally   (d) seemingly

3. (a) judged   (b) inferred
   (c) seen   (d) analysed

4. (a) dipped   (b) cut down
   (c) dropped   (d) slipped

5. (a) initiated   (b) erected
   (c) raised   (d) established

6. (a) lamentable   (b) regrettable
   (c) definable   (d) None of these

7. (a) admitted   (b) confessed
   (c) known   (d) understood

Passage – 4

It is difficult to ... 1 ... the future course of events. We cannot be ... 2 ... . I see some danger ... 3 ... . We cannot afford to ... 4 ... our efforts. We have to be prepared for every sacrifice. We ... 5 ... do without some ... 6 ... of life. It is the government's endeavour to provide the necessities of life of the people. But we cannot be too sure. We cannot say if our friends will continue to stand by us. Each one of us has, therefore, to be prepared for the biggest sacrifice. This should be constantly ... 7 ... in mind. As I said, truth and justice are on our side and victory shall be ours.

1. (a) depict   (b) predict
   (c) judge   (d) edict

2. (a) satisfied   (b) deficient
   (c) complacent   (d) implemented

3. (a) in front   (b) before
   (c) lead   (d) ahead

4. (a) lax   (b) relax
   (c) hoax   (d) None of these

5. (a) have to   (b) may have to
   (c) might have to   (d) will have to

6. (a) necessaries
   (b) necessities
   (c) vitalities
   (d) essentials

7. (a) kept   (b) retain
   (c) bore   (d) born

Passage – 5

Over the entire field of policy making, the problems facing the government are increasingly scientific and technological in ... 1 ... . Our decisions in defence and foreign ... 2 ... are increasingly governed by the developments in military and civil technology, ... 3 ... in such matters as armament and disarmament, the ... 4 ... of a new law for the seas or an international regime for space. The ... 5 ... field of industry and agriculture, education, health and welfare confronts us with a wide range of technological choices, and even decisions in such ... 6 ... non-scientific areas as taxation and procurement ... 7 ... affect the pace and ... 8 ... of the nation's technological progress.

1. (a) intent   (b) content
   (c) essence   (d) pith

2. (a) events   (b) happenings
   (c) affairs   (d) conditions

3. (a) in particular   (b) especially
   (c) virtually   (d) seemingly

4. (a) detail   (b) elaboration
   (c) spreading   (d) dimension

5. (a) complete   (b) entire
   (c) all   (d) whole

6. (a) obviously   (b) clearly
   (c) seemingly   (d) None of these

7. (a) willingly   (b) profoundly
   (c) superficially   (d) intensely

8. (a) quality   (b) caliber
   (c) talent   (d) intensity

Passage – 6

The ... 1 ... of education has also been a ... 2 ... instrument in emphasizing and shaping the underlying unity of mankind. The best ... 3 ... perhaps in which we can describe the present ... 4 ... is to call it a 'decade of promise'. The marvels of science, the immense ... 5 ... of harnessing nuclear energy for peaceful purposes and urge to ... 6 ... resources to their optimum level have all of them significantly contributed in tackling problems on a ... 7 ... scale rather than attempting to solve these baffling issues of ignorance, poverty and disease separately by individuals and nations.

1.   (a) need   (b) mode
       (c) spread   (d) development

2.   (a) effective   (b) defective
       (c) latest   (d) potent

3.   (a) form   (b) method
       (c) format   (d) manner

4.   (a) period   (b) decay
       (c) decade   (d) age

5.   (a) effects   (b) labour
       (c) possibilities   (d) capability

6.   (a) materialize   (b) utilize
       (c) synthesize   (d) pressurize

7.   (a) global   (b) globe
       (c) world   (d) universal

Passage – 7

Gandhiji had little sense of beauty or artistry in ... 1 ... objects though he ... 2 ... natural beauty. The Taj Mahal was for him an ... 3 ... of forced labour and little more. His sense of smell was ... 4 ... . And yet in his own way, he had ... 5 ... the art of living and had made of his life an artistic whole. Every ... 6 ... had meaning and grace without a ... 7 ... touch. There were no rough ... 8 ... or sharp ... 9 ... about him, no trace of ... 10 ... or commonness in which unhappily our middle classes ... 11 ... . Having found an inner peace he ... 12 ... it to others and ... 13 ... through life's ... 14 ... ways with firm and ... 15 ... steps.

1.   (a) man-made   (b) material
       (c) vulgar   (d) worldly

2.   (a) accepted   (b) appreciated
       (c) admired   (d) abhorred

3.   (a) building   (b) embodiment
       (c) explanation   (d) monument

4.   (a) limited   (b) meek
       (c) strong   (d) feeble

5.   (a) discovered   (b) invented
       (c) realized   (d) sensed

6.   (a) account   (b) gesture
       (c) indication   (d) word

7.   (a) false   (b) right
       (c) true   (d) benign

8.   (a) ground   (b) manners
       (c) edges   (d) words

9.   (a) contours   (b) ideas
       (c) weapons   (d) corners

10.   (a) capacity   (b) hostility
       (c) caprice   (d) vulgarity

11.   (a) excel   (b) sustain
       (c) follow   (d) dislike

12.   (a) absorbed   (b) released
       (c) radiated   (d) reflected

13.   (a) followed   (b) marched
       (c) peeped   (d) muddled

14.   (a) easy   (b) simple
       (c) ordinary   (d) tortuous

15.   (a) long   (b) tottering
       (c) undaunted   (d) quick

Passage – 8

There is a(n) ... 1 ... realization that the world is a single ... 2 ..., and the diversities that one notices are only ... 3 ... and not real. It is the spirit of universalism that is fast spreading to every ... 4 ... and corner of the earth. This spirit of ... 5 ... has become possible, thanks to the many discoveries and inventions which science and technology have made available to mankind during the last few years. We have, in a sense, today ... 6 ... time and space, and what occurs in one part of the universe finds its ... 7 ... in a matter of a few seconds in the other. What was considered to be mere ... 8 ... of imagination or fantasy, say, a quarter of a century ago, has become reality in our own lives.

1. (a) decreasing   (b) increasing
    (c) squeezing   (d) freezing

2. (a) unit   (b) unity
    (c) parity   (d) trinity

3. (a) superfluous   (b) superficial
    (c) surface   (d) imperial

4. (a) hook   (b) look
    (c) nook   (d) brook

5. (a) awakening   (b) quickening
    (c) hankering   (d) dwindling

6. (a) overcome   (b) contained
    (c) conquered   (d) handled

7. (a) duplicate   (b) echo
    (c) supplicate   (d) voice

8. (a) figment   (b) fiction
    (c) segment   (d) concerned

Passage – 9

The solution to the many ... 1 ... problems of present-day India in different fields — a challenging task to be ... 2 ... within the lifetime of a generation — most obviously will make many demands ... 3 ... the youth who are to ... 4 ... leadership of the nation in the coming years. Students have a deeper understanding of the problems ... 5 ... the country. Remember without hard and sustained work, dedicated ... 6 ... and fervour and, above all, without the collective discipline and national character the realization of our goals will neither be smooth nor easy.

1. (a) baffling   (b) squabbling
    (c) nibbling   (d) breathing

2. (a) completed   (b) done
    (c) accomplished   (d) accompanied

3. (a) on   (b) in
    (c) for   (d) at

4   (a) presume   (b) consume
    (c) assume   (d) take

5. (a) confronting   (b) lacing
    (c) defacing   (d) facing

6. (a) fervour   (b) zeal
    (c) seal   (d) weal

Passage – 10

India has for ... 1 ... given the lead in different fields and the impact of its civilization and culture has spread to the ... 2 ... corners. This has become possible, thanks to the lead given by her sages and saints, statesmen and scholars and poets and litterateurs. It is training and education that ... 3 ... contributed to her progress. As the Radhakrishnan Commission has rightly mentioned, "If India is to ... 4 ... the confusion of our times, she must ... 5 ... for guidance not to those who are lost in the mere exigencies of the passing hour, but to her men of letters. Her men of science, to her poets and artists and to her discoverers and inventors. These intellectual ... 6 ... of civilization are to be found and trained at the universities, which are the ... 7 ... of the inner life of the Nation."

1. (a) years   (b) periods
    (c) ages   (d) time

2. (a) furthest   (b) longest
    (c) farthest   (d) widest

3. (a) fundamentally (b) basically
    (c) eventually   (d) finally

4. (a) create   (b) remove
    (c) confront   (d) contribute to

5. (a) turn   (b) return
    (c) go   (d) move

6. (a) guardians   (b) perpetuation
    (c) dons   (d) pioneers

7. (a) epitome   (b) sanctuaries
    (c) temples   (d) None of these

Answer Keys

Passage - 1

1. (c)	**2.** (a)	**3.** (a)	**4.** (c)	**5.** (c)	**6.** (a)	**7.** (a)	**8.** (c)	**9.** (b)	**10.** (b)
11. (a)	**12.** (b)	**13.** (b)	**14.** (a)	**15.** (c)	**16.** (c)	**17.** (a)	**18.** (a)	**19.** (b)	**20.** (c)

Passage - 2

1. (b)	**2.** (c)	**3.** (d)	**4.** (a)	**5.** (b)	**6.** (c)	**7.** (b)	**8.** (b)	**9.** (d)	**10.** (c)
11. (a)	**12.** (b)	**13.** (c)	**14.** (a)						

Passage - 3

1. (c)	**2.** (c)	**3.** (b)	**4.** (c)	**5.** (d)	**6.** (b)	**7.** (a)

Passage - 4

1. (b)	**2.** (c)	**3.** (d)	**4.** (b)	**5.** (b)	**6.** (b)	**7.** (a)

Passage - 5

1. (b)	**2.** (c)	**3.** (b)	**4.** (b)	**5.** (b)	**6.** (c)	**7.** (b)	**8.** (a)

Passage - 6

1. (c)	**2.** (d)	**3.** (d)	**4.** (c)	**5.** (c)	**6.** (b)	**7.** (a)

Passage - 7

1. (a)	**2.** (c)	**3.** (b)	**4.** (d)	**5.** (a)	**6.** (b)	**7.** (a)	**8.** (c)	**9.** (d)	**10.** (d)
11. (a)	**12.** (c)	**13.** (b)	**14.** (d)	**15.** (c)					

Passage - 8

1. (b)	**2.** (a)	**3.** (b)	**4.** (c)	**5.** (a)	**6.** (c)	**7.** (b)	**8.** (a)

Passage - 9

1. (a)	**2.** (c)	**3.** (c)	**4.** (c)	**5.** (d)	**6.** (b)

Passage - 10

1. (c)	**2.** (c)	**3.** (b)	**4.** (c)	**5.** (a)	**6.** (d)	**7.** (b)

Solutions

Passage – 1

1. c The most appropriate option is 'come' as it is most idiomatically correct in this context.

2. a Options (c) and (d) are totally absurd with reference to the given passage. The best option here would be (a).

3. a The preposition 'of' fits in the sentence perfectly. Therefore, option (a) is the correct answer.

4. c An article would fit here. Between the two articles given 'the' is correct option.

5. c The line talks about two or three districts so the correct option here would be 'and'.

6. a The most appropriate option is 'become', which means to 'turn into'.

7. a 'Beauty' is the best option for describing nature.

8. c The word that fits here is 'walk'. Options (a), (b) and (d) do not fit in with the passage.

9. b The most appropriate option is 'be' as 'be alone' is the correct phrase to be used here.

10. b Looking at the passage, the option that would be suitable for this blank is 'well'.

11. a The obvious answer is 'used' as a comparison is being made in this sentence and the word 'used' is being reiterated.

12. b As the line talks about new recruits in the army so the best option here would be 'men'.

13. b Army men are trained and not taught or tutored and as the word 'for' is used later, that is why the most suitable option is (b).

14. a We can 'use' a place and not 'regard', adjust or desire a place. Thus, (a) is the correct option.

15. c Grammatically the best option is 'find'.

16. c The line already mentions mind, so the options (a), (b) and (d) are ruled out because they are more or less synonyms. The correct option to be used here is 'body'.

17. a The option that fits here the best is 'most'. Option (b) makes to sense and using option (d) would be assuming too much.

18. a 'Indeed' gives the necessary stress needed in the sentence., Therefore, option (a) is the most appropriate option.

19. b The best conjunction to fit here is 'and'.

20. c (c) is the best option here as the author wants the reader to go ahead and not worry about studying climbing techniques.

Passage – 2

1. b The best option is (b) as it means to a large extent.

2. c The correct option is (c) because the line mentions debt, so somebody owes 'a debt' and 'not offers' or 'feels it'. Thus, (c) is correct.

3. d Options (c) and (d) are quite close but the more suitable option is (d).

4. a Here (a) is the correct option because its intended meaning here is hard work which goes very well with sacrifices.

5. b 'Useful' is the correct option because the discoveries and inventions prove to be 'useful' to the common man in day-to-day life.

6. c The best option here is (c) as it means to make pain easy to bear and lessen.

7. b As the line mentions pain so the option that goes best with it is discomfort.

8. b Impossible is the correct option because to measure human feelings is not possible.

9. d Option (a) and (c) are irrelevant. The best option here is 'value' - meaning 'worth or importance' as opposed to option (b), which means 'pertinence to a matter at hand'.

10. c A person who is suffering from pain and discomfort gets 'relief' and not rest or peace.

11. a 'Large' is the correct option here as it here implies to a 'great extent'.

12. b The best option here is 'labour' as it here means 'physical toil'.

13. c The correct option is fortunate as we later discover that the previous generation suffered much hardship which has been removed to a large extent today.

14. a The correct option here is 'subjected' as it here means that the men were put under severe physical strain.

Passage – 3

1. c Though the options (a) and (b) are quite close but the better option here is (c).

2. c Option (c) - 'Vitally' which means 'to an important degree' is the best options that fits here. The other options fail to give the appropriate meaning.

3. b One is drawing conclusions from the fact that the average expectancy of life has increased. Therefore, the most appropriate answer here is (b) - inferred

4. c The options (a) and (c) are quite close but the better option here is (c).

5. d An institution is 'established' and not erected or initiated. Thus, (d) is the correct option.

6. b 'Regrettable' is the suitable option because the absence and lack of doctor is regretted.

7. a (a) is the most appropriate option, as it must be 'acknowledged' or 'admitted that constant efforts are being made.

Passage – 4

1. b The future is always predicted which means to foretell. Thus, (b) is correct.

2. c The correct option is (c) because it means relaxed or satisfied. But as the previous line says that future cannot be always predicted. So we need to stay alert and not complacent.

3. d Though (a) and (d) have similar meaning but 'ahead' is more suitable to fit here.

4. b The best option is (b) - 'relax' which means to 'slacken or reduce in intensity'. Option (a) 'Lax' which means 'something that is lacking in firmness' does not fit in with the sentence.

5. b (a) and (d) are not correct because we are not fully sure that it is going to happen the way we think. Thus, (b) is the correct option.

6. b The correct answer is (b) as it means something which is required in day-to-day life and we cannot do without it.

7. a 'Kept' is the best option which here means that it should be constantly remembered and not forgotten.

Passage – 5

1. b The correct option is 'content'. The other options do not fit in properly.

2. c (c) seems to be the most appropriate option though (a) is also close.

3. b 'Especially' is the best option that fits here as it gives the proper stress that is necessary.

4. b The suitable option that fits here is (b) - 'elaboration', meaning 'addition of extra material or clarifying detail'.

5. b 'Entire' is the best option as it covers everything.

6. c Option (c) - 'seemingly', which means 'in appearance but not necessarily in actuality' fits in the sentence perfectly.

7. b 'Profoundly' is the best option here because here it means deeply.

8. a 'Quality' goes very well here with pace and also fits exactly in the context of the paragraph.

Passage – 6

1. c Here the best option would be 'spread' of education because it talks about the unity of mankind. And all mankind can be united only when education is present everywhere. Thus, the spread is important.

2. d (a) and (d) are close options but (a) is ruled out as before the blank there is 'a' so option (a) is ruled out. Thus, (d) is correct.

3. d The best way of deserbing the present is being talked in the sentence so, option (d) seems to be the more appropriate choice.

4. c The sentence mentions decade of promise. So we can easily infer from that the answer is (c).

5. c 'Possibilities' is the best option as nuclear energy still has not been used for peaceful purposes. So it would be used in future is a possibility.

6. b (b) is the best option as it means here to use resources to the utmost.

7. a We are talking about a wordwide scale and hence, option (a) 'global' is the best option here.

Passage – 7

1. a The answer is man-made because it mentions that Gandhiji preferred natural beauty instead of man-made objects.

2. c Although (b) and (c) are quite close but (c) is the better option here.

3. b (b) is the best option here as it means a concrete form.

4. d Option (d) is the most appropriate option, meaning 'limited'.

5. a Gandhiji was not the one to invent the art of living so option (b) is ruled out. Rather he had discovered it. So (a) is the correct option.

6. b The sentence talks about touch so the best option that would go with it is 'gesture'.

7. a (a) is the best option. The other options are irrelevant in this context.

8. c 'Rough edges' gives the correct phrase. Therefore, (c) is the most appropriate option.

9. d Because the previous option talks about rough edges, here the suitable option is corners.

10. d In the context of the passage the correct option is (d). Moreover, 'vulgarity' which means 'the quality of lacking taste and refinement' matches with the 'commonness' mentioned.

11. a We are talking about the negative qualities in which the middle class people surpass others. So option (a) - 'excel' seems to be the only option that fits here.

12. c Here the sentence means that he propagated his knowledge to other people. Thus, the correct option is (c).

13. b Options (c) and (d) are absurd and are ruled out. The best option that fits in the blank is (b).

14. d As life is supposed to be very easy that is why it describes life's ways as tortuous.

15. c The sentence mentions firm steps. So the word that goes with it is 'undaunted' which means 'bold and fearless'.

Passage – 8

1. b 'Increasing' is the correct option here as in the next sentence it is mentioned that it is spreading. So we can easily infer that if it is spreading it has to increase.

2. a The passage talks about the world being a single undvided entry or whole and therefore, option (a) - 'Unit' is the best option.

3. b As the sentence mentions it is not real so the correct option is 'superfluous' because it also means the same.

4. c It is a commonly used term nook and corner, so the correct answer is 'nook'.

5. a The most logically correct option is 'awakening' - which means 'the start of a feeling or awareness'.

6. c The best option here is 'conquered' as the author talks of having taken control of time and space with the help of science and technology.

7. b An echo sounds exactly the same as the original and returns back after a few seconds. It is thus compared to the events here.

8. a Here figment means a notion perceived in mind or a fabrication.

Passage – 9

1. a The correct option here is baffling as it means puzzling.

2. c A task is accomplished so the correct option is (c).

3. c Apart from (c) the rest of the options are absurd as we always make a demand 'for' something.

4. c The correct option is 'assume'. Just as we assume responsibility we assume leadership.

5. d Although options (a) and (d) are close but the more appropriate option is (d).

6. b (a) cannot be used as it is already mentioned. (c) and (d) are absurd. The correct option is 'zeal' as it means 'enthusiasm'.

Passage – 10

1. c In this opening line, the author is talking about a length by time. Therefore, 'ages' is the most appropriate option.

2. c 'Farthest' is the correct option because it means the corner at the extreme far.

3. b The chief contributor to India's, progress was 'training and education'. Therefore, in this context, the most appropriate answer would be option (b) - which means 'chiefly or for the most part'.

4. c The answer is 'confront' as it means to face boldly.

5. a 'Turn for guidance' is the right statement just as we say turn for help, which means look or ask for help or guidance.

6. d The correct option is pioneers as it means innovators or one who initiates.

7. b In the context of the passage, the correct option is (b).

Practice Test : Worksheets

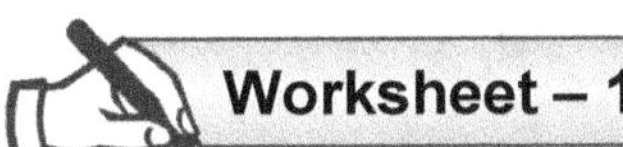

Worksheet – 1

Exercise – 1

Directions: Match the words in column A to their **closest** meaning or synonyms in column B.

Column – A	Column – B
1. Abandon	A. Forsake
2. Abase	B. Suspension
3. Abbreviate	C. Rebuke
4. Abeyance	D. Scorn
5. Acumen	E. Condense
6. Admonish	F. Humiliate
7. Affront	G. Alert
8. Agile	H. Astuteness
9. Alienate	I. Entice
10. Allure	J. Estrange

Exercise – 2

Directions: Match the words in column A to their **closest** meaning or synonyms in column B.

Column – A	Column – B
1. Bedlam	A. Warlike
2. Banter	B. Engaged
3. Bastion	C. Chaos
4. Bellicose	D. Dim
5. Betrothed	E. Teasing
6. Bleary	F. Defense
7. Buttress	G. Savage
8. Breach	H. Support
9. Bestial	I. Abundant
10. Bounteous	J. Violation

Exercise – 3

Directions: Match the words in column A to their **closest** meaning or synonyms in column B.

Column – A	Column – B
1. Cacophony	A. Warning
2. Camouflage	B. Force
3. Capitulate	C. Assist
4. Caveat	D. Discord
5. Coerce	E. Unrefined
6. Connive	F. Hide
7. Contemptuous	G. Surrender

8. Crass	H. Patriotism	5. Genesis	E. Stop
9. Chauvinism	I. Quack	6. Haggard	F. Gaudy
10. Charlatan	J. Scornful	7. Hiatus	G. Rumours
		8. Hinder	H. Kind
		9. Hearsay	I. Break
		10. Humane	J. Courage

Exercise – 4

Directions: Match the words in column A to their **closest** meaning or synonyms in column B.

Column – A	Column – B
1. Daft	A. Delay
2. Dainty	B. Lessen
3. Defer	C. Debase
4. Demean	D. Hard-working
5. Denizen	E. Foolish
6. Depreciate	F. Tremble
7. Diligent	G. Disagree
8. Dissent	H. Inactive
9. Dodder	I. Beautiful
10. Dormant	J. Citizen

Exercise – 6

Directions: Match the words in column A to their **closest** meaning or synonyms in column B.

Column – A	Column – B
1. Jaded	A. Young
2. Judicious	B. Grief
3. Juvenile	C. Wise
4. Jeremiad	D. Spoilsport
5. Killjoy	E. Worn-out
6. Kin	F. Acclaim
7. Kudos	G. Tear
8. Ken	H. Relative
9. Lacerate	I. Gap
10. Lacuna	J. Range

Exercise – 5

Directions: Match the words in column A to their **closest** meaning or synonyms in column B.

Column – A	Column – B
1. Garish	A. Exhausting
2. Grovel	B. Origin
3. Gruelling	C. Weary
4. Gumption	D. Cringe

Exercise – 7

Directions: Match the words in column A to their **closest** meaning or synonyms in column B.

Column – A	Column – B
1. Macabre	A. Adjust

2. Magnanimous
3. Malady
4. Masquerade
5. Mandatory
6. Modulate
7. Mediocre
8. Melee
9. Mollify
10. Mercenary

B. Compulsory
C. Average
D. Fight
E. Generous
F. Gruesome
G. Soothe
H. Illness
I. Venal
J. Disguise

Exercise – 8

Directions: Match the words in column A to their **closest** meaning or synonyms in column B.

Column – A	Column – B
1. Qualm	A. Irritate
2. Quaintness	B. Restless
3. Rankle	C. Uneasiness
4. Rapport	D. Odd
5. Recapitulate	E. Meeting
6. Rendezvous	F. Harmony
7. Replete	G. Repeat
8. Refractory	H. Full
9. Restive	I. Cut down
10. Retrench	J. Obstinate

Exercise – 9

Directions: Match the words in column A to their **closest** meaning or synonyms in column B.

Column – A	Column – B
1. Skinflint	A. Optimistic
2. Solicitude	B. Fragments
3. Sanguine	C. Miser
4. Saucy	D. Appearance
5. Smithereens	E. Outstanding
6. Taciturn	F. Impudent
7. Salient	G. Concerned
8. Theatrical	H. Careful
9. Semblance	I. Reserved
10. Scrupulous	J. Dramatic

Exercise – 10

Directions: Match the words in column A to their **closest** meaning or synonyms in column B.

Column – A	Column – B
1. Waylay	A. Clown
2. Zany	B. Greedy
3. Vertiginous	C. Attack
4. Voracious	D. Dizzy
5. Zephyr	E. Gusto
6. Vestige	F. Remains
7. Vilify	G. Breeze
8. Zest	H. Malign
9. Virulent	I. Green
10. Verdant	J. Deadly

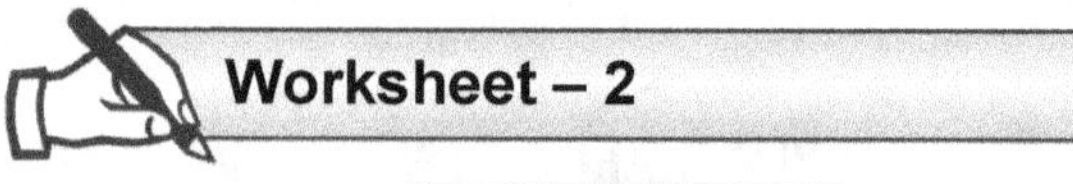

Worksheet – 2

Exercise – 1

Directions: Match the words in column A to their **most opposite** meanings or antonyms in column B.

Column – A	Column – B
1. Amiable	A. Adoration
2. Anathema	B. Obtuse
3. Annul	C. Enforce
4. Antipathy	D. Sullen
5. Assiduous	E. Gentle
6. Aplomb	F. Learned
7. Astute	G. Sympathy
8. Audacious	H. Lazy
9. Anomaly	I. Normality
10. Asinine	J. Diffidence

Exercise – 2

Directions: Match the words in column A to their **most opposite** meanings or antonyms in column B.

Column – A	Column – B
1. Beguile	A. Calm
2. Bawdy	B. Desert
3. Bashful	C. Intelligent
4. Benevolence	D. Escort
5. Berserk	E. Decent
6. Berate	F. Depressed
7. Bolster	G. Bold
8. Bovine	H. Praise
9. Bravado	I. Animosity
10. Buoyant	J. Cowardice

Exercise – 3

Directions: Match the words in column A to their **most opposite** meanings or antonyms in column B.

Column – A	Column – B
1. Cadence	A. Sympathetic
2. Callous	B. Hypocritical
3. Callow	C. Confined
4. Candid	D. Cacophony
5. Capacious	E. Mature
6. Cardinal	F. Lethargy
7. Celestial	G. Uncertain
8. Celerity	H. Minor
9. Certitude	I. Open
10. Clandestine	J. Earthly

Exercise – 4

Directions: Match the words in column A to their **most opposite** meanings or antonyms in column B.

Column – A	Column – B
1. Earthy	A. Pandemic
2. Ebullient	B. Misery
3. Embellish	C. Serious
4. Empirical	D. Success
5. Endemic	E. Tarnish

6. Farce   F. Fruitful

7. Felicity   G. Refined

8. Fiasco   H. Hypothetical

9. Futile   I. Honest

10. Fraudulent   J. Dejected

4. Laudable   D. Stiff

5. Jocular   E. Sanctuary

6. Lithe   F. Love

7. Livid   G. Incomprehensible

8. Loathe   H. Leaders

9. Lucid   I. Contemptible

10. Laggard   J. Calm

Exercise – 5

Directions: Match the words in column A to their **most opposite** meanings or antonyms in column B.

Column – A	Column – B
1. Hoi polloi	A. Genius
2. Hostile	B. Extrovert
3. Humdrum	C. Interesting
4. Ignoramus	D. Fact
5. Immaculate	E. Friendly
6. Introvert	F. Peaceful
7. Illusion	G. Certainty
8. Impetus	H. Elite
9. Incertitude	I. Impediment
10. Irate	J. Tarnished

Exercise – 7

Directions: Match the words in column A to their **most opposite** meanings or antonyms in column B.

Column – A	Column – B
1. Malice	A. Zenith
2. Malign	B. Cunning
3. Nadir	C. Kindness
4. Naive	D. Impartiality
5. Nepotism	E. Praise
6. Notorious	F. Preserve
7. Obliterate	G. Attractive
8. Odious	H. Good
9. Opportune	I. Orient
10. Occident	J. Untimely

Exercise – 6

Directions: Match the words in column A to their **most opposite** meanings or antonyms in column B.

Column – A	Column – B
1. Jeopardy	A. Energetic
2. Lackadaisical	B. Rejoice
3. Lament	C. Serious

Exercise – 8

Directions: Match the words in column A to their **most opposite** meanings or antonyms in column B.

Column – A	Column – B
1. Pacifist	A. Ephemeral
2. Perennial	B. Unite

3. Polarize   C. Irrelevant

4. Pertinent   D. Inequality

5. Pragmatic   E. Extremist

6. Perfunctory   F. Dedicated

7. Parity   G. Unrealistic

8. Quaintness   H. Restore

9. Ransack   I. Meager

10. Rampant   J. Modern

Exercise – 9

Directions: Match the words in column A to their **most opposite** meanings or antonyms in column B.

Column – A	Column – B
1. Sacrosanct	A. Discord
2. Tardy	B. Calm
3. Unison	C. Condone
4. Turbulent	D. Unholy
5. Unhinged	E. Prompt
6. Upbraid	F. Urban
7. Unilateral	G. Sane
8. Uprising	H. Transparent
9. Sylvan	I. Bilateral
10. Turbid	J. Submission

Exercise – 10

Directions: Match the words in column A to their **most opposite** meanings or antonyms in column B.

Column – A	Column – B
1. Zeal	A. Honest

2. Zenith   B. Denounce

3. Venal   C. Base

4. Verbose   D. Indifferent

5. Verve   E. Precise

6. Venerate   F. Impractical

7. Viable   G. Depression

8. Voracious   H. Quiet

9. Vindictive   I. Moderate

10. Vociferous   J. Forgiving

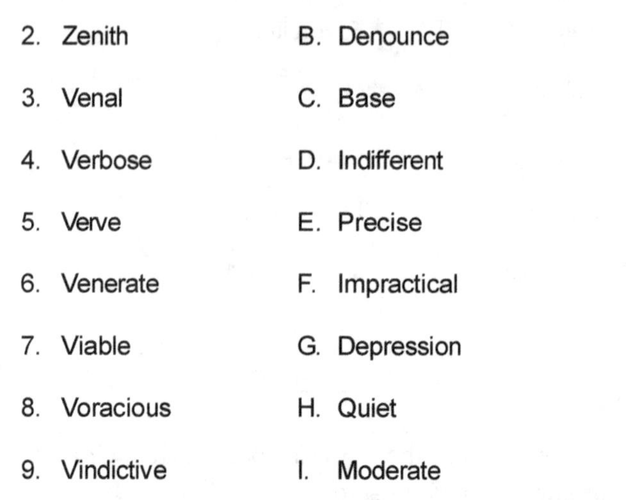

Worksheet – 3

Directions: For each of the following questions, choose which of the following groups is represented by the given set of words.

(a) humans   (b) animals
(c) birds   (d) objects

1. tables , chairs, stones, oil

2. leopard, panther, anteater, duck-billed platypus

3. eagles, hawks, condor, ostrich

4. Australians, Canadians, Dutch, Swedes

5. naga, kuki, hutus, pygmies

6. fridge, toaster, car, helicopter

7. chain, belt, jewellery, wardrobe

8. deer, lion, sheep, jaguar

9. turtle, porpoise, mongoose, hyena

10. Indians, Pakistanis, Chinese, Mongols

11. Aryans, Dravidians, Caucasians, aborigines

12. kiwi, dodo, albatross, emu

13. spacecraft, reel, books, gadgets

14. Europeans, Asians, Malaysians, Arabs

15. notebook, mobile phone, computer, pad

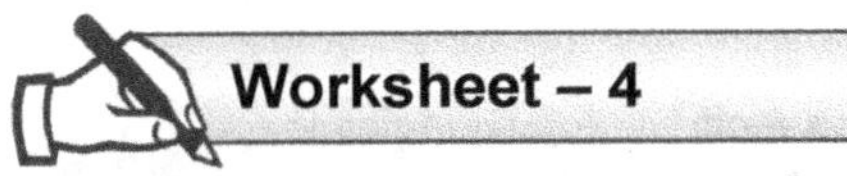

Worksheet – 4

Directions: For each of the following questions, choose the feminine gender of the given word.

1. mr.

   (a) mrs.   (b) countess
   (c) woman   (d) girl

2. peacock
   (a) egret   (b) she peacock
   (c) peacow   (d) peahen

3. wolf
   (a) vermin   (b) vixen
   (c) varmint   (d) vampire

4. gander
   (a) quack   (b) geese
   (c) goose   (d) eyrie

5. stag
   (a) doe   (b) dray
   (c) ox   (d) hinnie

6. duke
   (a) duchess   (b) countess
   (c) marquis   (d) lady

7. ram
   (a) saturn   (b) sheep
   (c) sun   (d) sanguine

8. stallion
   (a) mire   (b) mere
   (c) moiré   (d) mare

9. colt
   (a) filly   (b) filter
   (c) dray   (d) druid

10. knight
    (a) dame   (b) lady
    (c) countess   (d) viscount

11. lord
    (a) dame   (b) lady
    (c) countess   (d) viscount

12. tiger
    (a) dray   (b) lioness
    (c) tigress   (d) egret

13. monk
    (a) munic   (b) mun
    (c) nun   (d) sati

14. bachelor
    (a) sphinx   (b) spinster
    (c) sobriquet   (d) siphon

15. Monsieur
    (a) Lady   (b) Zarine
    (c) Madam   (d) Madonna

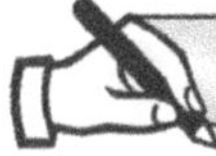

Worksheet – 5

Directions: Choose the option which best explains the given word.

1. level-headed

   (a) plain headed person

   (b) wild person

   (c) intractable person

   (d) sensible and reasonable person

2. cliché

   (a) an overused phrase or idea

   (b) unknown phrase or idea

   (c) spicy and interesting phrase or idea

   (d) foreign phrase or idea

3. barter

   (a) trade involving foreign currencies

   (b) trade involving exchange of goods

   (c) trade involving speculation

   (d) to mash and squeeze something

4. bizarre

(a) commonplace
(b) strikingly odd in shape or appearance
(c) reasonable and understandable
(d) lovable

5. clique
(a) a defunct group
(b) a ruling military group
(c) a small exclusive group
(d) a hosiery shop

6. junta
(a) a defunct group
(b) a small exclusive group
(c) a ruling military group
(d) a hosiery shop

7. margarine
(a) butter made from animal or vegetable fat
(b) type of fruit jam
(c) alcoholic pastry
(d) alcoholic chocolate

8. peignoir
(a) type of woman's nightgown
(b) woman's razor
(c) animal's bed
(d) butcher's knife

9. pulchritude
(a) impertinence   (b) abject misery
(c) with great speed   (d) beauty

10. catamaran
(a) type of boat
(b) type of cannon
(c) Jewish place of worship
(d) Zoroastrian place of worship

11. microcosm
(a) a small space   (b) a sample
(c) very stealthy   (d) deadly

12. paradox
(a) embarrassing or humiliating
(b) churlish
(c) self-contradictory but true
(d) charlatan

13. discredit
(a) make an account   (b) damage reputation of
(c) withdraw money   (d) praise a person

14. foray
(a) a short raid   (b) make advances
(c) build a road   (d) have an appetiser

15. impart
(a) satisfy oneself   (b) be invisible
(c) to give or bestow (d) be partial

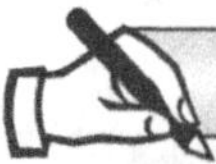

Worksheet – 6

Directions: Each of the following questions has four items, three of which are related to each other in some way. Find the item that does not belong to this group. Be perceptive and sharp, but also work fast and use your common sense and gut-feeling.

1. (a) Exercycle   (b) Unicycle
   (c) Bicycle   (d) Tricycle

2. (a) Doberman   (b) Spaniel
   (c) Canine   (d) Labrador

3. (a) Pencil   (b) Eraser
   (c) Sharpener   (d) Lead

4. (a) Eraser   (b) Ink
   (c) Lead   (d) Paint

5. (a) Delete   (b) Insert
   (c) Clear screen   (d) Space bar

6. (a) Rouge   (b) Glow
   (c) Sparkle   (d) Blush

7. (a) Applaud   (b) Love
   (c) Praise   (d) Appreciate

8. (a) Tennis   (b) Volleyball
   (c) Table tennis   (d) Squash

9. (a) Badminton   (b) Hockey
   (c) Tennis   (d) Football

10. (a) Confront   (b) Arrest
    (c) Effigy   (d) Fight

11. (a) Shoot   (b) Forecast
    (c) Omen   (d) Prediction

12. (a) Abode   (b) Shelter
    (c) Home   (d) Dwelling

13.   (a) Keynes   (b) Love
       (c) Amartya Sen   (d) Say

14.   (a) Forest   (b) Verdant
       (c) Disdain   (d) Sylvan

15.   (a) Rue   (b) Ruthless
       (c) Cruel   (d) Brutal

16.   (a) Ingenious   (b) Clever
       (c) Intelligent   (d) Gullible

17.   (a) Opulent   (b) Needy
       (c) Wealthy   (d) Rich

18.   (a) Salubrious   (b) Wholesome
       (c) Saline   (d) Health-giving

19.   (a) Seedy   (b) Superb
       (c) Shabby   (d) Shaggy

20.   (a) Cadaverous   (b) Cynosure
       (c) Pale   (d) Ghostly

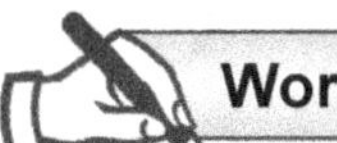

Worksheet – 7

Directions: Each of the following questions has four items, three of which are related to each other in some way. Find the item that does not belong to this group. Be perceptive and sharp, but also work fast and use your common sense and gut-feeling.

1.   (a) Leave   (b) Depart
     (c) Fire   (d) Move

2.   (a) Scent   (b) Perfume
     (c) Flavour   (d) Fragrance

3.   (a) Artificial   (b) Man-made
     (c) Synthetic   (d) Natural

4.   (a) Contradict   (b) Corroborate
     (c) Counter   (d) Controvert

5.   (a) Attention   (b) Apathy
     (c) Awareness   (d) Vigilance

6.   (a) Intrinsic   (b) Inherent
     (c) Innate   (d) Ornate

7.   (a) Ambitious   (b) Ambiguous
     (c) Ambidextrous   (d) Ambivalent

8.   (a) Reticent   (b) Reserved
     (c) Shy   (d) Aloof

9.   (a) Blush   (b) Sanguine
     (c) Inky   (d) Scarlet

10.   (a) Into   (b) Until
     (c) Upon   (d) Onto

11.   (a) Thought   (b) For
     (c) Since   (d) Because of

12.   (a) It   (b) Pit
     (c) Spit   (d) Spite

13.   (a) Abstract   (b) Conceptual
     (c) Material   (d) Idea

14.   (a) Bone   (b) Ring
     (c) Finger   (d) Hand

15.   (a) Caprice   (b) Whim
     (c) Unpredictable   (d) Canter

16.   (a) Abate   (b) Allay
     (c) Alleviate   (d) Aggravate

17.   (a) Tipsy   (b) Bibulous
     (c) Alcoholic   (d) Teetotaller

18.   (a) Puerile   (b) Juvenile
     (c) Immature   (d) Mature

19.   (a) Ribald   (b) Vulgar
     (c) Decent   (d) Lewd

20.   (a) Revelry   (b) Partial
     (c) Party   (d) Jamboree

Worksheet – 8

Directions: Each of the following questions has four items, three of which are related to each other in some way. Find the item that does not belong to this group. Be perceptive and sharp, but also work fast and use your common sense and gut-feeling.

1. (a) Hatched   (b) Birth
    (c) Germinate   (d) Propaganda

2. (a) Giggle   (b) Chuckle
    (c) Snigger   (d) Guffaw

3. (a) Fingers   (b) Knees
    (c) Ankles   (d) Hair

4. (a) Bolted   (b) Crawled
    (c) Whirled   (d) Flew

5. (a) Scintillating   (b) Dim
    (c) Lucid   (d) Dazzling

6. (a) Scoff   (b) Dough
    (c) Touch   (d) Chafe

7. (a) Formal   (b) Terrifying
    (c) Dangerous   (d) Fearful

8. (a) Fortune   (b) Treasure
    (c) Mandatory   (d) Riches

9. (a) Fur   (b) Coat
    (c) Belt   (d) Bright

10. (a) Lively   (b) Supernatural
    (c) Vivacious   (d) Chirpy

11. (a) Crisp   (b) Chilling
    (c) Soft   (d) Smooth

12. (a) Row   (b) Bicker
    (c) Argue   (d) Blow

13. (a) Sum   (b) Home
    (c) Product   (d) Divisor

14. (a) Harmony   (b) Opera
    (c) Rhythm   (d) Tune

15. (a) Rodent   (b) Asinine
    (c) Vulpine   (d) Bovine

16. (a) Thin   (b) Faint
    (c) Remembrance   (d) Vague

17. (a) Excise duty   (b) Sales tax
    (c) Octroi   (d) Quotation

18. (a) Equestrian   (b) Neigh
    (c) Derby   (d) Bark

19. (a) Abstract   (b) Concrete
    (c) Real   (d) Practical

20. (a) Ring   (b) Call
    (c) Fork   (d) Dial

Worksheet – 9

Directions: Each of the following questions has four items, three of which are related to each other in some way. Find the item that does not belong to this group. Be perceptive and sharp, but also work fast and use your common sense and gut-feeling.

1. (a) Ravenous   (b) Hungry
    (c) Swan   (d) Famished

2. (a) Curly   (b) Wavy
    (c) Straight   (d) Purr

3. (a) In a soup   (b) In a fix
    (c) In a rut   (d) In dire straits

4. (a) Vapour   (b) Floe
    (c) Icicle   (d) Hail

5. (a) Albatross   (b) Cuckoo
    (c) Goof   (d) Parrot

6. (a) Brush   (b) Paint
    (c) Draw   (d) Sketch

7. (a) Square   (b) Quadrilateral
    (c) Rectangle   (d) Pentagon

8. (a) Seismology   (b) Astronomy
    (c) Geology   (d) Astronaut

9. (a) Apache   (b) Tundra
    (c) Eskimo   (d) Polar

10. (a) Hoped   (b) Prayed
    (c) Wished   (d) Hypothesised

11. (a) Oil   (b) Benzoic acid
    (c) Paraffin wax   (d) Diesel

12.   (a) Soar   (b) Dart
      (c) Glide   (d) Converge

13.   (a) Lead   (b) Antimony
      (c) Chromium   (d) Cast iron

14.   (a) Inch   (b) Quart
      (c) Foot   (d) Metre

15.   (a) Uranus   (b) Venus
      (c) Saturn   (d) Sun

16.   (a) End   (b) Prelude
      (c) Finish   (d) Retire

17.   (a) Nice   (b) Effluent
      (c) Great   (d) Kind

18.   (a) Bulky   (b) Large
      (c) Tiny   (d) Tall

19.   (a) Influential   (b) Affluent
      (c) Creme de la creme (d) Paranoid

20.   (a) Arise   (b) Hinder
      (c) Stop   (d) Crib

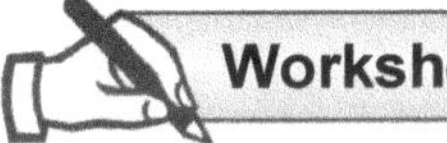

Worksheet – 10

Directions: Each of the following questions has four items, three of which are related to each other in some way. Find the item that does not belong to this group. Be perceptive and sharp, but also work fast and use your common sense and gut-feeling.

1.   (a) Increased   (b) Intensified
      (c) Aggravated   (d) Cushioned

2.   (a) Plummeting   (b) Falling
      (c) Declining   (d) Flourishing

3.   (a) Assuring   (b) Promising
      (c) Pledging   (d) Litigating

4.   (a) Stunned   (b) Terrified
      (c) Horrified   (d) Rueing

5.   (a) Supernatural   (b) Extraterrestrial
      (c) Discomfiture   (d) Surreal

6.   (a) Changed   (b) Caricature
      (c) Vacated   (d) Stated

7.   (a) Extinction   (b) Dissolution
      (c) End   (d) Mutated

8.   (a) Amicable   (b) Amiable
      (c) Philanthropic   (d) Affable

9.   (a) Delusion   (b) Lunacy
      (c) Deranged   (d) Dementia

10.   (a) On   (b) Like
      (c) Upon   (d) In

11.   (a) Handshake   (b) Kick
      (c) Salute   (d) Greet

12.   (a) Contract   (b) Dealing
      (c) Agreement   (d) Substitute

13.   (a) Delude   (b) Deceive
      (c) Hoax   (d) Forfeiture

14.   (a) Slacker   (b) Waster
      (c) Rebel   (d) Shirker

15.   (a) Truthful   (b) Sly
      (c) Virtuous   (d) Pensive

16.   (a) Tiger   (b) Leopard
      (c) Panther   (d) Elephant

17.   (a) Badminton   (b) Volleyball
      (c) Football   (d) Basketball

18.   (a) Time   (b) Clock
      (c) Theater   (d) Minute

19.   (a) Ohm   (b) Watt
      (c) Ampere   (d) Metre

20.   (a) Autocracy   (b) Bureaucracy
      (c) Diplomacy   (d) Democracy

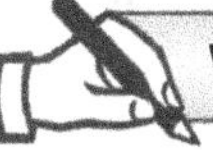

Worksheet – 11

Directions: Find the odd word in each of the following set of words.

1.   (a) sanguine   (b) optimistic
      (c) hopeful   (d) despondent

2.   (a) cadaverous   (b) deathly
     (c) pale   (d) sanguine

3.   (a) abhor   (b) detest
     (c) dislike   (d) cathartic

4.   (a) naive   (b) puerile
     (c) simple   (d) sly

5.   (a) haggard   (b) weathered
     (c) gnarled   (d) chagrin

6.   (a) exalted   (b) flustered
     (c) flabbergasted   (d) embarrassed

7.   (a) gentle   (b) soft
     (c) warm   (d) vicious

8.   (a) abase   (b) debase
     (c) humiliate   (d) urchin

9.   (a) inscrutable   (b) vivacious
     (c) gregarious   (d) sociable

10. (a) abate   (b) alleviate
     (c) attenuate   (d) attune

11. (a) acclimatize   (b) attune
     (c) attenuate   (d) adjust

12. (a) hermit   (b) ascetic
     (c) saint   (d) gourmand

13. (a) fastidious   (b) fussy
     (c) easygoing   (d) choosy

14. (a) valor   (b) courage
     (c) cowardice   (d) bravery

15. (a) reckless   (b) prudent
     (c) careful   (d) conscious

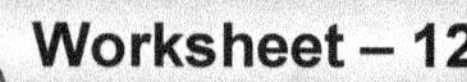 **Worksheet – 12**

Directions: Each of the following sentences contains an idiom (which is underlined). Pick the correct meaning of the idiom from the answer choices.

1.   The authorities <u>took him to task</u> for his negligence.
     (a) gave him additional work
     (b) suspended his assignment
     (c) reprimanded him
     (d) forced him to resign

2.   I am sure they will fight <u>tooth and nail</u> for their rights.
     (a) with all their might
     (b) without any other weapon
     (c) resort to violence
     (d) are cowards

3.   The detective <u>left no stone unturned</u> to trace the culprit.
     (a) took no pains
     (b) did very irrelevant things
     (c) resorted to illegitimate practices
     (d) used all available means

4.   <u>He was in high spirits</u> when I met him in the restaurant.
     (a) He was in a drunken state
     (b) He was very cheerful
     (c) He talked incoherently
     (d) He was deeply engrossed in thoughts

5.   Harassed by repeated acts of injustice, he decided <u>to put his foot down</u>.
     (a) not to yield
     (b) to give up
     (c) to accept the proposal unconditionally
     (d) to withdraw

6.   There has been <u>bad blood</u> between the two communities even before the shooting.
     (a) impure blood
     (b) ill-feeling
     (c) bloody fights
     (d) frequent quarrels

7.   He acts so much like his father, truly, he is <u>a chip off the old block.</u>
     (a) outdated in mannerisms
     (b) very similar to his father
     (c) a good actor
     (d) an honourable man

8.   Do not imagine that Dharmendra is really sorry that his wife died. Those are only <u>crocodile tears</u>.
     (a) pretended sorrow
     (b) tears of a crocodile
     (c) weeping crocodile
     (d) mild regret

9.   He <u>struck several bad patches</u> before he made good.
     (a) came across bad soil
     (b) had a difficult and tiring journey
     (c) went through many illness
     (d) had many professional difficulties

10. Mohan always <u>keeps to himself</u>.
    (a) is too busy
    (b) is selfish
    (c) is unsociable
    (d) does not take sides

11. He never liked the idea of keeping his wife <u>under his thumb</u> and so he let her do what she liked.
    (a) pressed down
    (b) unduly under control
    (c) below his thumb
    (d) under tyrannical conditions

12. It is no longer easy <u>to strike gold</u> in Shakespeare's research since much work has already been done on him.
    (a) hit a golden spot
    (b) come across gold
    (c) come across the word 'gold'
    (d) uncover or find a valuable line of argument or information

13. You cannot <u>have your cake and eat it too</u>.
    (a) enjoy for ever
    (b) have it both ways
    (c) run away from responsibility
    (d) absolve yourself of guilt

14. You have to be a <u>cool customer</u> and be patient if you want to get the best buys.
    (a) be calm and not be excitable
    (b) have a cool head
    (c) be uncommunicative
    (d) be choosy

15. In his youth, he was practically <u>rolling in money</u>.
    (a) spending more then his income
    (b) borrowing money liberally
    (c) very rich
    (d) wasting a lot of money

16. Noble has a <u>chequered career</u> since I first knew him as an officer assistant in the insurance company.
    (a) career marked by lots of ups and downs
    (b) career which helped him make lot of money
    (c) career where he signed a lot of cheques
    (d) did no jobs

17. Veena has <u>bitten off more than she can chew</u>.
    (a) is trying to do too much
    (b) is very greedy
    (c) is always hungry
    (d) has little regard for others.

18. I felt that it was a <u>tall order</u> to expect Kanchan to go home at twelve in the night.
    (a) difficult   (b) too much
    (c) customary   (d) simple

19. Reeni might scream <u>blue murder</u> but I feel Anita should get a promotion since she is better qualified for the job.
    (a) that someone has been murdered with some blue liquid
    (b) someone is being murdered and has become blue
    (c) blue murder is a type of murder
    (d) make a great deal of noise and object vehemently

20. Some kids <u>get a kick</u> from smoking cigarettes as a gesture of revolt against adult domination.
    (a) are kicked for   (b) get a thrill
    (c) kick a ball   (d) are punished

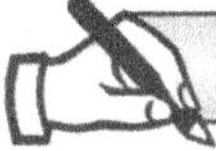

Worksheet – 13

Directions: Each of the following sentences contains an idiom (which is underlined). Pick the correct meaning of the idiom from the answer choices.

1. Though she herself was <u>as ugly as sin</u>, she had the audacity to criticise the looks of her companion.
   (a) sinfully ugly   (b) not ugly
   (c) exceptionally ugly (d) quite ugly

2. It was surprising to see that she looked quite pretty <u>at close quarters</u>.
   (a) very near
   (b) government quarters
   (c) close confinement
   (d) close examination

3. She was at that <u>awkward age</u> when she did not want to be seen playing with her dolls.
   (a) period of early adolescence
   (b) clumsy
   (c) uncomfortable
   (d) unsure

4. He is a plain, simple and sincere man, he will always <u>call a spade a spade</u>.
   (a) find meaning or purpose in your action
   (b) be outspoken in language
   (c) avoid controversial situations
   (d) desist from making controversial statement

5. He does not like to be friendly with Sunita, he always gives her a <u>cold shoulder</u>.
    (a) pushes her with his shoulder whenever they meet

    (b) insults her in the presence of others

    (c) argues with her on any issue

    (d) tries to be unfriendly by taking no notice of her

6. He always <u>cuts both ways</u>.
    (a) behaves dishonestly
    (b) works for both sides
    (c) creates discordance among friends
    (d) argues in support of both sides of the issue

7. When the police came, the thieves <u>took to their heels</u>.
    (a) were taken by surprise
    (b) took shelter in a tall building
    (c) shivered in fright
    (d) took to flight

8. I cannot <u>put up</u> with that nasty fellow.
    (a) praise   (b) forgive
    (c) endure   (d) control

9. If he goes on drinking like that, <u>as sure as eggs is eggs</u>, he'll have no liver left.
    (a) in course of time   (b) quite certainly
    (c) unfortunately   (d) sincerely

10. It is better to have one friend who is <u>as true as steel</u>, than to have fifty acquaintances who refuse to recognise you in your hour of need.
    (a) who is strong
    (b) who is with you
    (c) who is very loyal and dependable
    (d) who always speaks the truth

11. Mohan could not go to Kolkata for a vacation since he was <u>banking on</u> his arrears of pay which he however did not get in time.
    (a) depending on his bank
    (b) sloping on
    (c) relying on
    (d) falling on

12. I cannot <u>conceive of a time</u> when I was without a refrigerator.
    (a) imagine   (b) give birth
    (c) understand   (d) depend

13. The point that you have raised <u>has no bearing</u> on the issue we are discussing.
    (a) no relation to
    (b) not affected by
    (c) no impact on
    (d) no movement to

14. Whether Pakistan will ever become a democracy continues to be <u>the burning question</u>.
    (a) the question on fire
    (b) the question which is burning
    (c) the issue which is hotly debated
    (d) speculative

15. The two women are so jealous, that <u>at the drop of a hat</u> they start insulting each other.
    (a) when a hat falls
    (b) when anyone drops a hat
    (c) for no reason at all
    (d) on some occasions

16. <u>The bare bones</u> of the half-hour conversation was that he hated my guts.
    (a) the main line
    (b) just bones
    (c) with flesh removed
    (d) the naked truth

17. Her house is always <u>in apple-pie order</u> and is quite unlike mine.
    (a) like an apple-pie
    (b) tasty like an apple
    (c) neat and tidy
    (d) untidy

18. Baron Muchausen is famous for his <u>tall stories</u>, which however improbable, are very entertaining.
    (a) exaggerated and impossible stories
    (b) long tales
    (c) high buildings
    (d) simple stories

19. The community tried to <u>bring to book</u> all the rowdy elements but its attempts were foiled by the squad.
    (a) to book   (b) enter in a book
    (c) to imprison   (d) to punish

20. The trial was so important that the entire proceedings were held <u>in camera</u>.
    (a) photographed
    (b) made into a film
    (c) secret
    (d) not open to the public

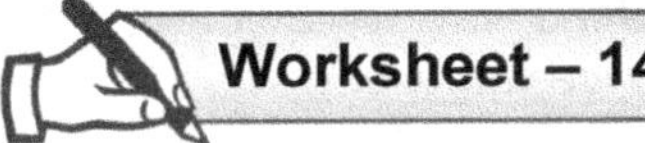

Worksheet – 14

Directions: Each of the following sentences contains an idiom (which is underlined). Pick the correct meaning of the idiom from the answer choices.

1. The only daughter of the rich baron would always have her way by <u>leading</u> her father <u>by the nose</u>.
   (a) throwing a tantrum
   (b) blackmailing into submission
   (c) cajoling into compliance
   (d) misleading through deceit

2. It is Shobha who <u>wears the trousers</u> in their house and he timidly allows it.
   (a) wears pants
   (b) wears off the trousers
   (c) quarrels
   (d) the dominant partner in a marriage

3. It is time that India and Pakistan <u>bury the hatchet</u> and work together to make this a healthier subcontinent.
   (a) stop arguing
   (b) bury their dead
   (c) come to friendly and peaceful terms
   (d) start a war and kill many people

4. Though he was not very intelligent <u>by dint of</u> hard work, he managed to do well in the examinations.
   (a) by the cause of
   (b) as a result of
   (c) with reference to
   (d) in accordance with

5. She <u>holds the purse strings</u>, whereas I merely earn the money.
   (a) decides how money is to be spent
   (b) keeps the purse
   (c) holds the strings of a purse
   (d) keeps an empty purse

6. Since he knew what would happen I would let him <u>stew in his own juice</u> if I were you.
   (a) make a stew
   (b) boil
   (c) suffer for his own act
   (d) suffer in his own juice

7. It was his <u>maiden speech</u> and it was memorable.
   (a) like a maiden
   (b) first woman's speech
   (c) first speech in that particular forum
   (d) first word

8. She is easy to talk with since she has such a <u>gift of the gab</u>.
   (a) gifted
   (b) present of chattering
   (c) a good conversationalist
   (d) a chatterbox

9. Now that prices have risen too much it is better <u>to go dutch while having a party</u>.
   (a) go to Holland
   (b) bear all the expense
   (c) each person pays his own share of the expenses
   (d) bear the cost of an outgoing

10. Since Spencer can be boring, teaching his works is not every lecturer's <u>cup of tea</u>.
    (a) what one likes and can do well
    (b) refreshing drink
    (c) something that most people do not like
    (d) a routine work

11. Smuggling can get you <u>easy money</u> and it may also easily put you in jail.
    (a) money to make someone lazy
    (b) money which can be easily spent
    (c) money gained after very little work
    (d) money earned from smuggling

12. Though Rahul tries to be humorous most of his jokes <u>fall flat</u>.
    (a) fall to the ground
    (b) gets flattered
    (c) do not have the expected effect
    (d) are very effective

13. She is too fond of her <u>creature comforts</u> to take the trouble to go on the long train journey.
    (a) be a comfortable creature
    (b) comfortable pets
    (c) amenities which provide day-to-day physical needs
    (d) home

14. He has not been quite the <u>prodigal</u> son returning, since he brought with him a lot of money.
    (a) rich son
    (b) poor son
    (c) extravagant son
    (d) step-son

15.   It is of no use <u>splitting hairs on this</u> issue since the Act has been passed and the Muslim women will have to lump it with their religion.
       (a) taking down fine details
       (b) making hairs finer
       (c) arguing on the minor points
       (d) hotly debating major issues

16.   My wife rarely behaved <u>like a fishwife</u> when we disagreed.
       (a) a wife who sold fish
       (b) shouted loudly or abusively
       (c) pretended to be a fish-wife
       (d) was quarrelsome

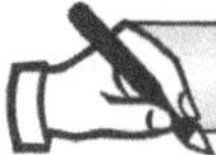

Worksheet – 15

Directions: Each of the following sentences contains an idiom (which is underlined). Pick the correct meaning of the idiom from the answer choices.

1.   After <u>sowing his wild oats</u>, Terry has decided to stick to the straight and narrow path in future.
       (a) becoming a gardener
       (b) becoming a farmer
       (c) going through a period of irresponsible pleasure-seeking
       (d) a period of wildness

2.   Mavis was <u>down in the mouth</u> when her husband told her that he was going to leave her.
       (a) put her mouth down
       (b) looked down
       (c) happy
       (d) felt depressed

3.   He put us <u>in a fix</u> when he didn't turn up to pick us up.
       (a) put us in a difficult situation
       (b) put us in a bad mood
       (c) made us feel bad
       (d) made us feel awkward

4.   It is time to <u>draw a veil over</u> last year's incidents and try to shape a happier future.
       (a) cover up
       (b) cover the face
       (c) sketch a veil
       (d) call it closed and forgotten

5.   He <u>cut the ground from under my feet</u> by offering to take her home.
       (a) dug up the ground
       (b) cut with a knife
       (c) broke the surface
       (d) made my plan ineffective

6.   His sob story explaining why he could not meet me yesterday <u>cut no ice with me</u>.
       (a) had no effect
       (b) could not persuade
       (c) did not charm
       (d) dissuaded

7.   Students are to some extent <u>a captive audience</u> since they have no option but to buy the books included in their syllabus.
       (a) captured by the book-sellers
       (b) held captive
       (c) have little freedom of choice
       (d) are captive viewers of plays

8.   Gopal was <u>ill at ease</u> in his house because they really had nothing to talk about and the silence was becoming oppressive.
       (a) was ill
       (b) was becoming more ill as she was trying to relax
       (c) was uncomfortable
       (d) was feeling disturbed

9.   I do not like to be <u>at the beck and call</u> of anyone.
       (a) very obedient and subservient
       (b) answer the call
       (c) running around
       (d) being beckoned and called

10.   Subhash was truly <u>in his element</u> and he easily impressed the gathering with his erudition.
       (a) was elemental
       (b) was at his worst
       (c) feeling happy and confident
       (d) unusually confident

11.   It was <u>out of place</u> for him to talk on politics when the seminar was arranged to discuss recent trends in literature.
       (a) strange   (b) inappropriate
       (c) unnatural   (d) foolish

12.   Robert was so sure of himself that he would often <u>be a law unto himself</u> without any fears of the society.
       (a) set rigid laws for himself
       (b) ignore laws and rules.
       (c) be the judge of his own actions
       (d) take the law in his own hands and punish others

13. Some people feel that apartheid is <u>on its last legs</u> now and the blacks will soon have a say in the government.
(a) on its last pair of legs
(b) on one leg
(c) about to collapse
(d) about to revive

14. His phenomenal success shows that he has got <u>the Midas touch</u>.
(a) ability to succeed in all projects
(b) superhuman ability
(c) miraculous touch
(d) a powerful backer

15. Samuel Johnson never forgave Lord Chesterfield for making him <u>cool his heels</u> in his house.
(a) rest after a long walk
(b) give relief to his heels
(c) wait fruitlessly and at the cost of his dignity
(d) made to wait for a long time before being given relief

16. Her absent-mindedness <u>cost her dear,</u> for her food had burnt and she had to do with a sandwich she disliked.
(a) cost her dear life
(b) made her suffer much
(c) cost her a lot
(d) was expensive

17. The Pakistani commandos failed <u>to strike while the iron was hot</u>, and as a result many innocent passengers lost their lives.
(a) make timely use of an opportunity
(b) strike the iron to shape it
(c) strike with a hot iron
(d) shoot and kill

18. The police are so much used to seeing the same <u>seamy side of life</u> that the sight of a prostitute soliciting rarely bothers them.
(a) creamy side of life
(b) life where the seams show
(c) unpleasant or immoral aspects of society
(d) criminal society

19. It is time that government <u>seized the nettle and stopped parleying</u> with the separatists.
(a) get a hold of the thorns
(b) seized property
(c) dealt firmly
(d) overcame the difficulties

20. He wished to <u>rub shoulders</u> with the glitterati in Hong Kong.
(a) elbow push
(b) intimidate
(c) socialize
(d) punish

Worksheet – 16

Directions: Complete the following idioms.

1. look before you ___
(a) jump   (b) plunge
(c) take the plunge   (d) leap

2. strike while the iron is ___
(a) cool   (b) cold
(c) warm   (d) hot

3. early bird catches the ___
(a) worm   (b) germ
(c) jelly   (d) jam

4. every cloud has a silver ___
(a) line   (b) lining
(c) statue   (d) border

5. to be born with a silver ___ in the ___
(a) bowl, palm   (b) bowl, hand
(c) spoon, mouth   (d) plate, hand

6. to grease someone's ___
(a) wheels   (b) engine
(c) motor   (d) palms

7. to take leave of one's ___
(a) senses   (b) job
(c) faculties   (d) family

8. to have an itching ___
(a) palm   (b) hand
(c) back   (d) ear

9. to join ___ with
(a) issue   (b) battle
(c) war   (d) hands

10. to go to pigs and ___
(a) whistles   (b) cows
(c) dogs   (d) hen

11. a square peg in a ___ hole
(a) triangular   (b) square
(c) rectangular   (d) round

12. to blow one's own ___
     (a) horn   (b) bell
     (c) flute   (d) trumpet

13. actions speak louder than ___
     (a) sound   (b) gestures
     (c) words   (d) vice

14. to bury the ___
     (a) hatchet   (b) axe
     (c) sword   (d) pick

15. to get your ___ together
     (a) brace   (b) act
     (c) might   (d) trial

Worksheet – 17

Directions: In the following questions, there are four words of which only one is with the correct spelling. Find the word with correct spelling. Try to find the answer, but also work by eliminating wrong choices easily.

1.   (a) Recommend   (b) Recomend
     (c) Reccomend   (d) Reccommend

2.   (a) Marrige   (b) Marraige
     (c) Marriage   (d) Mariage

3.   (a) Setlement   (b) Setalment
     (c) Settleement   (d) Settlement

4.   (a) Editter   (b) Editor
     (c) Edittor   (d) Editer

5.   (a) Accurate   (b) Acurate
     (c) Accuratte   (d) Acurrate

6.   (a) Diapharagm   (b) Diapharam
     (c) Diaphragm   (d) Diapphragm

7.   (a) Pemegranate   (b) Pomegranate
     (c) Pommogrante   (d) Pomegrannate

8.   (a) Emibicie   (b) Imbicile
     (c) Imbicille   (d) Imbecile

9.   (a) Judecious   (b) Judiceous
     (c) Judicious   (d) Juditious

10. (a) Persuation   (b) Persuasion
     (c) Perssuasion   (d) Persuassion

11. (a) Insight   (b) Insite
     (c) Insiet   (d) Insitte

12. (a) Replete   (b) Repleet
     (c) Riplete   (d) Repleat

13. (a) Fictitious   (b) Fictious
     (c) Fictitiuos   (d) Fictutious

14. (a) Pertentious   (b) Pretentious
     (c) Pretencious   (d) Pretantious

15. (a) Expedient   (b) Expediant
     (c) Expidient   (d) Expendiant

16. (a) Forbidden   (b) Forbiden
     (c) Forrbide   (d) Forbidan

17. (a) Anual   (b) Annual
     (c) Anuall   (d) Annuel

18. (a) Infinnite   (b) Infynite
     (c) Infinate   (d) Infinite

19. (a) Requissets   (b) Requisite
     (c) Requasite   (d) Requisette

20. (a) Disillution   (d) Disliusion
     (c) Disillusion   (d) Dissillusion

21. (a) Commendable   (b) Commendible
     (c) Comendable   (d) Comendablle

22. (a) Oblivous   (b) Obleevious
     (c) Oblivious   (d) 0bilivious

23. (a) Assimmilate   (b) Assimillate
     (c) Asimmilate   (d) Assimilate

24. (a) Grieved   (b) Greived
     (c) Greeved   (d) Grived

25. (a) Electoral   (b) Electeral
     (c) Ellecterel   (d) Elecrol

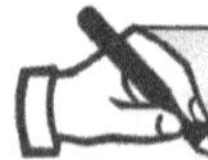

Worksheet – 18

Directions: In the following questions, there are four words of which only one is with the correct spelling. Find the word with correct spelling. Try to find the answer, but also work by eliminating wrong choices easily.

1.   (a) Controversey   (b) Controverssey
     (c) Controversy   (d) Contraversy

2.   (a) Rebellion   (b) Rebelion
    (c) Rebbellion   (d) Rebelleon

3.   (a) Sureptitious   (b) Surreptious
    (c) Surreptitiuos   (d) Surreptitious

4.   (a) Incorregible   (b) Incorigible
    (c) Incorrigible   (d) Incorregible

5.   (a) Connoisseur   (b) Connoiseur
    (c) Connoisieur   (d) Connoissure

6.   (a) Humilation   (b) Humilliation
    (c) Humiliation   (d) Hummilliation

7.   (a) Morronq   (b) Moron
    (c) Moroon   (d) Morroon

8.   (a) Mortgage   (b) Mortagage
    (c) Mortguage   (d) Mortgaige

9.   (a) Asistance   (b) Assistanse
    (c) Assisstanse   (d) Assistance

10.   (a) Alaination   (b) Alination
    (c) Alienation   (d) Alienaton

11.   (a) Dureabilety   (b) Durbilety
    (c) Durabelity   (d) Durability

12.   (a) Committment   (b) Commitment
    (c) Comitment   (d) Committmant

13.   (a) Enthral   (b) Entrall
    (c) Enthroll   (d) Enthrall

14.   (a) Applase   (b) Applause
    (c) Applauze   (d) Appllause

15.   (a) Intersperse   (b) Intersparse
    (c) Intersperce   (d) Intersparce

16.   (a) Refutetation   (b) Refutasion
    (c) Refutation   (d) Refutassion

17.   (a) Pueraile   (b) Puerile
    (c) Purile   (d) Pureile

18.   (a) Intermvel   (b) Interval
    (c) Intarval   (d) Intarvel

19.   (a) Pageantry   (b) Pagentry
    (c) Pagentary   (d) Pageantary

20.   (a) Cataclysemic   (b) Catacliesmic
    (c) Cataclysmic   (d) Cataclismic

21.   (a) Imbroglio   (b) Embroglio
    (c) Imbrogleo   (d) Imbrogloi

22.   (a) Cedulous   (b) Sedulous
    (c) Sedulus   (d) Cedulus

23.   (a) Knaiv   (b) Knaive
    (c) Knave   (d) Knaeve

24.   (a) Phanton   (b) Phainton
    (c) Phantom   (d) Fantom

25.   (a) Domiscile   (b) Domicile
    (c) Domisile   (d) Domiciale

✎ Worksheet – 19

Directions: In the following questions, there are four words of which only one is with the correct spelling. Find the word with correct spelling. Try to find the answer, but also work by eliminating wrong choices easily.

1.   (a) Conspicous   (b) Conspicuous
    (c) Conspicious   (d) Conspisious

2.   (a) Effervescent   (b) Efervescent
    (c) Ephervescent   (d) Efervesent

3.   (a) Inadverdently   (b) Inadvertently
    (c) Inadvertaintly   (d) Inadverdaintly

4.   (a) Recomendation   (b) Recommandation
    (c) Recommendation   (d) Reccomendation

5.   (a) Increduluous   (b) Incredolous
    (c) Incredulous   (d) Incredulus

6.   (a) Cohorts   (b) Coherts
    (c) Coharts   (d) Cuhorts

7.   (a) Retoric   (b) Rhetorric
    (c) Retorric   (d) Rhetoric

8.   (a) Indigenous   (b) Indegenious
    (c) Inidigenious   (d) Indegenous

9.   (a) Promiscuisity   (b) Promiscuty
     (c) Promicuity   (d) Promiscuty

10. (a) Citadal   (b) Citadale
     (c) Citadel   (d) Citadail

11. (a) Ignoramous   (b) Ignoramus
     (c) Ignoramuse   (d) Ignoremus

12. (a) Pedectrian   (b) Pedestarion
     (c) Pedestrian   (d) Pediatrician

13. (a) Anatema   (b) Anathema
     (c) Anatemma   (d) Annathema

14. (a) Jeorpardise   (b) Jeopardise
     (c) Jeorpardize   (d) Jeoparadise

15. (a) Illusons   (b) Illuesions
     (c) Illuscions   (d) Illusions

16. (a) Phelgm   (b) Phlegm
     (c) Phlegam   (d) Phelgam

17. (a) Superceed   (b) Supersede
     (c) Superseed   (d) Superced

18. (a) Irevocacable   (b) Irrivocable
     (c) Irrevocable   (d) Irivocable

19. (a) Judiciary   (b) Judiaciary
     (c) Judiciery   (d) Judicairy

20. (a) Rheumatic   (b) Reumatic
     (c) Rheomatic   (d) Reomatic

21. (a) Undetered   (b) Undettered
     (c) Undeterred   (d) Undetterred

22. (a) Condemn   (b) Condem
     (c) Condeme   (d) Condmn

23. (a) Mileston   (b) Milistone
     (c) Milestone   (d) Millstone

24. (a) Duration   (b) Durasion
     (c) Duretion   (d) Durassion

25. (a) Erossion   (b) Erosion
     (c) Eroesion   (d) Erotion

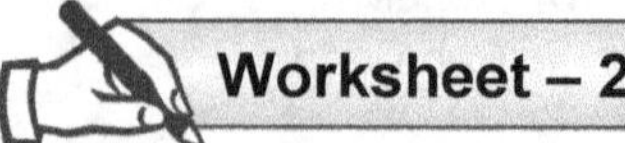

Worksheet – 20

Directions: In the following questions, there are four words of which only one is with the correct spelling. Find the word with correct spelling. Try to find the answer, but also work by eliminating wrong choices easily.

1.   (a) Forecast   (b) Forcast
     (c) Furecast   (d) Forecaste

2.   (a) Perceevable   (b) Percievable
     (c) Perceivable   (d) Percevable

3.   (a) Contemptible   (b) Contemtible
     (c) Contimptible   (d) Copntemptable

4.   (a) Ostantation   (b) Ostentation
     (c) Ostaintation   (d) Ostentasion

5.   (a) Laudabal   (b) Lawdable
     (c) Laudeble   (d) Laudable

6.   (a) Espionege   (b) Espionage
     (c) Aspionage   (d) Espionaige

7.   (a) Prieminenece   (b) Preemininence
     (c) Preeminence   (d) Preminenc

8.   (a) Lassitude   (b) Lasitude
     (c) Lassitute   (d) Lessetude

9.   (a) Cinematography   (b) Cinematografy
     (c) Cinemmatograpy   (d) Cinematograffy

10. (a) Benkruptcy   (b) Bankruptcy
     (c) Bankrptcie   (d) Bankrupticy

11. (a) Emmalient   (b) Emollient
     (c) Emolient   (d) Emolleint

12. (a) Aberation   (b) Aberetion
     (c) Aberration   (d) Abberation

13. (a) Daged   (b) Doged
     (c) Dagged   (d) Dogged

14. (a) Plaumment   (b) Plaument
     (c) Plunment   (d) Plummet

15. (a) Moeroocasm   (b) Macroccosm
     (c) Macrocosm   (d) Marcocasme

16. (a) Dispansionate   (b) Dispanssionate
     (c) Dispassionate   (d) Dispanssiante

17. (a) Metoric   (b) Meteoric
     (c) Meteroic   (d) sMeteoroic

18. (a) Arthodontist   (b) Orthodontiest
     (c) Orthodontist   (d) Orthodentist

19. (a) Moeroocasm   (b) Myread
     (c) Myriad   (d) Miriad

20. (a) Specalative   (b) Speculative
     (c) Spaculative   (d) Spaculative

21. (a) Imutable   (b) Immutable
     (c) Imuttable   (d) Immuttable

22. (a) Magnanimity   (b) Magnimity
     (c) Magnanimitty   (d) Magnanimitic

23. (a) Luxurios   (b) Lukxurious
     (c) Luxurious   (d) Luksurious

24. (a) Counterpoint   (b) Conterpoint
     (c) Countarpoint   (d) Contoorpont

25. (a) Voluptuous   (b) Valptuous
     (c) Vaulptous   (d) Valuptous

Answer Keys

Worksheet - 1

Exercise - 1

1. (A)   2. (D)   3. (E)   4. (B)   5. (H)   6. (C)   7. (F)   8. (G)   9. (J)   10. (I)

Exercise - 2

1. (C)   2. (E)   3. (F)   4. (A)   5. (B)   6. (D)   7. (H)   8. (J)   9. (G)   10. (I)

Exercise - 3

1. (D)   2. (F)   3. (G)   4. (A)   5. (B)   6. (C)   7. (J)   8. (E)   9. (H)   10. (I)

Exercise - 4

1. (E)   2. (I)   3. (A)   4. (C)   5. (J)   6. (B)   7. (D)   8. (G)   9. (F)   10. (H)

Exercise - 5

1. (F)   2. (D)   3. (A)   4. (J)   5. (B)   6. (C)   7. (I)   8. (E)   9. (G)   10. (H)

Exercise - 6

1. (E)   2. (C)   3. (A)   4. (B)   5. (D)   6. (H)   7. (F)   8. (J)   9. (G)   10. (I)

Exercise - 7

1. (F)   2. (E)   3. (H)   4. (J)   5. (B)   6. (A)   7. (C)   8. (D)   9. (G)   10. (I)

Exercise - 8

1. (C)   2. (D)   3. (A)   4. (F)   5. (G)   6. (E)   7. (H)   8. (J)   9. (B)   10. (I)

Exercise - 9

1. (C)	2. (G)	3. (A)	4. (F)	5. (B)	6. (I)	7. (E)	8. (J)	9. (D)	10. (H)

Exercise - 10

1. (C)	2. (A)	3. (D)	4. (B)	5. (G)	6. (F)	7. (H)	8. (E)	9. (J)	10. (I)

Worksheet - 2

Exercise - 1

1. (D)	2. (A)	3. (C)	4. (G)	5. (H)	6. (J)	7. (B)	8. (E)	9. (I)	10. (F)

Exercise - 2

1. (D)	2. (E)	3. (G)	4. (I)	5. (A)	6. (H)	7. (B)	8. (C)	9. (J)	10. (F)

Exercise - 3

1. (D)	2. (A)	3. (E)	4. (B)	5. (C)	6. (H)	7. (J)	8. (F)	9. (G)	10. (I)

Exercise - 4

1. (G)	2. (J)	3. (E)	4. (H)	5. (A)	6. (C)	7. (B)	8. (D)	9. (F)	10. (I)

Exercise - 5

1. (H)	2. (E)	3. (C)	4. (A)	5. (J)	6. (B)	7. (D)	8. (I)	9. (G)	10. (F)

Exercise - 6

1. (E)	2. (A)	3. (B)	4. (I)	5. (C)	6. (D)	7. (J)	8. (F)	9. (G)	10. (H)

Exercise - 7

1. (C)	2. (E)	3. (A)	4. (B)	5. (D)	6. (H)	7. (F)	8. (G)	9. (J)	10. (I)

Exercise - 8

1. (E)	2. (A)	3. (B)	4. (C)	5. (G)	6. (F)	7. (D)	8. (J)	9. (H)	10. (I)

Exercise - 9

1. (D)	2. (D)	3. (A)	4. (B)	5. (G)	6. (C)	7. (I)	8. (J)	9. (F)	10. (H)

Exercise - 10

1. (D)	2. (C)	3. (A)	4. (E)	5. (G)	6. (B)	7. (F)	8. (I)	9. (J)	10. (H)

Worksheet - 3

1. (d)	2. (b)	3. (c)	4. (a)	5. (a)	6. (d)	7. (d)	8. (b)	9. (b)	10. (a)
11. (a)	12. (c)	13. (d)	14. (a)	15. (d)					

Worksheet - 4

1. (a)	**2.** (d)	**3.** (b)	**4.** (c)	**5.** (a)	**6.** (a)	**7.** (b)	**8.** (d)	**9.** (a)	**10.** (a)
11. (b)	**12.** (c)	**13.** (c)	**14.** (b)	**15.** (c)					

Worksheet - 5

1. (d)	**2.** (a)	**3.** (b)	**4.** (b)	**5.** (c)	**6.** (c)	**7.** (a)	**8.** (a)	**9.** (d)	**10.** (a)
11. (b)	**12.** (c)	**13.** (b)	**14.** (a)	**15.** (c)					

Worksheet - 6

1. (a)	**2.** (c)	**3.** (d)	**4.** (a)	**5.** (c)	**6.** (a)	**7.** (b)	**8.** (b)	**9.** (d)	**10.** (c)
11. (a)	**12.** (b)	**13.** (b)	**14.** (c)	**15.** (a)	**16.** (d)	**17.** (b)	**18.** (c)	**19.** (b)	**20.** (b)

Worksheet - 7

1. (c)	**2.** (c)	**3.** (d)	**4.** (b)	**5.** (b)	**6.** (d)	**7.** (a)	**8.** (d)	**9.** (c)	**10.** (b)
11. (a)	**12.** (d)	**13.** (c)	**14.** (b)	**15.** (d)	**16.** (d)	**17.** (d)	**18.** (d)	**19.** (c)	**20.** (b)

Worksheet - 8

1. (d)	**2.** (c)	**3.** (d)	**4.** (b)	**5.** (b)	**6.** (b)	**7.** (a)	**8.** (c)	**9.** (d)	**10.** (b)
11. (b)	**12.** (d)	**13.** (b)	**14.** (b)	**15.** (a)	**16.** (c)	**17.** (d)	**18.** (d)	**19.** (a)	**20.** (c)

Worksheet - 9

1. (c)	**2.** (d)	**3.** (c)	**4.** (a)	**5.** (c)	**6.** (a)	**7.** (d)	**8.** (d)	**9.** (a)	**10.** (d)
11. (b)	**12.** (d)	**13.** (d)	**14.** (b)	**15.** (d)	**16.** (b)	**17.** (b)	**18.** (c)	**19.** (d)	**20.** (a)

Worksheet - 10

1. (d)	**2.** (d)	**3.** (d)	**4.** (d)	**5.** (c)	**6.** (b)	**7.** (d)	**8.** (c)	**9.** (a)	**10.** (b)
11. (b)	**12.** (d)	**13.** (d)	**14.** (c)	**15.** (d)	**16.** (d)	**17.** (a)	**18.** (c)	**19.** (d)	**20.** (c)

Worksheet - 11

1. (d)	**2.** (d)	**3.** (d)	**4.** (d)	**5.** (d)	**6.** (a)	**7.** (d)	**8.** (d)	**9.** (a)	**10.** (d)
11. (c)	**12.** (d)	**13.** (c)	**14.** (c)	**15.** (a)					

Worksheet - 12

1. (c)	**2.** (a)	**3.** (d)	**4.** (b)	**5.** (a)	**6.** (b)	**7.** (b)	**8.** (a)	**9.** (d)	**10.** (c)
11. (b)	**12.** (d)	**13.** (b)	**14.** (a)	**15.** (c)	**16.** (a)	**17.** (a)	**18.** (b)	**19.** (d)	**20.** (b)

Worksheet - 13

1. (c)	**2.** (d)	**3.** (a)	**4.** (b)	**5.** (d)	**6.** (d)	**7.** (d)	**8.** (c)	**9.** (b)	**10.** (c)
11. (c)	**12.** (a)	**13.** (a)	**14.** (c)	**15.** (c)	**16.** (d)	**17.** (c)	**18.** (a)	**19.** (d)	**20.** (a)

Worksheet - 14

1. (c)	**2.** (d)	**3.** (c)	**4.** (b)	**5.** (a)	**6.** (c)	**7.** (c)	**8.** (c)	**9.** (c)	**10.** (a)
11. (c)	**12.** (c)	**13.** (c)	**14.** (c)	**15.** (a)	**16.** (b)				

Worksheet - 15

1. (c)	2. (d)	3. (a)	4. (d)	5. (d)	6. (a)	7. (c)	8. (c)	9. (a)	10. (c)
11. (b)	12. (b)	13. (c)	14. (a)	15. (c)	16. (b)	17. (a)	18. (c)	19. (c)	20. (c)

Worksheet - 16

1. (d)	2. (d)	3. (a)	4. (b)	5. (c)	6. (d)	7. (a)	8. (a)	9. (a)	10. (a)
11. (d)	12. (d)	13. (c)	14. (a)	15. (b)					

Worksheet - 17

1. (a)	2. (c)	3. (d)	4. (b)	5. (a)	6. (c)	7. (b)	8. (d)	9. (c)	10. (b)
11. (a)	12. (a)	13. (a)	14. (b)	15. (a)	16. (a)	17. (b)	18. (d)	19. (b)	20. (c)
21. (a)	22. (c)	23. (d)	24. (a)	25. (a)					

Worksheet - 18

1. (c)	2. (a)	3. (d)	4. (c)	5. (a)	6. (c)	7. (b)	8. (a)	9. (d)	10. (c)
11. (d)	12. (b)	13. (d)	14. (d)	15. (a)	16. (c)	17. (b)	18. (b)	19. (a)	20. (c)
21. (a)	22. (b)	23. (c)	24. (c)	25. (b)					

Worksheet - 19

1. (b)	2. (a)	3. (b)	4. (c)	5. (c)	6. (a)	7. (d)	8. (a)	9. (b)	10. (c)
11. (b)	12. (c)	13. (b)	14. (b)	15. (d)	16. (b)	17. (b)	18. (c)	19. (a)	20. (a)
21. (c)	22. (a)	23. (c)	24. (a)	25. (b)					

Worksheet - 20

1. (a)	2. (c)	3. (a)	4. (b)	5. (d)	6. (b)	7. (c)	8. (a)	9. (a)	10. (b)
11. (b)	12. (c)	13. (d)	14. (d)	15. (c)	16. (c)	17. (b)	18. (c)	19. (c)	20. (b)
21. (b)	22. (a)	23. (c)	24. (a)	25. (a)					

Solutions

Practice Test : Worksheets

Worksheet – 1

Exercise – 1

1. A   Both Abandon and Forsake mean to give up completely, renounce.

2. D   Abase means to belittle or lower, as in rank or esteem. The only word matching in column B is scorn, which means contempt or disdain felt towards a person.

3. E   Both the words abbreviate and condense mean to shorten.

4. B   The word Abeyance means a temporary suspension.

5. H   Both the words Acumen and Astuteness more or less mean keenness of mind, insight.

6. C   Admonish means to reprove. And rebuke too, means the same.

7. F   Affront and Humiliate, both mean to insult openly.

8. G   Agile means to be mentally quick or alert.

9. J   Alienate means to become unfriendly or hostile. Estrange means exactly the same.

10. I   Both Allure and Entice mean to attract or tempt with something desirable.

Exercise – 2

1. C   Bedlam means a situation of noisy uproar and confusion. Chaos from column B, which means the same is the perfect synonym.

2. E   Banter is to speak in a playful or teasing manner.

3. F   Bastion is stronghold - a well-fortified position. So, the appropriate synonym from column B will be Defense.

4. A   Bellicose means to be warlike in manner or temperament.

5. B   Betrothed means engaged to be married.

6. D   Both bleary and dim mean blurred or not very clear.

7. H   Buttress is a structure built for support.

8. J   Breach means a violation (of law promise)

9. G   Both the words have the same meaning - wild barbaric.

10. I   Bounteous means to give generously and abundantly.

Exercise – 3

1. D   Both Cacophony and Discord mean unpleasant or harsh or jarring sounds.

2. F   Camouflage is the method of concealment by disguise. In simple terms, it means to hide.

3. G   Capitulate means to surrender or to stop resisting.

4. A   Caveat means a warning.

5. B   Coerce mean to force or to compel.

6. C   Connive means to collude or plot. So the appropriate synonym matching in column B is Assist.

7. J   Both the words contemptuous and scornful mean to be full of contempt.

8. E   Crass is crude and unrefined behaviour.

9. H   Chauvinism is fanatical and unreasonable belief.

10. I   A character is a fraud person. A quack also means the same.

Exercise – 4

1. E   Daft means stupid or foolish.

2. I   Dainty means something which is pretty and delicate and beautiful.

3. A   Both the words - Defer and Delay mean to postpone.

4. C   Demean means to lower in dignity, status, to degrade. Debase also, means the same.

5. J   Denizen means an inhabitant or a resident. So the appropriate synonym will be citizen.

6. B   Depreciate means to lessen in value.

7. D   Diligent means hardworking and preserving.

8. G   Dissent means to differ in opinion. Disagree means the same.

9. F   Dodder means to shake or tremble.

10. H   Dormant means something which is not active, that is, inactive.

Exercise – 5

1. F Garish means loud and flashy. Gaudy means the same.

2. D Grovel means to cringe - that is, to behave in a servile demeaning manner.

3. A Gruelling means something physically or mentally demanding. Exhausting means the same.

4. J Gumption means courage and determination.

5. B Both Genesis and Origin mean creation or beginning of something.

6. C Haggard means to appear worn and exhausted. Weary means the same.

7. I Hiatus means a gap or a break.

8. E Hinder means to keep back or to stop.

9. G Both Hearsay and Rumour mean gossip - information passed around by word of mouth gossip.

10. H Humane means to be characterized by kindness and compassion.

Exercise – 6

1. E Jaded means to have a worn-out and wearied look.

2. C Judicious means to show good judgment, to be wise.

3. A Juvenile mean not fully grown - young.

4. B Jeremiad means a tale of lament & woe. So the appropriate synonym from column B will be grief.

5. D A killjoy is one who spoils the pleasure or enjoyment of others, in short, a spoilsport.

6. H Kim means family. So, the appropriate synonym is relative.

7. F Both kudos and acclaim mean praise.

8. J Ken means the range of vision.

9. G Lacerate mean to rip, cut or tear

10. I Lacuna means an empty space or gap.

Exercise – 7

1. F Both macabre and gruesome means something that is horrible and upsetting, usually involving death and decay.

2. E Magnanimous means to be unselfish and generous.

3. H A malady is a disease or illness.

4. J Masquerade means to wear a mask or disguise.

5. B Both mandatory and compulsory means something that is required, obligatory.

6. A Modulate means to adapt or adjust.

7. C Mediocre means something that is ordinary or average.

8. D Melee means confused brawl or fight.

9. G Mollify means to appease, to calm or soothe.

10. I Mercenary means someone who does work for money only. Venal means a person who is open to bribery.

Exercise – 8

1. C Qualm means uneasiness.

2. D Quaint means something that is odd, especially in an old-fashioned way.

3. A Rankle means to annoy or irritate.

4. F Rapport means good bond, understanding and harmony between people.

5. G Recapitulate means to repeat (usually the most important points or to summarize).

6. E Rendezvous means a prearranged meeting.

7. H Replete means full, abundant.

8. J Refractory means resistance to authority obstinate.

9. B Restive means someone who is impatient. Restless also means the same.

10. I Retrench means to lessen or to cut-down (specially expenses).

Exercise – 9

1. C Skinflint means a person who is reluctant to spend money i.e. a miser.

2. G Solicitude means to be concerned for someone.

3. A Sanguine means to be cheerfully confident or optimistic.

4. F Saucy means to be impertinent. impudent means the same.

5. B Smithereens means bits or fragments.

6. I Taciturn means one who is not talkative and reserved.

7. E   Salient means prominent and conspicuous. Outstanding means the same.

8. J   Theatrical means to be dramatic.

9. D   Semblance outward form or appearance.

10. H   Scrupulous means to be careful of details and principled.

Exercise – 10

1. C   Waylay means to wait for someone on the way, especially in order to attack.

2. A   Zany means a comical person, a clown

3. D   Vertiginous means causing a dizzying effect.

4. B   A voracious person is a person who eats more or has greed for food.

5. G   Zephyr means a gentle breeze.

6. F   Vestige means remains of something which once existed.

7. H   Vilify is to make defamatory statements.

8. E   Zest means spirited enjoyment or gusto.

9. J   Virulent means malignant and deadly.

10. I   Verdant means green (usually green growth-vegetation)

Worksheet – 2
Exercise – 1

1. D   Amiable means good-natured, sociable while its opposite is sullen or gloomy.

2. A   Anathema is a detested person or one who is not liked, while the opposite is adorable.

3. C   Annul is to make something void, while its antonym is enforce.

4. G   Antipathy is dislike or aversion, while the opposite is sympathy.

5. H   Assiduous is hardworking. So the apposite would be lazy.

6. J   Aplomb means self-confidence, while the opposite is diffident or timid.

7. B   Astute means very cunning and crafty, while obtuse means mentally slow.

8. E   Audacious means recklessly daring, while the opposite is gentle.

9. I   Anomaly means irregular or not normal, while opposite is normality.

10. F   Asinine means stupid. Therefore, the opposite will be learned.

Exercise – 2

1. D   Beguile means to mislead, while its antonym is escort.

2. E   Bawdy means indecent and very flashy, while its opposite is decent.

3. G   Bashful means timid or shy, while the opposite is bold.

4. I   Benevolence means generosity, kindness while the opposite is animosity.

5. A   Berserk means wild or frenzied, while opposite is calm and tranquil.

6. H   Berate means to scold, so the antonym would be to praise.

7. B   Bolster means to reinforce or support, while the opposite is desert.

8. C   Bovine means slow and stupid, while its opposite is intelligent.

9. J   Bravado is false bravery. So the opposite is cowardice.

10. F   Buoyant means high-spirited, while the antonym is depressed.

Exercise – 3

1. D   Cadence means rhythmic, while cacophony is harsh sound.

2. A   Callous means hard-hearted, while the opposite is sympathetic.

3. E   Callow means immature. So the opposite is mature.

4. B   Candid means frank, honest and its antonym is hypocritical.

5. C   Capacious means roomy and spacious, while confined means limited space.

6. H   Cardinal means chief or most important, while minor is its antonym.

7. J   Celestial means out of this world or of the heavens and the sky. So, its antonym is Earthly.

8. F   Celerity means speed or swiftness, while opposite is lethargy.

9. G   Certitude means certain. So, the appropriate antonym from column B is uncertain.

10. I   Clandestine means secret or hidden. So, the opposite will be open.

Exercise – 4

1. G   Earthy means unrefined. So, the opposite will be refined.

2. J   Ebullient means excited, while antonym is dejected or depressed.

3. E   Embellish means to decorate or adorn, while tarnish is to spoil.

4. H   Empirical means practical, or something that can be proved by experiment or observation. So, the matching opposite will be hypothetical which means something that is assumed or thought to exist.

5. A   Endemic means confined, while pandemic means extensive or widespread.

6. C   Farce means absurd or humorous, while the opposite is serious.

7. B   Felicity means happiness and joy, while antonym is misery.

8. D   Fiasco means disaster, while opposite is success.

9. F   Futile means in vain or useless, while opposite is useful.

10. I   Fraudulent means deceitful or fraud. So the antonym will be honest.

Exercise – 5

1. H   Hoi polloi means the common people or masses, while elite is the opposite.

2. E   Hostile means unfriendly. So, the opposite is friendly.

3. C   Humdrum means boring. There, the appropriate antonym would be interesting.

4. A   Ignoramus is a foolish or ignorant person, while the opposite is genius.

5. J   Immaculate means pure and clean, while tarnished means unclean or spoilt.

6. B   Introvert means a reserved person, while an extrovert is a person who speaks to everyone,

sociable.

7. D   Illusion is something which is unreal, while a fact is the truth and is real.

8. I   Impetus means the driving force or momentum, while impediment means something which stops the momentum.

9. G   Incertitude means doubtful, while the opposite is certain.

10. F   Irate means angry, while the antonym is peaceful.

Exercise – 6

1. E   Jeopardy means risky, while the opposite is sanctuary or security.

2. A   Lackadaisical means showing lack of interest, while its antonym is energetic.

3. B   Lament means to express sorrow, while its opposite would be to rejoice.

4. I   Laudable means praiseworthy, while antonym is contemptible.

5. C   Jocular means giving to joking. So its antonym will be serious.

6. D   Lithe is flexible, while the opposite is stiff.

7. J   Livid is furiously angry, while its antonym is calm.

8. F   Loathe means to detest or hate, while its opposite is to love.

9. G   Lucid means clear. So, the opposite will be something that is difficult to understand - incomprehensible.

10. H   Laggard means a person who always lags behind, while the opposite would be a leader that is, someone who leads.

Exercise – 7

1. C   Malice means grudge or hatred, while the opposite is kindness.

2. E   Malign means to speak bad about someone. So, the appropriate antonym would be praise.

3. A   Nadir means the lowest point, while zenith means pinnacle or the highest point

4. B   Naive means innocent, while the opposite is cunning.

5. D   Nepotism means favouritism, while its antonym is impartiality.

6. H   Notorious means ill-famed, while opposite is good or virtuous.

7. F   Obliterate means to erase or blot out, while its antonym is to preserve or build.

8. G   Odious means disgusting, while the antonym is attractive.

9. J   Opportune means appropriate, while the opposite is untimely.

10. I   Occident means the West, while Orient means the East.

Exercise – 8

1. E   A Pacifist is a person who is opposed to war or violence. So, its antonym would be an extremist – a violent person.

2. A   Perennial means longlasting, while ephemeral means short-lived.

3. B   Polarize means to split or divide, while the opposite is unite.

4. C   Pertinent means relevant. So, the appropriate antonym will be irrelevant.

5. G   Pragmatic means practical or realistic. So, the opposite is unrealistic.

6. F   Perfunctory is careless, while opposite is dedicated or sincere.

7. D   Parity means equality as in amount, status or value. Its opposite therefore is inequality.

8. J   Quaintness means odd and old-fashioned. Its opposite is modern.

9. H   Ransack means to plunder, while its antonym is to restore.

10. I   Rampant means widespread, while the opposite is limited or meager.

Exercise – 9

1. D   Sacrosanct means sacred or holy. So, its perfect antonym would be unholy.

2. D   Tardy means delayed, while its antonym is prompt.

3. A   Unison means harmony, agreement while the opposite is discord.

4. B   Turbulent is stormy. So, the appropriate antonym would be calm.

5. G   Unhinged means mentally unstable, while the opposite is sane or normal.

6. C   Upbraid means to rebuke and scold, while opposite is to condone or forgive.

7. I   Unilateral means involving just one side, while its opposite is bilateral which means to involve two sides.

8. J   Uprising means revolt. So, the appropriate antonym will be submission.

9. F   Sylvan means rural, while its antonym is urban.

10. H   Turbid means muddy, thick while the opposite is transparent.

Exercise – 10

1. D   Zeal means enthusiasm while the opposite is to be indifferent or apathetic.

2. C   Zenith means the highest point and the antonym is base or the lowest point.

3. A   Venal means corrupt. So, the appropriate antonym is honest.

4. E   Verbose means elaborate and wordy while its opposite is precise.

5. G   Verve means enthusiasm, while the antonym is depression.

6. B   Venerate means to regard with respect, while its opposite is to denounce or insult.

7. F   Viable means practical. So, the perfect antonym is impractical.

8. I   Voracious means excessively greedy, while the opposite is moderate.

9. J   Vindictive means revengeful. Forgiving means just the opposite.

10. H   Vociferous means noisy. So, it appropriate antonym is quiet.

Worksheet – 6

1. a   Option (a) is not used as a mode of transport but (b), (c) and (d) are all used for conveyance, the difference between them being the number of wheels.

2. c   Option (c) means anything related to dogs while the options (a), (b) and (d) are specific breed of dogs.

3. d   While (a), (b) and (c) are not components of anything else, option (d) is a component of a pencil.

4. a   While options (b), (c) and (d) are used in writing or for marking; option (a) is used to remove those.

5. c   Options (a), (b) and (d) are all keys present on the computer keyboard while (c) is not.

6. a   While (b), (c) and (d) are various facial expressions, (a) is powdery substance applied on the face.

7. b   While (b), (c) and (d) are positive form of emotions, (a) is a negative form.

8. b   (b) is played with hand while (a), (c) and (d) are played using a racquet.

9. d   (a), (b) and (c) are played with the help of a racquet or stick while (d) is played with foot.

10. c   (a), (b) and (d) are verbs signifying aggressive behaviour while (c) is a dummy of a person.

11. a   Options (b), (c) and (d) are synonyms while (a) is not.

12. b   (b) is a place where people usually stay on a temporary basis usually to protect oneself from danger or weather but (a), (c) and (d) are permanent places to live.

13. b   (a), (c) and (d) are famous economists while (b) is a feeling.

14. c   Options (a), (b) and (d) are related to greenery, trees etc., while (c) means dislike.

15. a   (b), (c) and (d) are synonyms which mean someone who is barbaric and causes pain while (a) means to feel sorry for one's doing.

16. d   Options (a), (b) and (c) are synonyms which mean wise while (d) means someone who can be fooled easily.

17. b   Options (a), (c) and (d) are synonyms meaning people having lots of money while (b) means person who needs money or other things.

18. c   Options (a), (b) and (d) are all related to health in one way or another while (c) means salty water.

19. b   Options (a), (c) and (d) are synonyms which mean untidy and dirty while superb is their antonym.

20. b   Option (b) means a person or thing that is the centre of attention while (a), (c) and (d) mean pale or feeble looking.

Worksheet – 7

1. c   (a), (b) and (d) are in one way or the other related to movement while (c) does not have any relation to them.

2. c   (a), (b) and (d) are related to smell while (c) is related to taste.

3. d   (d) is natural which means that it is not made or caused by people. While the rest are its antonyms.

4. b   (a), (c) and (d) mean to argue against something or to have opposite views while (b) means to support something.

5. b   Options (a), (c) and (d) are synonyms while (b) is not.

6. d   Options (a), (b) and (c) are synonyms while (d) is not.

7. a   While in options (b), (c) and (d) 'ambi' signifies two or both while in (a) it does not.

8. d   (a), (b) and (c) are people who keep things to themselves and do not speak much but (d) means a person who stays away from people and does not like to mix.

9. c   (a), (c) and (d) are samehow related to the colour red. (c) is the odd word out.

10. b   Options (a), (c) and (d) are prepositions while (b) is a conjunction.

11. a   Options (b), (c) and (d) are prepositions while (a) is not.

12. d   In options (a), (b) and (c) a series is made in which a letter is added to the beginning of a sentence while in (d) it is added at last.

13. c   (a), (b) and (d) are all in the mind which means that they do not have a solid form while material is just the opposite.

14. b   While (a), (c) and (d) are together joined and connected to each other naturally, (b) is an external thing.

15. d   (a), (b) and (c) are thoughts or actions which are not thought of or are not deliberate while (d) is the way a horse walks.

16. d   (a), (b) and (c) signify decrease in their respective meanings while in (d) there is an increase.

17. d   (a), (b) and (c) describe people who consume alcohol while (d) does not take alcohol at all.

18. d   (a), (b) and (c) means related to children while (d) is the opposite.

19. c   The options (a), (b) and (d) are all synonyms of indecent while (c) is their antonym.

20. b (a), (c) and (d) are synonyms of festivity, celebration, party but (b) means incomplete or existing only in part.

Worksheet – 8

1. d (a), (b) and (c) are all related to growth or coming into the world while (d) means the spread of some information.

2. c (a), (b) and (d) are forms of laughter in which the laugh is in a positive manner and is not rude while (c) is laughing quietly in a disrespectful rude manner.

3. d Options (a), (b) and (c) are all related to joints while (d) is not and does not contain any joint.

4. b The movements (a), (c) and (d) are all quick movements and occur very quickly while (b) is a slow motion activity.

5. b While in options (a), (c) and (d) sparkle or shine is involved; option (b) is just the opposite.

6. b Options (a), (c) and (d) are activities or actions performed by humans while (b) is not.

7. a The options (b), (c) and (d) are synonyms while option (a) is not.

8. c The options (a), (b) and (d) are related to money while the option (c) means compulsory.

9. d Options (a), (b) and (c) refer to clothes while (d) is not.

10. b Options (a), (c) and (d) are synonyms which mean cheerful, while (b) is not.

11. b Options (a), (c) and (d) more or less mean having no roughness and pleasant to touch while option (b) is different.

12. d Options (a), (b) and (c) are synonyms while (d) is not.

13. b Options (a), (c) and (d) are mathematical terms while (b) is not.

14. b Options (a), (c) and (d) are the various terms used in music. While option (b) is a musical play.

15. a Options (b), (c) and (d) are terms used to describe stupid or sluggish people while (a) is the term used for a particular group of mammals, e.g. rat.

16. c Options (a), (b) and (d) are synonyms while (c) is not.

17. d (a), (b) and (c) are types of taxes while (d) is not the same.

18. d Options (a), (b) and (c) are terms related to horses while (d) is related to dogs.

19. a Options (b), (c) and (d) are all synonyms while (a) is their antonym.

20. c Options (a), (b) and (d) are all terms related to a telephone while option (c) is not.

Worksheet – 9

1. c Options (a), (b) and (d) are synonyms of hunger while option (c) is not.

2. d Options (a), (b) and (c) are all hairstyles while (d) is not.

3. c Options (a), (b) and (d) mean to have a problem while (c) does not mean the same.

4. a Options (b), (c) and (d) are all forms of ice while (a) is not.

5. c (a), (b) and (d) are all birds while (c) is not.

6. a Options (b), (c) and (d) are the processes used to produce a picture diagram etc., while (a) is the tool used to do so.

7. d (d) has five sides while the rest have four.

8. d (a), (b) and (c) are the studies of various branches of science while (d) is not.

9. a Options (b), (c) and (d) are all terms related to the Arctic region or very cold regions while (a) is not.

10. d (a), (b) and (c) are all synonyms while (d) means a proposed explanation.

11. b (a), (c) and (d) are all used as fuels while (b) is not.

12. d Options (a), (b) and (c) are all forms of motion while (d) is not.

13. d (a), (b) and (c) are all metals which are found in their original form, while (d) has to be processed and made.

14. b (a), (c) and (d) are units for measuring length while (b) is for measuring liquids.

15. d (a), (b) and (c) are planets while (d) is not.

16. b While (a), (c) and (d) denote an end to something (b) denotes a beginning.

17. b (a), (c) and (d) are human qualities while (b) is not.

18. c (a), (b) and (d) refer to a big amount in their respective terms while (c) is a small amount.

19. d   (a), (b) and (c) refer to the upper class of society while (d) is a mental state.

20. a   (b), (c) and (d) all mean to restrain, to stop while (a) does not.

Worksheet – 10

1. d   In (a), (b) and (c) there is an increase in some way or the other while in (d) it is not.

2. d   (a), (b) and (c) mean going down or a decrease while it is not in (d).

3. d   Options (a), (b) and (c) are synonyms while (d) is not.

4. d   Options (a), (b) and (c) are synonyms while (d) is not.

5. c   (a), (b) and (d) mean which are out of this world, bizarre while (c) does not mean the same.

6. b   Options (a), (c) and (d) are verbs while (b) is not.

7. d   Options (a), (b) and (c) are all synonyms meaning the end while (d) means to change form.

8. c   (a), (b) and (d) more or less mean friendly while (c) means generous.

9. a   (b), (c) and (d) are all states of mental disorder while option (a) is a belief or an impression.

10. b   Options (a), (c) and (d) are prepositions while (b) is not.

11. b   Options (a), (c) and (d) are all forms of greetings while (b) is not.

12. d   (a), (b) and (c) are all synonyms while (d) is not.

13. d   (a), (b) and (c) are all terms related to deceit while (d) is not.

14. c   Options (a), (b) and (d) are all synonyms of lazy while (c) is not.

15. d   Options (a), (b) and (c) are all the types of qualities a person can have while (d) is not.

16. d   (a), (b) and (c) are all members of the cat family while (d) is not.

17. a   Games (b), (c) and (d) all involve a ball while in (a) a shuttle is used.

18. c   Options (a), (b) and (d) are terms related to time while (c) is not.

19. d   Options (a), (b) and (c) are all units of electricity while (d) is a unit of length.

20. c   (a), (b) and (d) are all systems of government while (c) is a skill.

Worksheet – 11

1. d   'Despondent' meaning dejected is the odd one. The rest – options (a), (b) and (c) are all synonyms.

2. d   Options (a), (b) and (c) have the same meaning – to look dull and deathly. Therefore, option (d), which means 'of a healthy colour' is the odd one here.

3. d   Option (d) means something that induces catharsis (a purging or cleansing of emotions). The rest are synonyms meaning - to dislike, i.e. to regard someone with distaste and aversion.

4. d   The first three options have the same meaning – juvenile, immature and simple. Option (d), which means 'cunning' is the odd one.

5. d   Option (d) means a keen feeling of unease, as of annoyance or disappointment. The rest are synonyms meaning – having a weary and worn appearance.

6. a   'Exalted' means to be elevated (in rank or status). The rest of the options have a similar meaning.

7. d   Option (d) meaning spiteful and evil is the obvious odd one here. The rest are all synonyms having a positive connotation.

8. d   Options (a), (b) and (c) – all have the same meaning – to lower in rank, dignity, esteem. 'Urchin' which means 'a mischievous youngster' is the odd word in this case.

9. a   Option (a) meaning something that is difficult to understand or fathom is the odd one. The rest are synonyms. They refer to someone who is lively and enjoys the company of others.

10. d   Options (a), (b) and (c) have the same meaning – to reduce or lessen. 'Attune' which means to adjust or acclimatize is the odd word.

11. c   The odd word is 'attenuate' is the odd word. It means to weaken or lessen. The rest are all synonyms, meaning 'to adapt'.

12. d   The first three options have a similar meaning – someone who has given up all pleasures. Option (d) is just the opposite. It refers to someone who loves food.

13. c   Options (a), (b) and (d) refers to a person who is difficult to please. An 'easygoing' person on the other hand is someone who is not demanding.

14. c   Options (a), (b) and (d) are synonyms. Option (c) is the antonym and hence the odd one out.

15. a   Options (b). (c) and (d) have a similar meaning. They refer to a person who is careful. 'Reckless' is the opposite. Its means a heedless or careless person.

Worksheet – 12

1. c   The idiom – to 'take someone to task' means to admonish, to rebuke.

2. a   The idiom 'tooth and nail' means to do everything possible and use all the force available.

3. d   The idiom is 'leave no stone unturned'. It means to use all the resources available and to try out everything.

4. b   The idiom 'in high spirits' means to be cheerful and very happy.

5. a   'To put your foot down' means not to yield or come under pressure or force anymore.

6. b   The idiom 'bad blood' means ill feeling or bitterness among individuals or groups of people.

7. b   The idiom refers to a child whose appearance or character closely resembles that of one parent or another.

8. a   'Crocodile tears' means an insincere display of grief.

9. d   'Struck several bad patches' means to come across professional difficulties.

10. c   To 'keep to himself' means to be unsociable.

11. b   The idiom 'under (one's) thumb' means to keep someone unduly under control.

12. d   'To strike gold' means to find something useful or valuable.

13. b   The idiom 'have your cake and eat it too' means to have your say both ways.

14. a   'Cool customer' refers to a person who is calm and relaxed.

15. c   'Rolling in money' means to be very rich.

16. a   To have a 'chequered career' means to have lots of ups and downs in career.

17. a   The idiom is 'bite off more than you can chew'. It means trying to do more than one is capable of.

18. b   'Tall order' means to be expecting too much from someone.

19. d   To 'scream blue murder' means to object loudly and create a scene.

20. b   The idiom 'get a kick' means to get excitement and thrill from something.

Worksheet – 13

1. c   The idiom means to be exceptionally ugly.

2. d   'At close quarters' means to look closely.

3. a   The 'awkward age' refers to the period of early adolescence.

4. b   The idiom 'to call a spade a spade' means to speak the truth bluntly and without hesitation.

5. d   'Cold shoulder' means to avoid someone or to be indifferent.

6. d   To 'cut both ways' means to argue in support of both the sides.

7. d   The idiom is 'take to one's heels'. It means to run away.

8. c   'Put up' means to be unable to endure.

9. b   The idiom 'sure as eggs is eggs' means quite certainly.

10. c   'As true as steel' means to be loyal and trustworthy.

11. c   To 'bank on' someone means to rely on that person.

12. a   'Conceive of a time' means to imagine or think of a time.

13. a   To have no bearing means to have no relation at all.

14. c   The burning question refers to the current issue which is hotly debated.

15. c   The idiom 'at the drop of a hat' means for no reason at all.

16. d   The idiom 'bare bones' means the naked truth.

17. c   To be in 'apple-pie order' means to be in perfect order and condition.

18. a   'Tall stories' means exaggerated and fabricated stories.

19. d   The idiom 'to bring to book' means to punish someone.

20. a   'In camera' means to be photographed.

Worksheet – 14

1. c   To 'lead someone by the nose' means to make some one do unquestioningly all of ones wishes; to dominate.

2. d   The idiom 'to wear the trousers' refers to the person in a relationship who makes all the important decisions.

3. c   'Bury the hatchet' means to forget the past and reconcile.

4. b   The idiom 'by dint of hard work' means 'as a result of'.

5. a   The idiom 'hold the purse strings' refers to a person who controls the spending of a family's or an organization's money.

6. c   'Stew in your own juice' means to let someone suffer for their own doings.

7. c   The first speech is known as the maiden speech.

8. c   The idiom 'gift of the gab' means the ability to speak easily and confidently.

9. c   To 'go dutch while having a party' means that each person pays for his expenses.

10. a   The idiom 'cup of tea' refers to someone's chosen or preferred thing or task.

11. c   'Easy money' refers to the money made with little effort, sometimes even dishonestly.

12. c   To 'fall flat' means that they do not produce the expected effect or result.

13. c   'Creature comforts' refers to material things or luxuries that help to provide for one's bodily comforts.

14. c   The 'prodigal son' refers to a person who spends lavishly and extravagantly.

15. a   The idiom 'split hairs' means to make petty distinctions or to argue about details.

16. b   To behave like a fishwife means to be loud and abusive.

Worksheet – 15

1. c   The idiom 'to sow one's wild oats' means to do wild and foolish things in one's youth.

2. d   To be 'down in the mouth' is to be unhappy or depressed.

3. a   To put someone 'in a fix' is to put the person in a difficult situation.

4. d   To 'draw a veil over' a subject means that a person does not want to talk about it anymore.

5. d   To 'cut the ground from under someone's feet' is to anticipate someone's action or argument and thus make it irrelevant or meaningless.

6. a   The idiom means to fail to make an impression.

7. c   'Captive audience' refers to those listeners or onlookers who have no choice but to attend.

8. c   'Ill at ease' means not to feel comfortable.

9. a   The idiom 'at the beck and call' means to be ready to obey someone's orders instantly.

10. c   To be 'in one's element' means to be in a comfortable situation; to feel happy.

11. b   To be 'out of place' means inappropriate.

12. b   The idiom is 'law unto oneself'. It refers to someone who sets his/her own standards of behaviour; someone who ignores laws and rules.

13. c   'On its last legs' means to be at the last stage; about to end.

14. a   'Midas touch' means to succeed in whatever one does.

15. c   The idiom 'cool one's heels' means to be kept waiting for a long time.

16. b   If something that someone does, costs them dear, it means that it has caused them lots of problems.

17. a   The idiom 'to strike while the iron is hot' means to do something at the appropriate time.

18. c   The 'seamy side of life' means the least pleasant aspect of life.

19. c   The idiom means to deal firmly and strictly.

20. c   To 'rub shoulders' means to walk at the same level, to socialise.

Worksheet – 16

1. d   The correct idiom is 'look before you leap. It means to be careful before taking any decision.

2. d   'Hot' is the correct option. To 'strike while the iron is hot' means to make use of opportunities.

3. a   The idiom is 'early bird catches the worm'. It means that the early starter gets the best opportunities.

4. b   'Lining' is the correct option. The idiom means that there is light at the end of the tunnel, i.e. there is something good even in an unpleasant situation.

5. c   The correct idiom is 'to be born with a silver spoon in the mouth'. It means to be born in a very rich family.

6. d   'Palms' is the correct option. The idiom means to bribe someone.

7. a   The idiom is 'to take leave of one's senses'. It means to lose control of oneself and to become irrational.

8. a   'Itching palm' means a desire for money' greed; also wanting a bribe.

9. a   The correct idiom is 'to join issue with'. It means to enter into a controversy.

10. a   'To go pigs and whistles' means to be ruined completely.

11. d   The correct idiom is 'a square peg in a round hole'. It means to be a misfit.

12. d   'Trumpet' is the correct option. It means to boast.

13. c   The idiom is 'actions speak louder than words'. It means that the acts of a person are more important then what he says (or promises).

14. a   The correct option is (a) – hatchet. The idiom means to settle old enmity and start afresh.

15. b   The idiom is 'to get your act together'. It means that someone needs to do the right things (improve), especially because they are inefficient or disorganized.

PART – III : LANGUAGE

Grammar

I. Use of articles

Common Usage of 'a / an' (indefinite articles) and 'the' (definite article).

'a' is used before consonants when we do not refer to a specific object. So when we say 'a case', we mean any case. We would say 'the case' when we are referring to a particular case.

'an' is used before vowels, and some consonants (when we do not pronounce the first letter, as in an hour, where 'h' is silent).

a/an are used in expressions of frequency or quantity as in "thrice a week" or "four times an hour".

'the' is used :

- Where there is only one of its kind, as in "the sun";
- In superlatives, as in "the best", "the fattest";
- When we refer again to something that has been referred to once before, as in
  "Gone with the Wind is a book worth reading. The book is a masterpiece";
- To indicate groups or classes of people as in "the youth" and "the Indians";
- Before oceans, seas, rivers, islands, mountain chains, deserts, countries with plural names, and noun forms of points of the compass as in "the Atlantic Ocean" or "the North";
- Before any noun that the listener or reader already knows about, as in " My car is a Maruti. The Maruti is a reliable car."
- Before names of hotels, newspapers, musical instruments and large organisations. For eg. "the Hiltons", "the Indian Express", "the UN", etc

Practice articles:

Fill in the blanks in the following sentences using the code given below:

(a) an, a	(b) the, a
(c) a, no article	(d) an, the
(e) the, the	

1. Someone with _______ beard had come to meet _______ you.
2. If _______ trial is on today, why have you not sent me _______ case papers?
3. _______ Rajdhani Express now stops at _______ few more stations.
4. It is truly _______ honour to meet _______ President of India.
5. It is not at all unusual for _______ editor to tamper with _______ writer's manuscript.

[Answers: 1.(c), 2.(e), 3(b), 4.(d), 5.(a)]

II. Different Parts of Speech

(a) Nouns

A noun is the name of a person, place, animal or thing. Nouns are naming words.

E.g.

> **Akbar** was a great **king**.
> **Kolkata** is on the banks of the **Hooghly**.
> The **sun** shines brightly.
> His **courage** won him **honour**.

- **Nouns that are used only in the singular form:**
  - (a) Scenery, information, furniture, advice, machinery, stationery, news, poetry, business, mischief, fuel, issue, repair, bedding, etc.
    E.g. The *scenery* of Kashmir *is* very beautiful.
    The *information* in the newspapers *is* adequate.

(b) Physics, Mathematics, Economics, Classics, ethics, athletics, innings, gallows, etc.
E.g. *Physics* is *a* subject that needs to be studied very intently.
These days, the *ethics* of politicians *is* deplorable.

(c) Brick, bread, fruit, word (as 'promise')
E.g. Let me buy some *fruit*. He was true to his *word*.

(d) Words like dozen, score, hundred, thousand, million; when preceded by a numeral
E.g. Before going abroad my friend bought four pairs of shoes and two *dozen* shirts.

(e) Expressions such as a ten-rupee note, a six-hour journey, a two-mile walk, a five-year plan, a one-man show, etc
E.g. It was *a one-man show* when Amit had to compere, act, sing and dance on stage.

- **Nouns that are used only in the plural form:**

(a) Cattle, police, poultry, people, gentry, peasantry, artillery, etc.
E.g. The *police have* caught the culprit. *Cattle are* grazing in the field.

(b) Alms, scissors, trousers, stockings, spectacles, shorts, remains, riches, goods, measles, etc
E.g. The *scissors are* very blunt. The goods shipped were in perfect condition.

- **Nouns that are used both in the singular and plural forms:**

(a) Deer, sheep, fish, apparatus, wages
E.g. The *deer* in the park *was* chewing at sweets thrown by the children. *Deer are* very attractive animals.
The *wages* of sin *is* death. The *wages* of the workers *have* been raised.
I saw a *sheep* grazing in the field. *Sheep are* sold cheaper than goats.

(b) Collective nouns such as jury, public, team, audience, committee, government, congregation, orchestra, etc.
E.g. The *team are* looking fit and fine. The *team has* not yet scored a goal.

(b) Adjectives

An adjective is a word that says something more about a noun. Adjectives are describing words.
E.g.

Ramesh is a **brave** boy.
There are **twenty** students in the class.

Comparison of adjectives

Positive / Absolute	Comparative (-er)	Superlative (-est)
Bright	Brighter	Brightest
Slim	Slimmer	Slimmest
Weak	Weaker	Weakest
Doubling of final consonant		
Fat	Fatter	Fattest
Big	Bigger	Biggest
For –e, add –r and – st		
Fine	Finer	Finest
True	Truer	Truest
For –y, add –ier and –iest		
Dry	Drier	Driest
Happy	Happier	Happiest
Exception:		
Gay	Gayer	Gayest
-ful / -ing / - ive / - less / -ous /	**more -**	**most -**
Beautiful	More beautiful	Most beautiful
Attractive	More attractive	Most attractive
Boring	More boring	Most boring
Irregular adjectives		
Good	Better	Best
Bad	Worse	Worst
Little	Less	Least
Far	Farther/further	Farthest / furthest

- The adjectives ending in – ior (prior, junior, senior, inferior, anterior, posterior, etc) take 'to' and not 'than' after them. E.g. He is senior *to* me.

- Some adjectives like unique, ideal, perfect, extreme, complete, universal, infinite, perpetual, chief, entire, round, impossible are **not** compared. E.g. It is a unique book.
- Comparative degree is used in comparing two things or persons, while the superlative compares more than two things or persons. E.g. Ramesh is the better of the two brothers. Ramesh is the tallest boy in his class.
- <u>Double comparatives and double superlatives must not be used</u>. E.g. He is more taller than his brother (incorrect). He is taller than his brother (correct). Examples of double superlative are most perfect, most correct, etc.
- When two qualities in the same person or thing are compared, the comparative ending with–er is not used. E.g. You are wiser than old (incorrect). You are more wise than old (correct).
- When two adjectives in the superlative or comparative degree are used together, the one formed by adding 'more' or 'most' must follow the other adjective. E.g. He is more intelligent and wiser than his brother (incorrect). He is wiser and more intelligent than his brother (correct).
- When two adjectives with differing degrees of comparison are used, they should be complete in themselves. E.g. He is as wise, if not wiser than his brother (incorrect). He is as wise as, if not wiser than his brother (correct).
- When a comparative degree is used in its superlative sense, it is followed by 'any other'. E.g. Kapil is better than any bowler (incorrect). Kapil is better than any other bowler (correct).
- When two or more comparatives are joined by 'and' they must be in the same degree. E.g. Russel was one of the wisest and most learned men of the world.

Commonly Confused Adjectives:

- **Less** refers to quantity or non-countable nouns, **Fewer** denotes number or countable nouns.
- **Last** is the final one; **Latest** is last up to the present.
- **Little** means not much and expresses negative quantity, **A little** means 'at least some' and expresses positive quantity. The same is true for 'few' and 'a few'.
- **Farther** means 'more distant'.
- **Latter** means the second of the two things discussed. (former and latter).

(c) Pronouns

Pronouns are words used to replace nouns or noun groups.
E.g.   Harish is absent because **he** is ill.
      The books are where **you** left **them**.

Whenever you use a pronoun in place of a noun, ensure that it is using the same form as the noun that it is replacing. Gender and number often get confused.
E.g.   "Rashmi has borrowed **my** book and passed **it** on to the Desai family. **She** should get **it** back from **them** and return **it** to **me**." This sentence makes it very clear who has to do what.

- The pronoun 'one' must be followed by 'one's'. E.g. **One** must do **one's** duty diligently. Alternatively 'one' can be followed by 'oneself'. E.g. **One** should always prepare **oneself** for the worst.
- When 'one' means 'one in number', the pronoun for it is (his, her, its). E.g. **One** of them has given up **his/her** studies.
- 'Everybody' or 'everyone' must be followed by 'his/her'. E.g. **Everyone** should love **his /her** mother tongue.
- 'Each', 'every', 'anyone', 'anybody' must be followed by the singular pronoun of their person. E.g. **Anyone** can do this exercise if **he/she** tries.
- 'Let' is followed by a pronoun in the objective case. E.g. **Let** him go wherever **he** wants to.
- 'But' and 'except' are followed by the pronoun in the objective case. E.g. Everyone attended the party **except him/her**.
- Verbs like enjoy, avail, pride, resign, apply, acquit, assert, absent, etc are usually followed by reflexive pronouns. E.g. The boy **absented himself** from class very often. We **enjoyed ourselves** at the party.
- 'Who' denotes subject and 'whom' denotes object. E.g. **Who** do you think will win the match? **Whom** did you abuse?
- 'Who' is used for persons and 'which' for lifeless objects. E.g. This is the house **which** I was talking about. My brother married Sunitha **who** is a lawyer.
- 'each other' is used for two; 'one another' for more than two. E.g. Rahul and Rani loved **each other** dearly. The villagers helped **one another**.
- The complement of the verb 'to be', when it is expressed by a pronoun, should be in the nominative case. E.g. It was **he** who stole the show. If I were **he**, I would not go there again.
- When the same person is the subject and object, it is necessary to use reflexive pronouns. E.g. **I** cut **myself** while shaving this morning.
- When a pronoun is the object of a verb or a preposition, it should be in the objective case. E.g. These books are for **you** and me. Don't worry, there is perfect understanding between **him** and **me**.
- Always use the possessive form of the pronoun before gerunds (nouns in the -ing form).

E.g. My parents object to me working late nights. (incorrect) My parents object to **my** working late nights (correct).

Subject Pronouns	Object Pronouns	Possessive Pronouns	Reflexive Pronouns
I	Me	My	Myself
We	Us	Our	Ourselves
You	You	You	Yourself
He	Him	His	Himself
She	Her	Her	Herself
They	Them	Their	Themselves
Who	Whom	Whose	--

Directions for questions: Select the appropriate pronouns in the given sentences.

1.   It was she/her at the window.

2.   Payal and she/her have quit BL.

3.   They asked he/him and I/me to join the academic team.

4.   That call was for I/me, not he/him.

5.   An invitation was sent for he/him and she/her.

[Answers: 1. she; 2. she; 3. him, me, 4; me, him; 5. him, her]

(d) Verbs

A verb is a word used to express an action or state of being.

E.g.   I **wrote** a letter to my cousin.
Bangalore **is** a big city.
Iron and copper **are** useful metals.

Subject – Verb Agreement.

The verb must always agree with the subject.

- Singular subjects must have a singular verb. E.g. He **writes**. I **write**.
- Plural subjects must have a plural verb. E.g. **They write. We write.**
- Two subjects joined by 'and' will always take a plural verb. E.g. The doctor **and** the nurse **work** together.
- Two singular subjects joined by 'or' or 'nor' will take a singular verb. E.g. The boy **or** the girl **is** coming to the party.
- A singular subject and a plural subject joined by 'or' or 'nor' will take a singular or plural verb, depending on which subject is nearer the verb. E.g. Neither my father **nor** my **brothers are** attending the meeting. Neither his friends **nor** Deepak **is** joining the tour.

- Indefinite pronouns such as someone, somebody, each, nobody, anyone, anybody, one, no one, everyone, every one, everybody, either, neither, etc. always take a singular verb. E.g. **Each** of my friends **calls** me every day. **Nobody is** missing the class.

- Indefinite pronouns that indicate more than one (several, few, both, many, etc) always take plural verbs. E.g. **Both** the books **are** useful for exams. **Several** of the fielders **run** four or five miles a day.

- Collective nouns (fleet, army, committee, etc) are singular when the group works together as a unit and hence, take singular verbs. E.g. The **jury has** announced its verdict. The **team functions** smoothly.

- Collective nouns are plural when the members of the group are acting individually and hence, take plural verbs. E.g. The **jury have** argued for five hours.

- Words such as news, measles, mumps, etc that end in –s, but represent a single unit need singular verbs. E.g. The **8 o'clock news is** about to begin. **Mumps has** rather serious side effects. **Mathematics is** his favourite subject.

- Titles of books that end in –s needs singular verbs. E.g. *Great Expectations* is a wonderful book. *Tom Jones* **is** a book of Fielding.

- If two subjects are joined together by 'as well as' the verb will act according to the first subject. E.g. The **students as well as the teacher are** in the class. **He as well as his brothers** is sitting for the exam.

- If two subjects are joined by 'with', 'together with', 'along with', 'accompanied by', 'as well as', 'combined with' the verb will be according to the first subject. E.g. The **Principal together with his students was** watching the play. The **students together with the Principal were** watching the match.

- The subject 'Many a …' is always followed by a singular verb. E.g. **Many a man was** drowned in the sea.
- If the subject is 'The number of …' use a singular verb. E.g. **The number of books in the library is** very small. Note: In case the sentence begins with the phrase 'A large number…', then the verb should be in the plural form. E.g. **A large number of cars were** parked in the playground.
- Confusion often arises while using words like 'either', 'neither', 'everyone', as they appear to be in the singular but actually are in the plural form. "Neither of them likes to be corrected." This sentence means that there are two people and both of them do not like to be corrected.

(e)   Adverbs

An Adverb is a word used to add something to the meaning of a verb, an adjective or another adverb.

E.g.   The child worked out the problem **quickly.**

This flower is **very** beautiful.

She spelt all the words **quite** correctly.

- **Adverbs of frequency** (never, often, usually, always, rarely, already, most, just, quite, nearly, hardly, etc) are normally put between the subject and the verb.
  - E.g. My father **often** goes abroad.
    I **quite** agree with you.
- The adverb 'enough' is placed after the adjective. E.g. She is cunning **enough** to tackle her friend.
- 'Ever' is sometimes used incorrectly for 'never'. E.g. He seldom or ever tells a lie (incorrect). He seldom or never tells a lie (correct).
- The adverb 'not' should not be used with words having negative meaning. E.g. The teacher forbade me not to go (incorrect). The teacher forbade me from going (correct).
- The word' only' should be placed immediately before the word it modifies. E.g. Harish answered **only** two questions.

(f)   Prepositions

A preposition is a word that begins with a prepositional phrase and shows the relationship between its object and another word in the sentence. A preposition must always have an object. A prepositional phrase starts with a preposition, ends with an object, and may have modifiers between the preposition and the object of the preposition. Here is a list of common words that can be used as prepositions:

about,	*above,*	*across,*	*after,*
against,	*along,*	*among,*	*around,*
at,	*before,*	*behind,*	*below,*
beneath,	*beside,*	*besides,*	*between,*
beyond,	*but (when it means except),*		
by,	*concerning, down,*		*during,*
except,	*for,*	*from,*	*in,*
inside,	*into,*	*like,*	*near,*
of,	*off,*	*on,*	*out,*
outside,	*over,*	*past,*	*since,*
through,	*to,*	*toward,*	*under,*
until,	*up,*	*upon,*	*with,*
within,	*and*	*without.*	

These words can be used as other parts of speech as well. What part of speech a given word belongs to depends on how it is used in a given sentence.

Many of the common words used as **prepositions can be used as adverbs**. Words are prepositions if they have an object to complete them. If a noun or a pronoun answers the question regarding the object, the word in question is a **preposition**.

Example: The boy stood up and ran down the street.

Up what? There is no object; therefore *up* is not a preposition. *Down* what?

'Street' answers the question; therefore, *down* is a preposition. 'Down the street' is the prepositional phrase starting with the preposition down and ending with the object *street* with a modifier *the* in between.

Dimensions and Prepositions

Prepositions differ according to the **number of dimensions** they refer to. These can be grouped into three classes using concepts from geometry: **point, surface and area or volume**.

1.   **Point:** Prepositions in this group indicate that the noun that follows them is treated as a point in relation to which another object is positioned.

Example:

My car is **at** the house.

The preposition 'at' used here, locates a car in relation to a house, which is understood as a fixed point.

2. **Surface:** Prepositions in this group indicate that the position of an object is defined with respect to a surface on which it rests.

    Example:

    There is a new roof **on** the house. The house has been treated here as a surface upon which another object, the roof, is placed. Thus, the preposition 'on' is used.

3. **Area/Volume:** Prepositions in this group indicate that an object lies within the boundaries of an area or within the confines of a volume.

    For Example:

    The house is **in** the National Capital Region. (The house has been located within a geographical area.)

    There are four rooms in the house, which has a lovely staircase in the living room. (The house has been treated as a three-dimensional structure that can be divided into smaller volumes, namely rooms, inside one of which is an object, the staircase.)

In light of these descriptions, 'at', 'on', and 'in' can be classified as follows:

at .... point

on .... surface

in .... area/volume

The preposition *'at'* has a great variety of uses. Here are some of them:

Location: Vidisha is waiting for her sister *at* the bank. (The bank can be understood as a point defining Vidisha's location)

Rahul spent the whole afternoon *at* the book fair. (Since book fairs are usually spread out over a fairly large area, it makes little sense to think of a fair as a point. At is used in this case just because it is the least specific preposition; it defines Rahul's location with respect to the fair rather than some other place.)

Destination: We arrived *at* the house. ('At' exhibits cause/effect relationship. 'to' cannot be used here because arrival at a place is the result of going to it).   The waiter was *at* our table immediately.

Direction: The policeman leaped at the robber.

The dog jumped at my face and really scared me.

1. **Nouns denoting enclosed spaces, such as a field or a window, take both 'on' and 'in'.**

    The prepositions have their normal meanings with these nouns. 'on' is used when the space is considered as a surface, 'in' when the space is presented as an area.

    Anika and her friends are practicing *on* the field. (surface)

All my buffaloes are grazing *in* the field. (area)

The frost made patterns *on* the window. (surface)

A face appeared *in* the window. (area)

2. **When the area has metaphorical instead of actual boundaries, such as when field means "academic discipline," 'in' is used:**

    Radhika is a leading researcher *in* the bioengineering field.

3. **'In' and 'on' are also used with means of transportation: in is used with a car and on with public or commercial means of transportation:**

    in the car

    on the bus, plane or train or ship

4. **Prepositions of Direction:** Apart from to, on, onto, in, into there are a number of prepositions that can be used to show direction and movement around the floor plan. Some of them are across, between, out of, past, round, through and towards.

    Examples:

    Walk *through* the exit of room two and enter *into* building number one.

    Walk *across* the indoor garden to reach room number *six*.

    Walk *past* the side entrance to reach the main entrance.

Relationships expressed by prepositions

Place:	at, on, in, inside, within, by, near, behind, beyond, among, between, above, below, beneath, over, under to, towards, from, into, out (of), off, onto, across, along, down, past, round, through
Time:	at, on, in, during, for, after, before, by, since, till, throughout, until
Reason:	because of, despite, for
Similarity:	as, like, unlike, than
Addition:	with, without
Means:	by, with

Usage of 'For', 'Which' and 'During'

'For' is used with a period of time to express the duration or 'how long' something has happened:

for three weeks, *for* many years

'While' is used with a verb form as in the following cases:

While I was watching TV

While I lived in Mumbai

'During' is used with a noun to express the time 'when' something happened.

During the class

During my exams

There are some words that demand particular prepositions. These verb phrases have a special meaning and must be used as it is, e.g:

depend on	cope with
marriage to	tired of
averse to	long for
battle against or with	reason for
trouble with	angry at
bored with	live on

Usage

Some of the most common prepositional phrases are:

Under: Under the influence, under no obligation, under his thumb, under consideration.

At: At times, at last, at first, at once, at a profit, at risk, at any rate, at least.

By: By all means, by chance, by no means, by name, by now, by then, by sight, by and by.

For: For now, for instance, for a change, for example, for ages, for better or worse.

Without: Without warning, without success, without fail, without notice, without exception.

From: From then on, from bad to worse, from now on, from my point of view.

Prepositions of place: [at and in]

We use **at** with a position, an address, an activity, a journey etc. We use **in** with something big enough to be all around a person, a road, a building, a city and a country.

e.g. I live **at** 54 Cross Roads.

We were **at** the theatre.

Vanita was **in the garden.**

It was dark **in** the theatre.

Prepositions of time: [on, at and in]

e.g. I had my breakfast **at** 8 O' clock.

I got up early **in** the morning.

We graduated **in** the year 2000.

I met him **on** Wednesday morning.

Prepositions of time: [before, during, after, till, until and by]

e.g. I'm always busy **during** the day.

We had to leave immediately **after** the speech.

The children were very excited **before** the show began.

I am very busy **until** Sunday.

We shall be returning home **by** the weekend.

Prepositions meaning transportation and communication: [by]

e.g. Will we go **on** foot or **by** car?

We can inform them **by** post.

Describing: [with and in]

eg. It's number 54, the house **with** the bamboo door.

The photographer is looking for a tall model **with** long hair.

Using: [like and as]

e.g. He's just **like** his father.

I like to use my house **as** my office.

In the case of nouns, adjectives and verbs prepositions combine and form idioms or phrases,

Prepositions + Nouns

By

e.g. I paid **by** cheque / credit card.

(to pay by credit card)

I broke the mirror **by** mistake.

(To do something by accident)

There has been a fall **in** prices recently.

(A decrease in something)

For

e.g. Let's go **for** a walk.

(to go for a walk)

We went **for** a swim as soon as we arrived.

I had a hamburger **for** lunch.

Noun + Prepositions

e.g.

Belief in: His **belief in the** superstition was unjustified.

Confusion about: There was confusion **about** the schedule.

Participation in: His **participation in** the cultural programme was negligible.

Verb + Preposition

Phrasal Verbs:

The verbs with prepositions are called **phrasal verbs.**

e.g.

Apologize for: He **apologized for** his blunder.

Prepare for: They are **preparing for** the CAT.

Look up: When in doubt, always **look up** the dictionary.

Pay for: Atul had to **pay for** his haste.

Position:

At the back of, at the bottom of, at the top of, behind, in the corner of, in the middle of, next to the left of, on the side of, on top of e.g.   The smallest room is **located to the left of** the building.

Direction:

Across, between, into, out of, past, round, through, towards.

e.g.   We went *across* the road to meet out friends.

The passage *through* the market was unapproachable.

Blow up: explode

The militants **blew up** the tracks.

Bring up :   mention a topic

They were forced to **bring up** a distasteful topic.

Call off :   cancel

We had to **call off** the meet.

Hold up: delay

There was a **hold up** on the highway.

Make up: invent a story

The boys **made up** a convincing story.

Put off: postpone

The trip was **put off** due to external pressure.

Put on :   wear

The girls **put on** their new dresses.

Set up: to arrange

The hall was **set up** to welcome the delegates.

Talk over: discuss

The students wanted to **talk over** the examination schedule.

Catch up with : keep abreast

The friends were trying to *catch up with* the office gossip.

Come up with : to contribute

Everybody *came up with* some unique suggestions.

Cut down on : curtail

We should *cut down on* our expenses.

Keep up with : maintain pace with

The athletes were very / too quick; we all found it difficult to *keep up with* them.

Look down on : despise

Fanatics *look down on* other religions.

Run out of : exhaust supply

The canteen had *run out of* sandwiches

Walk out on: Abandon

The girl *walked out on* her boyfriend.

Fill in the correct preposition:

1.   Some people believe that in emotional maturity men are inferior .... women.

     (a) Than   (b) To

     (c) From   (d) Against

2.   My father was annoyed .... me.

     (a) Towards   (b) Against

     (c) With   (d) Upon

3.   Some orthodox persons are averse .... drinking liquor.

     (a) Against   (b) For

     (c) In   (d) To

4.   The Cinema Hall was on fire and the Cinema owner had to send .... the Fire Brigade.

     (a) For   (b) Through

     (c) Off   (d) In

5.   He was not listening .... I was saying.

     (a) That   (b) Which

     (c) To what   (d) What

[Answers: 1.(b), 2.(c), 3.(d), 4.(a), 5.(c)]

(g) Conjunctions

A conjunction is a word used to join words or sentences.

E.g.   Amit **and** Arjun are twins.

I ran fast **but** missed the train.

Coordinating Conjunctions	and / as well as / both … and / or / nor / neither … nor / not only … but also / so / for / therefore / consequently / accordingly / but / still / yet / nevertheless / however
Subordinating Conjunctions	As / as if / as though where / wherever
Subordinating Conjunctions	As / as soon as / since / when / wherever / while / before / after / till / until
Subordinating Conjunctions	Because / since / now that /
Subordinating Conjunctions	(so) that/ in order that / lest … should / for fear that / so that … not
Subordinating Conjunctions	so … that / such … that
Subordinating Conjunctions	if / if … not / unless / as long as / on condition that / provided (that) / in case
Subordinating Conjunctions	although / (even) though / even if / no matter / in spite of / however (badly/hard/much/well)
Subordinating Conjunctions	than / as … as / (not) so … as / such … as

- "Scarcely" or "hardly" is followed by "when". E.g. **Scarcely/Hardly** had I entered the hall **when** the teacher called my name.
- "No sooner" is followed by "than". **No sooner** <u>did I reach</u> the office **than** I had to attend to a phone call. **No sooner** <u>had I reached</u> the office **than** I had to attend to a phone call.
- "Not only" is followed by "but also". One must **not only** prepare diligently for the exams **but also** attempt the questions in a quick manner.
- "Lest" is followed by "should". Cover all the cut fruit **lest** flies **should** sit on them.
- "Both" is followed by "and". **Both** Arun **and** Arjun came to receive me at the airport.
- "So …. as" is used in the negative sentences; whereas "as …. as" is used for affirmative ones. E.g. Rahul is **not so** tall **as** Rajesh. Rajesh is **as tall as** his brother.
  Reading English is not **so** tough **as** studying French. Learning French is **as** tough **as** learning Latin.
- "As" and "since" are used to express reason. E.g. **As / Since** I was very busy I could not have my lunch on time.
- "Neither" is followed by "nor". E.g. **Neither** the child **nor** her teacher is on time today.
- "Either" is followed by "or". E.g. **Either** my friend **or** his cousin is coming for the party.

- "Unless", "until" are negative in sense and hence should not be negated. E.g. You can't go out to play **unless** you finish your work.
- "Such" is followed by "as". E.g. We talked about **such** things **as** the weather, books, etc.
- "If" is used in the conditional sense, "whether" is used in the case of uncertainty. E.g. **If** I do not get the tickets in time, I may have to cancel the trip. I do not know **whether** I'll get the tickets.

Identify the part of speech of the underlined words in the given sentences:

1.   A kindly person is one who behaves <u>kindly</u>.
    (a) noun   (b) preposition
    (c) adverb   (d) verb

2.   He is not normally a <u>very</u> fast runner, but he runs fast in major events.
    (a) adverb   (b) adjective
    (c) verb   (d) noun

3.   I must <u>perfect</u> the operation to make the perfect robot.
    (a) verb   (b) adverb
    (c) adjective   (d) noun

[Answers: 1.(c), 2.(b), 3(a)]

III. Tense

Grammatical tense is a temporal linguistic quality expressing the time at, during, or over which a state or action denoted by a verb occurs.

Tense is one of at least five qualities, along with mood, voice, aspect and person which verb forms may express.

There are 3 types of tenses:
I.   Present tense
II.   Past tense
III. Future tense

I. Present Tense

Present indefinite tense

It is used;
1.   To describe permanent truths and habitual or customary activities. It is found with such adverbs as:
      a. Generally, usually, frequently, often, always, rarely
      b. With adverbial phrases as everybody, once, a week, etc.
      E.g. The moon shines during the night.
      E.g. Your daughter speaks very well.
2.   When we speak of the events that will take place in future time but have been planned beforehand. Only a few verbs are used in this way; to be, open, close, begin, start, end, finish, arrive, come, leave, return.
      E.g. The train leaves at 8 p.m in the evening.
3.   In exclamatory sentences beginning with 'here' and 'there'.
      E.g. Here comes Mr. Sharma!
            There goes the shuttlecock!
4.   Used to express general truths such as scientific fact.
      E.g. Rectangles have four sides.

Present Progressive or continuous tense

It is used;
1.   For an action going on at the time of speaking.
      E.g. The students are writing an essay.
2.   For a temporary action which may not be actually happening at the time of speaking.
      E.g. I am reading a new book nowadays.
3.   For an action that is bound to take place in the near future
       E.g. I am coming there in an hour.
4.   For habitual actions, which continues in spite of a warning.
      E.g. You are always chatting on the Internet.

Present perfect tense

It is used;
1.   To indicate completed activities in the immediate past (with just).
      E.g. He has just eaten breakfast.
2.   For an action whose time is not definite
      E.g. Pinky has gone to Honolulu.
3.   For a past event whose effect is felt in the present.
      E.g. I have taken all the biscuits.
      (There aren't any left for you)

Present perfect continuous tense

It is used;
1.   To show that something started in the past and is continuing till now. "For five minutes," "for two weeks," and "since Tuesday" are all durations which can be used with the Present Perfect Continuous.
2.   With first person, second person and third person plural subjects always use:
      have been+participle;
3.   In case of third person singular subjects use always use has been+participle:
      E.g. I have been talking to my friend for three days.
      She has been sleeping since morning.

II. Past Tense

Past indefinite tense

It is used;
1.   For an action completed in the past.
      E.g. He watched a movie yesterday.
2.   For an action in the past (regular habit or event).
      E.g. He regularly wrote to me for two years.

Past continuous tense

It is used;
      To denote an action going on at some time in the past. It may not indicate the time of the action though.
      E.g. We were roaming around in the mall throughout the evening.

Past perfect tense

It is used;
      To describe a situation of two actions happening in the past in which one action happened earlier than the other.
      E.g. When I reached the station the train had already left.

Remember to use:
Had + past participle of the verb with all the persons both in the singular and the plural.
E.g. I had watched the movie before I read the review.

Past perfect continuous tense

It is used;

To show an action that began in the past before a certain point and also has continued up to that time.
E.g. I had been writing for 2 hours.
Remember that with all persons you must use had been + participle.
E.g. I had been reading the novel since morning.

III. Future tense

Future indefinite tense

It is used;
1. To express the future as a fact.
   E.g. I shall be 25 next Month.
2. To talk about what is expected to happen in the future.
   E.g. I think India will win the Samsung Series.

Rules
- To express you must use 'shall' or 'will' with the form of the verb (mostly, shall + first person and will + second and third person):
  E.g. We shall visit the fair.
- In negative sentences, you may use the following pattern:
  E.g. We shall not break the rules of the college.
- In interrogative sentences:
  Will or shall + subject + the first form of the verb
  e.g. Shall we complete the assignment?
  e.g. Will you walk down the road with me?

Future continuous tense

It is used;

For actions, which will be taking place at some time in the future.
E.g. I will be playing cricket in the evening.

Future perfect

It is used;
1. To show the completion of an action by a certain time in the future.
   E.g. By the month end, we shall have completed the process.

- Formation of negative and interrogative sentences follows the usual rules.
  She will not have played. Will she have played?

Future perfect continuous tense

It is used;
1. For an action that will be in progress over a period of time and will continue in the future.
   E.g. By next march we shall have been studying here for one year.
   Now Go through this …

Expressing the Future ….

Be Going To
1. It is used when the speaker is making a prediction based on evidence.
   - It's going to rain.
2. When the speaker already has an intention or plan.
   - We're going to enjoy the party tomorrow.

About to
It is used to talk about an impending event.
- He is about to make a change in the schedule.

Identify the appropriate verb form to fill the sentence with:

1. I meant to repair the radio, but _______ time to do it.
   (a) was not having   (b) haven't had
   (c) have no   (d) will not had

2. Our guests _______ they are sitting in the garden.
   (a) arrived   (b) have arrived
   (c) had arrived   (d) will not had

3. Even after a decade in the state, Sangram _______ mastered Tamil, but he can communicate.
   (a) has not   (b) have not
   (c) had not   (d) haven't had

4. I _______ my relatives across the border once in 1990 before I moved in with them in 2000.
   (a) have been visiling
   (b) had visited
   (c) had been visiting
   (d) haven't had

5. I _______ working all afternoon and have just finished the assignment.
   (a) will be   (b) have been
   (c) have   (d) would be

[Answers: 1.(b), 2.(b), 3.(a), 4.(b), 5.(b)]

IV. Parallelism

Whenever a sentence expresses a series of actions or ideas, it is important that they should be presented in the same format. In other words, words or phrases used in a series should belong to the same part of speech. Usually a comma separates the words or phrases. E.g.

- I like reading, writing and I enjoy drawing too (incorrect). I like reading, writing and drawing too.
- After you have turned over the soil, weeded and cultivating, you'll be ready to plant the sapling (incorrect). After you have turned over the soil, weeded and cultivated, you'll be ready to plant the sapling.
- A good worker is conscientious, reliable and efficiency (incorrect). A good worker is conscientious, reliable and efficient.
- Ladakh, one of the highest regions in the world, is made up of plains and it has deep valleys too (incorrect). Ladakh, one of the highest regions in the world, is made up of plains and deep valleys.

Quite simple, isn't it? The correct sentences tend to be simple. However, many people write the wrong kind, especially when they are writing in a hurry and have little time to review the construction of each sentence.

Now, correct the following sentence

She cooks, washes dishes, does her homework and <u>then she is relaxing</u>.

    (a) then relaxes
    (b) then relaxing
    (c) relaxing then
    (d) No correction required

[Answer: (a)]

V. Unnecessary Words

Sometimes an unnessary word that should not be present in a sentence is added to it. This may result in a double subject, a double negative, a repeated similar adjective or adverb, or an unnecessary preposition.

E.g. I went to the library to return back the book (incorrect). I went to the library to return the book.

While jogging strengthens your legs, push-ups they strengthen your arms (incorrect). While jogging strengthens your legs, push-ups strengthen your arms.

VI. Transformation of Sentences

You may be required to transform a sentence without changing its meaning. There are several ways to change the form of a sentence and to do so correctly, you have to be familiar with the variety of sentence structures in English; understand the essential meaning and implications of various sentence patterns; and be able to express yourself in a variety of forms.

While transforming one sentence into another form, remember NOT to change anything that does not require any change.

It is not possible to list all the sentence transformations possible, however, a list of the most common types is given below:

(a)   **Active to passive voice and vice-versa:**
e.g., 'The car was washed by the rain.' *becomes* 'The rain washed the car.'
'The team was reprimanded by the coach' becomes 'The coach reprimanded the team'.

VOICE CHART

ACTIVE VOICE	PASSIVE VOICE
Statements	
Vikram writes a letter	A letter is written by Vikram.
Vikram is writing a letter	A letter is being written by Vikram.
Vikram has written a letter.	A letter has been written by Vikram.
Vikram wrote a letter.	A letter was written by Vikram.
Vikram was writing a letter.	A letter was being written by Vikram.
Vikram had written a letter.	A letter had been written by Vikram.

Interrogative Statements	
How do we do it?	How is it done?
When do they wash their clothes?	When are their clothes washed?
Who wrote *Macbeth*?	By whom was **Macbeth** written?
Why do people laugh at the beggar?	Why is the beggar being laughed at?
Did his behaviour shock you?	Were you shocked by his behaviour?
Imperative Statements	
Shut the door.	Let the door be shut.
Obey your elders.	Let your elders be obeyed by you.
Please bring me a glass of water.	You are requested to bring me a glass of water.

Notes:

Whenever it is evident who the doer of the action is, it is unnecessary to mention him in the passive form as this omission gives a neater turn to the sentence. E.g. Someone picked my pocket. (Active) My pocket was picked (by someone).

(b) Interchanging parts of speech:

Reframing sentences by changing parts of speech e.g. *noun to adjective* as in 'The man is known to be generous.' *becomes* 'The man is known for his generosity.' OR *adjective to adverb* as in 'He is slow in his work.' *becomes* 'He works slowly.'

- **Replacing nouns by verbs:**
  - o The men put up a brave **fight**. The men **fought** bravely.
- **Replacing verbs and adjectives by nouns**:
  - o I **regretted** my rude behaviour. I expressed **regret** for my rude behaviour.
  - o She is neither **beautiful** nor **intelligent**. She has neither **beauty** nor **intelligence**.
- **Replacing nouns and adverbs by adjectives:**
  - o There is a possibility that he will **create problems**. It is possible that he will **become problematic**.
  - o You have argued very **convincingly**. You have put forth a very **convincing** argument.
- **Replacing nouns and adjectives by adverbs:**
  - o Handle these delicate clothes with **care**. Handle these delicate clothes **carefully**.
  - o Her behaviour was **courteous** and **sweet**. She behaved **courteously** and **sweetly**.

(c) Reported Speech:

Direct to indirect speech and vice-versa, e.g., "Please make an appointment for tomorrow," the advocate said *becomes* "The advocate told him to make an appointment for the next day."

1. Change of pronouns: (into second and third person)

DIRECT SPEECH	INDIRECT SPEECH	DIRECT SPEECH	INDIRECT SPEECH
I and you	He or she	We and you	They
Me and you	Him or her	Us and you	Them
My and your	His or her	Our and your	Their
Mine and yours	His or hers	Ours and yours	Theirs

2. Change of Tenses: (into the past tense)

DIRECT SPEECH	INDIRECT SPEECH
Write/s	Wrote
Is/am writing	Was writing
Are writing	Were writing
Has/have written	Had written
Wrote	Had written
Was/were writing	Had been writing
Shall/will write	Should/would write
Shall/will be writing	Should/would be writing
Shall/will have written	Should/would have written

Notes:

Had (the past tense of have) becomes had had in the Indirect Speech.

3. Change of Pointer words: (into distant words)

DIRECT SPEECH	INDIRECT SPEECH
Now	Then
Hence	Thence
Hither	Thither

Hereafter	Thereafter
Today, tonight	That day, that night
Yesterday	The day before / the previous day
The day before yesterday	Two days before
Ago	Before
Tomorrow	The next day / the following day
Next week, month, year, etc	The following ...
Last week, month, year, etc	The previous ...

Some useful hints for converting basic sentences into the Indirect Speech:

Statements	Use reporting verbs like **remark, observe, suggest, insist, add, reply, declare, assure, warn, confess, protest, deny, point out, plead, remind, repeat, explain,** etc.
Interrogation	Use reporting verbs like **wonder, want to know, inquire,** etc.
In questions opening with a question-word (who, where, why, when, where, whose and how)	Repeat the question-word in the Indirect Speech.
Imperatives	Use reporting verbs like ask, tell, order, command, beg, request, urge, advise, etc.
Exclamations	Use reporting verbs like exclaimed with ... (grief, joy, sorrow, surprise, etc according to the context)

(d)   Degrees of Comparison:
E.g. 'No other plane is as fast as the Concorde.' *becomes* 'The Concorde is faster than any other plane' or 'The Concorde is the fastest plane in the world.'

Sentences of proportionate Comparison or Contrast:
- As I read the book more, I like it more and more. The more I read the book, the more I like it.
- As I play football more, I like it less and less. The more I play football, the less I like it.
- As we grow older, we become wiser and wiser. The older we grow, the wiser we become

(e)   Interchange of Sentences:
E.g. "Everyone enjoyed the play." *becomes* "No one disliked the play." The changes can be among

assertive, interrogative and exclamatory patterns too, such as "This is a fine book" *can become* "Isn't this a fine book?" or "What a fine book this is!"

Basic Types of Sentences

Affirmative/ Assertive	My uncle drives his car very carefully.
Negative	My uncle does not drive his car carelessly.
Interrogative	Does my uncle drive his car very carefully?
Interrogative Negative	Doesn't my uncle drive his car carefully?

Interchange of Exclamatory and Assertive Sentences

If only I were young again!	I wish I were young again.
How beautiful is the night!	The night is very beautiful.

Interchange of Interrogative and Assertive Sentences

When can their glory fade?	Their glory can never fade..
Shall I ever forget those happy days?	I shall never forget those happy days.

(f)   Different ways of expressing a concession or contrast:
i.   **Though** I am poor, I will not beg.
ii.   **Poor as** I am I will not beg for my food.
iii. **However** poor I may be, I will not beg for my food.
iv.   I am poor, **all the same** I will not beg for my food.
v.   **Admitting** that I am poor, I will not beg for my food.
vi.   **Even if** I am poor, I will not beg for my food.
vii. **Notwithstanding** that I am poor, I will not beg for my food.
viii. I am poor **nevertheless,** I will not beg for my food.
ix.   I am poor **indeed**, but I will not beg for my food.

(g)   Interchanging conditionals:
Different ways of expressing a condition:
i.   **Just** try once more and you will succeed.
ii.   **If** you try once more, you will succeed.
iii. **Should** you try once more, you will succeed.
iv.   **Supposing** you try once more, you will succeed

v.   You will not succeed **unless** you attempt it once more.

vi. Just try it once more **and** you will succeed.

vii. **If you were to** try it once more, you would succeed.

(h) Using inversion:
E.g. No sooner had he reached the station than the train left. Here 'had' is used before the subject 'he'. This is called inversion of verb.

(i) Synthesis of Sentences:

- By using a participle:
  - He opened the front door. He entered the house. **Opening** the front door, he entered the house.
  - I finished my work. I went for a walk. **Finishing** my work I went for a walk.

- By using a noun or a phrase in apposition.
  - This is my aunt. Her name is Vidya. This is my **Aunt** Vidya.

- By using a preposition with a noun or gerund.
  - My friend was ill. Still he worked hard for the exam. **In spite of his illness** my friend worked hard for the exam.
  - The lights went out. The film had not ended. The lights went out **before** the end of the show.
  - Keats was a poet. He was a critic. **Besides** being a poet, Keats was also a critic.

Transformation of Sentences

1. I only realized the full implications of what had happened sometime later.
    It wasn't until later that I realized the full implications of what had happened.

2. We cannot invite an unlimited number of people because of space constraint.
    There is a space constraint due to which only a limited number of people can be invited.

3. Nobody could have done anything to prevent the problem from arising.
    Nothing that had been done could present the problem from arising.

4. One can be highly intelligent, but may not have much common sense.
    Having high intelligence does not always amount to having common sense.

5. He has been put in charge of reorganizing the department.
    He has been made the incharge of department reorganization.

(j) Sentence Starters:
E.g. Madhuri has been consistent in her studies. Her performance in the examination was nothing but excellent.

The optional starters are:

(a) Despite being consistent in her studies…

(b) Madhuri's performance in the examination was nothing but excellent because…

(c) Since Madhuri was only consistent and not intelligent her performance…

Answer Options

(i) Only (a)   (ii) Only (b) and (c)

(iii) Only (b)   (iv) All the above

In this kind of exercise we have to proceed carefully, eliminating the starters that do not make grammatically correct sentences or where the starters change the meaning of the given sentences.

Sentence Starter (a) – If this starter were to be used, the meaning of the sentences would change. This starter does not work.

Sentence Starter (b) – This would make a sentence that is grammatically correct and conveys the meaning of the sentence as in - Madhuri's performance in the examination was nothing but excellent because of her consistent study.

Sentence Starter (c) – This sentence adds information that is not provided in the sentences, hence cannot be correct.

Hence, only (b) is the correct sentence.

VII. Punctuation

Punctuation rules are the basic rules of using commas, colons, capitals, semicolons, full stops, ellipses, apostrophes and writing numbers.

The full stop: At the end of a sentence we put a full stop (.). It is also used after statements or imperatives. It is also called period.

Example: We went for a walk in the morning.
The questions mark (?) comes after a question.
It is also called a note of interrogation.

Example:

Do you like reading books?

An exclamation mark (!) after making an exclamation e.g. Hurrah! Wow! Yippee! Alas! Oh!

The Capital letter: A sentence always begins with a capital letter. Proper names are written in capital letters. Days and months are always written in Capital letters. 'I' is always written in capitals.

The Colon: Colons follow independent clauses and are used to draw attention to the information that comes after.

Colons come after the independent clause and before the word, phrase, sentence, quotation, or list it is introducing.

Examples:

Rani had only one thing on her mind : her career.

The Semi-colon: Semi-colons (;) are used between two main clauses when the second main clause is not linked grammatically to the first.

e.g. The father and his son start work at every morning; they get up early because there is always a lot to do.

The Comma: Commas are used to show shorter pauses than a semi-colon (;) or a full stop (.).

We usually put a comma between two main clauses, before but, and or, Commas are put after sub clauses and reported clauses.

Examples:

He looked for the book, but he couldn't find it.

Quotation marks: Quotation marks ("…") are put before and after direct speech. We put a comma before or after the direct speech.

Examples:

Sheen said, "It's time for the movie."

"It's time for the movie," Sheen said.

The Apostrophe: Apostrophes are used in the possessive form of nouns and short forms or contractions.

Some examples of **contractions**

We've	-	we have
Won't	-	will not
Aren't	-	are not
I'll	-	I will

Apostrophes show possession, they are placed before the 's' to show possession by the person/persons.

e.g. The girl's dress.	(singular)
The girls' dresses.	(plural)
Mr. Singh's house.	(house belongs to one Singh).
The Singhs' house.	(house belongs to the family Singh).

Ellipses: The Ellipses (…) consists of three evenly spaced dots. The Ellipses is used when you're quoting material and you want to omit some words. Use ellipses only when omitting words within citations.

Examples:

The ceremony honoured some … from the US.

Exercise

Exercise on Grammatical Errors

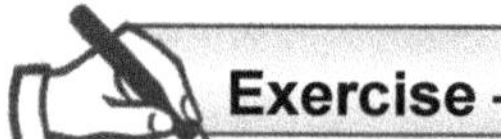

Exercise – 1

Directions for questions 1 to 25: In the following questions, a sentence is divided into 4 parts, mark the part that has an error.

1. (a) Part of the difference
    (b) between the films and its
    (c) relative achievements derives
    (d) from the source novels.

2. (a) The only child like creatures
    (b) are the Hobbits,
    (c) short of stature and
    (d) averse from responsibility.

3. (a) His movies (b) achieves what
    (c) the best fairy (d) tales don't.

4. (a) Climbing Everest is
    (b) as much a historic journey
    (c) it is a feat
    (d) of mountaineering.

5. (a) The early Sherpa climbers
    (b) fought not only their
    (c) own physical limitations
    (d) also cultural and religious barriers.

6. (a) I fully agree when you say
    (b) that India is hanging
    (c) his head
    (d) in shame.

7. (a) Why are clients and
    (b) advertising agencies
    (c) are making such a
    (d) lot of noise?

8. (a) Beside,
    (b) the problems faced
    (c) by them do not always
    (d) relate to money.

9. (a) It may take
    (b) at least
    (c) a generations to
    (d) change their perception.

10. (a) They must realize
    (b) that the fault
    (c) lie within
    (d) themselves.

11. (a) Analysts and columnists
    (b) agrees that such a
    (c) war of retaliation would
    (d) be a disaster.

12. (a) Neither America
    (b) or Europe
    (c) is that eager
    (d) to press the button.

13. (a) The countries present
    (b) at Bonn was
    (c) probably working with
    (d) good intentions.

14. (a) Provinces are
    (b) working for
    (c) its own
    (d) interests.

15. (a) He had built
    (b) almost nothing in America
    (c) but writing the fabulous
    (d) cult book 'Delirious New York'.

16. (a) Miuccia Prada is
    (b) the Italian designer
    (c) who turned her family business into
    (d) a globe fashion empire.

17. (a) He blurs
    (b) the distinctions
    (c) among
    (d) high art and commercialism.

18. (a) Fluent in
    (b) four languages,
    (c) he think and writes
    (d) about architecture in English.

19. (a) The best
    (b) idea can
    (c) come from the
    (d) newest persons.

20. (a) Few countries
    (b) has ever seen their
    (c) cultural heritage decimated as
    (d) rapidly as Afghanistan.

21. (a) Sandra agreed that
    (b) the government could not
    (c) constitutional make it a
    (d) crime to present young-looking adults as children.

22. (a) A positive
    (b) attitude
    (c) make the
    (d) biggest difference.

23. (a) You need to
    (b) feel the place,
    (c) visiting the ashrams,
    (d) know the people.

24. (a) Are we prepared for the consequences
    (b) who will follow when young,
    (c) impressionable minds
    (d) are poisoned?

25. (a) Children are
    (b) many more
    (c) open-minded
    (d) than adults.

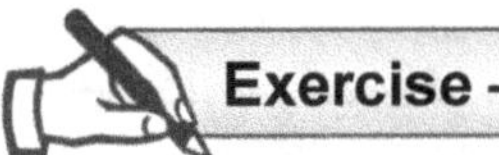 **Exercise – 2**

Directions for questions 1 to 25: The underlined part of the following questions may be grammatically erroneous. Replace the underlined portion of the sentence with an appropriate choice from among the given options.

1. Charles has received the information that virtually every British parent is <u>instinctive sympathetically.</u>
    (a) instinct sympathetic
    (b) instinctively sympathetic
    (c) instinctively sympathetically
    (d) instinctive sympathetically

2. Everyone in this class <u>receive bad feedback</u>.
    (a) has received bad feedback
    (b) have received bad feedback
    (c) receive bad feedback
    (d) have been receiving bad feedback

3. She keeps agonizing over <u>what to wear of the growing parade of awards shows.</u>
    (a) to wear at the growing parade of awards shows
    (b) what to wear of the growing parade of awards shows

   (c) what to wear with the growth parade of awards shows

   (d) what to wear at the growing parade of awards shows

4.   Further complicating the situation in the U.S. is the fact <u>that whatever decision is made can be ruled by the family</u>.

   (a) that whatever decision is made can be overruled by the family.

   (b) whatever decision is made can be overruled by the family.

   (c) that what decision is made can be overruled by the family.

   (d) that whatever decision is made can be ruled by the family.

5.   Once they get past infancy, <u>there is a number of children who aren't adopted and are left in homes</u>.

   (a) there is a number of children who aren't adopted and are left in homes.

   (b) there are a number of children who aren't adopted and are left in homes.

   (c) there are a number of children who isn't adopted and are left in homes.

   (d) there are a number of children who aren't adopted and is left in homes.

6.   Hakeem said the Muslims had been overlooked in <u>early peace bids which ended in disaster.</u>

   (a) early peace bidding ending in disaster

   (b) earliest peace bids which ended in disaster

   (c) early peace bids which ended in disaster

   (d) earlier peace bids which ended in disaster

7.   <u>Intelligent investors make their move</u> ahead of her.

   (a) Intelligence investors make their move

   (b) Intelligence investors make its move

   (c) Intelligent investors make their moves

   (d) Intelligent investors make their move

8.   Latin America has for long been a forgotten wasteland <u>to the politics controllers</u> Indian foreign policy.

   (a) to the politics controllers

   (b) to the politics controllers by

   (c) to the political controllers of

   (d) to the politics controllers in

9.   Few are aware of the sacrifices made by some, who since ancient times, <u>have silently worked in uplift human values</u>.

   (a) have silently worked to uplift human values

   (b) has silently worked to uplift human values

   (c) have silently worked in uplift human values

   (d) have silently worked to uplifting human values

10.   Ranbaxy made headlines around the world by <u>seeking to supply cheap drug to the developing world</u>.

   (a) seeking supply of cheap drug to the developed world.

   (b) seeking to supply cheap drugs to the developed world.

   (c) seeking to supply cheap drug to the developing world.

   (d) seeking to supply cheap drugs to the developing world

11.   Conservative political parties keep winning <u>policy debates then lose elections.</u>

   (a) policy debates and then lose elections

   (b) policy debates and then losing elections

   (c) policy debates and then losing election

   (d) policy debates then lose elections

12.   The diesel Mitsubishi Lancer is powered by a 2 liter, 8 valve engine <u>whose patented Super Silent Shaft technology make it</u> as noiseless as the petrol engine.

   (a) whose patented Super Silent Shaft technology makes it as noisy

   (b) whose patented Super Silent Shaft technology makes it as noiseless

   (c) who patented Super Silent Shaft technology makes it as noiseless

   (d) whose patented Super Silent Shaft technology make it as noiseless

13.   It often happens <u>when a party's ideas is triumphant it ends</u> up faring poorly in national elections.

   (a) when a party's ideas is triumphant it ends

   (b) which a party's idea are triumphantly end

   (c) that when a party's ideas are triumphant it ends

   (d) that when a party's ideas are triumphant it end

14.   Renaming historic places for military correctness <u>is as misguided as apologize for</u> the tangled past.

   (a) is as misguided as apologizing for

   (b) is misguided as apologizing for

   (c) is as misguided as apologizing to

   (d) is as misguided as apologize for

15.   The citizens of Bosnia and Herzegovina spoke <u>for themselves, pleasing neither the West or</u> international journalists.

   (a) by themselves, pleasing neither the West nor

   (b) for themselves, pleasing neither the West nor

   (c) for themselves, pleasing neither the West or

   (d) for himself, pleasing neither the West nor

16. Lasting peace <u>among blood brothers, as Indians and Pakistanis surely are, are</u> imperative.
    (a) among blood brothers, as Indians and Pakistanis surely are, is
    (b) between blood brothers, as Indians and Pakistanis surely are, is
    (c) among blood brothers, as Indians and Pakistanis surely is, is
    (d) among blood brothers, as Indians and Pakistanis surely are, are

17. The search <u>for answers begins with the fragmenting</u> of families.
    (a) for answers begins with the fragmentation
    (b) for answer begin with the fragmentation
    (c) for answers begin with the fragmentation
    (d) for answers begins with the fragmenting

18. A series <u>of Palestinian terrorist attack threatens</u> to destroy the hard-won peace accord signed at Wye.
    (a) in Palestinian terrorist attacks threatens
    (b) of Palestinian terrorist attack threatens
    (c) of Palestinian terrorist attacks threaten
    (d) of Palestinian terrorist attacks threatens

19. The sound was not <u>a harbinger to hope, but a prelude to</u> disaster.
    (a) a harbinger of hope, but a prelude to
    (b) harbinger of hope, but a prelude to
    (c) a harbinger to hope, but a prelude to
    (d) a harbinger of hope, but a prelude of

20. There are <u>too may dangers still lurking, to looting to food shortages</u> to epidemics.
    (a) to may dangers still lurking, from looting to food shortages
    (b) too many dangers still lurking, from looting to food shortages
    (c) too may dangers still lurking, from looting from food shortages
    (d) too may dangers still lurking, to looting to food shortages

21. One is Milford; <u>the others a sharp-eyed</u> old lady with cascading white hair.
    (a) the others a sharp-eyed
    (b) the other is a sharp-eyed
    (c) the others are a sharp-eyed
    (d) the others a sharp-eye

22. Her life was an incendiary cocktail of literary ambition, <u>famous, adventure</u> and addiction.
    (a) famous, adventurous
    (b) famous, adventure
    (c) fame, adventure
    (d) famously adventure

23. Bjork also grapples with a world that <u>is far lesser</u> enchanting than her imagination.
    (a) is far lesser
    (b) further less
    (c) are far lesser
    (d) is far less

24. The government <u>has been steadily pursuing significant economical and political</u> reforms for a year.
    (a) has been steadily pursuing significant economic and political
    (b) have been steadily pursuing significant economic and political
    (c) has been steadily pursuing significant economical and political
    (d) has steadily pursuing significant economic and political

25. He is the <u>less ideological man</u> I have met.
    (a) less ideological man
    (b) low ideology man
    (c) least ideological man
    (d) lesser ideology man

Exercise on Prepositions

Exercise – 1

Directions for questions 1 to 100: Fill in the blanks with the appropriate choice of prepositions.

1. He wanted to talk to me but I kept ___ working and refused to listen.
(a) on   (b) up   (c) out   (d) back

2. She is a good secretary but she is kept ___ by her ignorance of languages.
(a) on   (b) up   (c) out   (d) back

3. The country was in a state of rebellion and was only kept ___ by repressive measures.
(a) on   (b) down   (c) out   (d) back

4. Look ___ the baby while I am out.
(a) on   (b) up   (c) after   (d) back

5. She kept the children ___ all day because it was so wet and cold.
(a) on   (b) in   (c) out   (d) back

6. You must look ___ and make plans for the future.
(a) on   (b) up   (c) ahead   (d) back

7. "Keep ___!" he said. "Don't come any nearer."
(a) on   (b) up   (c) out   (d) back

8. If you look ___ it carefully, you will see the mark.
(a) on   (b) at   (c) out   (d) back

9. I told the children to keep ___ the room that was being painted.
(a) on   (b) up   (c) out of   (d) back

10. Looking ___ , I see now all the mistakes I made when I was younger.
(a) on   (b) up   (c) out   (d) back

11. I have started getting ___ at 5 a.m. to study but I don't know if I can keep this up.
(a) on   (b) up   (c) out   (d) back

12. He had an unhappy childhood and he never looks ___ on it with any pleasure.
(a) on   (b) up   (c) out   (d) back

13. The man walked so fast that the child couldn't keep ___ with him.
(a) on   (b) up   (c) out   (d) back

14. She looked ___ to see who was following her.
(a) on   (b) up   (c) out   (d) back

15. There were so many panes of glass broken that the windows couldn't keep ___ the rain.
(a) on   (b) up   (c) out   (d) back

16. I' ve been looking ___ a cup to match the one I broke.
(a) on   (b) up   (c) out   (d) for

17. Look ___ me at the station. I'll be at the bookstall.
(a) on   (b) up   (c) out for   (d) back

18. Look ___ ! You nearly knocked my cup out of my hand.
(a) on   (b) up   (c) out   (d) back

19. He was kept ___ in his research by lack of money.
(a) on   (b) up   (c) out   (d) back

20. Tom is looking ___ his first trip abroad.
(a) on   (b) foward to
(c) out   (d) back

21. Drop ___ on your way home and tell me what happened.
(a) on   (b) up   (c) out   (d) in

22. Before putting any money into the business, we must look very carefully ___ the accounts.
(a) on   (b) up   (c) into   (d) back

23. I look ___ her as one of the family.
(a) on   (b) up   (c) out   (d) back

24. My windows look ___ the garden.
(a) on   (b) on to   (c) out   (d) back

25. He asked me to look ___ the document and then sign it.
(a) on   (b) up   (c) over   (d) back

26. He looked ___ the book to see if he had read it before.
(a) on   (b) up   (c) out   (d) through

27. If you can afford a new car, your business must be looking ___ .
     (a) on   (b) up   (c) out   (d) back

28. You can always look ___ her address in the directory if you have forgotten it.
     (a) on   (b) up   (c) out   (d) back

29. He looked me ___ and ___ before he condescended to answer my question.
     (a) on ... on   (b) up ... down
     (c) up ... up   (d) back ... front

30. I am looking ___ seeing your new house.
     (a) foward to   (b) up to
     (c) out to   (d) back to

31. Children have a natural inclination to look ___ their parents.
     (a) foward to   (b) up to
     (c) out on   (d) back to

32. You will see I am right if you look ___ the matter from my point of view.
     (a) on   (b) at   (c) down   (d) back

33. He looks ___ me because I spend my holidays in Bournemouth instead of going abroad.
     (a) down at   (b) down on
     (c) out of   (d) back on

34. If he doesn't know the word he can look it ___ in a dictionary.
     (a) on   (b) up   (c) out   (d) back

35. The crowd looked ___ while the police surrounded the house.
     (a) on   (b) up   (c) out   (d) at

36. Since our quarrel, she looks ___ me whenever we meet.
     (a) at   (b) up to   (c) down   (d) through

37. It was some time before he came ___ after being knocked out.
     (a) round   (b) up   (c) on   (d) back

38. I had to wait for permission from the Town Council before I could go ___ with my plans.
     (a) round   (b) up
     (c) on   (d) back

39. He came ___ to my way of thinking after a good deal of argument.
     (a) round (b) up   (c) on   (d) back

40. The guard dog went ___ the intruder and knocked him down.
     (a) round (b) for   (c) on   (d) back

41. He had a sandwich and a cup of coffee, then went ___ working.
     (a) out   (b) up   (c) on   (d) back

42. It's no use trying to keep it secret; it's sure to come ___ in the end.
     (a) out   (b) up   (c) on   (d) back

43. I went ___ the proposal very carefully with my solicitors and finally decided not to accept their offer.
     (a) over   (b) up   (c) on   (d) off

44. The gun went ___ by accident and wounded him in the leg.
     (a) over   (b) up   (c) on   (d) off

45. The question of salary increases will come ___ at the next general meeting.
     (a) out   (b) up   (c) on   (d) off

46. Wearing black for mourning went ___ many years ago.
     (a) out   (b) up   (c) on   (d) off

47. She went ___ a beauty contest and got a prize.
     (a) in for (b) up for (c) on for (d) off

48. Those rust marks will come ___ if you rub them with lemon.
     (a) out   (b) up   (c) on   (d) off

49. The price of tomatoes usually goes ___ during summers in England.
     (a) out   (b) down   (c) on   (d) off

50. If there isn't enough soup to go ___, just put some hot water in it.
     (a) out   (b) round   (c) on   (d) off

51. Seeing me from across the room she came ___ me, and said that she had a message for me.
     (a) out to (b) up to   (c) on to   (d) off to

52. The early colonists of Canada went ___ many hardships.
    (a) out   (b) to   (c) through (d) off

53. You can't go ___ on your promise now; we are depending on you.
    (a) out   (b) back   (c) up   (d) down

54. I have changed my mind about marrying him; I simply can't go ___ with it.
    (a) on   (b) up   (c) through (d) off

55. The aeroplane crashed and went ___ in flames.
    (a) out   (b) up   (c) on   (d) off

56. He came ___ a fortune last year.
    (a) up   (b) into   (c) on   (d) off

57. Wait till the prices come ___ again before you buy.
    (a) low   (b) up   (c) on   (d) down

58. I refuse to go ___ now. I'm going on.
    (a) out   (b) up   (c) on   (d) back

59. They have gone ___ all the calculations again but they still can't find the mistake.
    (a) out   (b) over   (c) on   (d) off

60. The party went ___ very well; we all enjoyed ourselves.
    (a) out   (b) up   (c) on   (d) off

61. Come ___ ! It's far too cold to wait here any longer.
    (a) out   (b) up   (c) on   (d) off

62. Mary went ___ in such a hurry that she left her passport behind.
    (a) out   (b) up   (c) on   (d) off

63. The handle of the tea-pot came ___ in my hand as I was washing it.
    (a) out   (b) up   (c) on   (d) off

64. Why don't you go ___ for stamp collecting if you want a hobby?
    (a) out   (b) up   (c) in   (d) off

65. I came ___ a vase exactly like yours in an antique shop.
    (a) out   (b) upon   (c) on   (d) off

66. Her weight went ___ to 70 kilos when she stopped playing tennis.
    (a) out   (b) up   (c) on   (d) off

67. Don't go ___ food if you want to economize. Just drink less.
    (a) without (b) no   (c) on   (d) off

68. The sea has gone ___ considerably since last night's gale.
    (a) out   (b) down   (c) on   (d) off

69. I'm at home all day. Come ___ whenever you have time.
    (a) out   (b) up   (c) on   (d) round

70. She went ___ with her work after the interruptions.
    (a) out   (b) up   (c) on   (d) off

71. She goes ___ a lot. She hardly ever spends an evening at home.
    (a) out   (b) up   (c) on   (d) off

72. I suggested that we should all take a cut in salary. Naturally this didn't go ___ very well .
    (a) out   (b) up   (c) down   (d) off

73. I couldn't take ___ the lecture at all. It was too difficult for me.
    (a) out   (b) in   (c) on   (d) off

74. He is inclined to let his enthusiasm run ___ with him.
    (a) out   (b) up   (c) away   (d) off

75. When he offered me only $3, I was too taken ___ to say a word.
    (a) out   (b) back   (c) on   (d) aback

76. He has already run ___ the money his father left him two years ago.
    (a) out   (b) through (c) on   (d) off

77. Now he is catching ___ because he wants to pass.
    (a) out   (b) up   (c) on   (d) off

78. She took ___ riding because she wanted to lose weight.
    (a) out   (b) up   (c) on   (d) off

79. I can't start the car; the battery has run ___ .
    (a) out   (b) up   (c) down   (d) off

80. The policeman ran ___ the thief.
    (a) out   (b) up   (c) on   (d) after

81. He takes ___ his mother; he has blue eyes and brown hair.
    (a) out   (b) up   (c) on   (d) after

82. I forgot to turn off the tap and the wash basin ran ___ .
    (a) out   (b) up   (c) over   (d) off

83. That blouse is easy to make. You could run it ___ in an hour.
    (a) out   (b) up   (c) on   (d) off

84. I am sorry I called you a liar. I take it ___ .
    (a) out   (b) back   (c) on   (d) off

85. Reformers usually run ___ against opposition from all kinds of people.
    (a) out   (b) up   (c) on   (d) off

86. He took ___ going for a walk every night before he went to bed.
    (a) to   (b) up   (c) on   (d) off

87. Don't run ___ with the idea that Scotsmen are mean. They just don't like wasting money.
    (a) out   (b) away   (c) on   (d) off

88. I wish we could sell the grand piano; it takes ___ too much space here.
    (a) out   (b) up   (c) on   (d) off

89. She is always running ___ her friends behind their backs. She soon won't have any friends left.
    (a) out   (b) up   (c) down   (d) off

90. You'd better take ___ your coat if you're feeling too hot.
    (a) out   (b) up   (c) on   (d) off

91. Just run ___ the music of this song for me.
    (a) out   (b) over   (c) on   (d) off

92. We took ___ each other the first time we met and have been friends ever since.
    (a) to   (b) over   (c) on   (d) off

93. When his father died, Tom took ___ the business.
    (a) out   (b) up   (c) over   (d) off

94. What I saw in the water was only an old tree, I took it ___ the Loch Ness Monster.
    (a) out   (b) for   (c) on   (d) off

95. I ran ___ an old school friend in the tube today.
    (a) into   (b) up   (c) on   (d) off

96. I can't go more than 50 km/hr as this is a new car and I am still running it ___ .
    (a) out   (b) up   (c) in   (d) off

97. People often take me ___ my sister. We are very much alike.
    (a) out   (b) for   (c) about   (d) off

98. My neighbour is always running ___ of bread and borrowing some from me.
    (a) out   (b) up   (c) on   (d) off

99. He always takes ___ his false teeth before he goes to bed.
    (a) out   (b) up   (c) off   (d) on

100. I took ___ Tom at chess and beat him
    (a) out   (b) up   (c) on   (d) off

Exercise – 2

Directions for questions 1 to 15: Choose the correct preposition to fill the blanks in the given sentences.

1. We decided to carry ___ until midnight.
   (a) on   (b) forward
   (c) up   (d) before

2. ___ hindsight, it was a very ordinary decision.
   (a) In   (b) By
   (c) Through   (d) On

3. The hungry lion pounced ___ the cat.
   (a) into   (b) onto
   (c) upon   (d) under

4. The cat jumped ___ the cage.
   (a) on   (b) onto
   (c) in   (d) underneath

5. I decided to break ___ the jeweler's shop.
   (a) onto   (b) into
   (c) in   (d) forward

6. Always stay one step ___ of the game.
   (a) beside   (b) forward
   (c) ahead   (d) under

7. He earns a lot of money ___ the table.
   (a) under   (b) over
   (c) beside   (d) besides

8. At the age of 19, Martina Hingis is already a burn ___.
    (a) inward   (b) in
    (c) outward   (d) out

9. He lived ___ to the ripe old age of 97.
    (a) in   (b) on
    (c) over   (d) forward

10. Marlon Brando made a deep impression ___ my mind.
    (a) over   (b) in
    (c) on   (d) under

11. The little car jumped ___ the speed-breaker.
    (a) in   (b) under
    (c) into   (d) over

12. I decided to step ___ the gas.
    (a) on   (b) in
    (c) into   (d) over

13. Why is there a frown ___ his face?
    (a) of   (b) in
    (c) on   (d) to

14. Little details matter ___ us.
    (a) on   (b) to
    (c) in   (d) of

15. A wartime trail becomes a symbol ___ Vietnam's future.
    (a) in   (b) on
    (c) to   (d) of

Answer Keys

Exercise on Grammatical Errors

Exercise – 1

1. (b)	**2.** (d)	**3.** (b)	**4.** (c)	**5.** (d)	**6.** (c)	**7.** (c)	**8.** (a)	**9.** (c)	**10.** (c)
11. (b)	**12.** (b)	**13.** (b)	**14.** (c)	**15.** (c)	**16.** (d)	**17.** (c)	**18.** (c)	**19.** (d)	**20.** (b)
21. (c)	**22.** (c)	**23.** (c)	**24.** (b)	**25.** (b)					

Exercise – 2

1. (b)	**2.** (a)	**3.** (d)	**4.** (a)	**5.** (b)	**6.** (d)	**7.** (c)	**8.** (c)	**9.** (a)	**10.** (d)
11. (b)	**12.** (b)	**13.** (c)	**14.** (a)	**15.** (b)	**16.** (b)	**17.** (a)	**18.** (d)	**19.** (a)	**20.** (b)
21. (b)	**22.** (c)	**23.** (d)	**24.** (c)	**25.** (c)					

Exercises on Preposition

Exercise – 1

1. (a)	**2.** (d)	**3.** (b)	**4.** (c)	**5.** (b)	**6.** (c)	**7.** (d)	**8.** (b)	**9.** (c)	**10.** (d)
11. (b)	**12.** (d)	**13.** (b)	**14.** (d)	**15.** (c)	**16.** (d)	**17.** (c)	**18.** (c)	**19.** (d)	**20.** (b)
21. (d)	**22.** (c)	**23.** (a)	**24.** (b)	**25.** (c)	**26.** (d)	**27.** (b)	**28.** (b)	**29.** (b)	**30.** (a)
31. (b)	**32.** (b)	**33.** (b)	**34.** (b)	**35.** (a)	**36.** (d)	**37.** (a)	**38.** (c)	**39.** (a)	**40.** (b)
41. (c)	**42.** (a)	**43.** (a)	**44.** (d)	**45.** (b)	**46.** (a)	**47.** (a)	**48.** (a)	**49.** (b)	**50.** (b)
51. (b)	**52.** (c)	**53.** (b)	**54.** (c)	**55.** (b)	**56.** (b)	**57.** (d)	**58.** (d)	**59.** (b)	**60.** (d)
61. (c)	**62.** (d)	**63.** (d)	**64.** (c)	**65.** (b)	**66.** (b)	**67.** (a)	**68.** (b)	**69.** (d)	**70.** (c)
71. (a)	**72.** (c)	**73.** (b)	**74.** (c)	**75.** (d)	**76.** (b)	**77.** (b)	**78.** (b)	**79.** (c)	**80.** (d)
81. (d)	**82.** (c)	**83.** (b)	**84.** (b)	**85.** (b)	**86.** (a)	**87.** (b)	**88.** (b)	**89.** (c)	**90.** (d)
91. (b)	**92.** (a)	**93.** (c)	**94.** (b)	**95.** (a)	**96.** (c)	**97.** (b)	**98.** (a)	**99.** (c)	**100.** (c)

Exercise – 2

1. (a)	**2.** (a)	**3.** (c)	**4.** (b)	**5.** (b)	**6.** (c)	**7.** (a)	**8.** (d)	**9.** (b)	**10.** (c)
11. (d)	**12.** (a)	**13.** (c)	**14.** (b)	**15.** (d)					

Solutions

Exercise – 1

1. b 'Films' is plural and therefore option (b) should be - 'between the films and their'.

2. d 'averse from' is incorrect. Averse always takes the preposition 'to'. So, option (d) should have been 'averse to responsibility'.

3. b The 'movies' in option (a) will take the plural 'achieve' in option (b).

4. c Here, a comparison is being made between two activities. Therefore, the correct sentence should be – 'Climbing Everest is as much a historic journey as it is a feat of mountaineering'.

5. d The 'not only' in option (b) hints that there should be a 'but' in option (d). So, it should be - 'but also cultural and religious barriers'.

6. c 'his' in option (c) is incorrect. The name of a country (India in this example) in such cases takes the neuter gender 'its'.

7. c The second 'are' in option (c) is redundant. It should be 'making such a lot of noise'.

8. a 'Besides' should be used which means 'in addition to' or 'moreover'.

9. c 'a' in (c) refers to only one and therefore the use of the plural 'generations' is incorrect. It should be 'a generation'.

10. c The singular 'fault' will take the singular 'lies'. Therefore, option (c) should be 'lies with'.

11. b The 'agrees' in option (b) is incorrect. In option (a), 'Analysts and columnists' form two separate entities and so, the plural 'agree' should be used.

12. b 'Neither' takes 'nor'. Hence, option (b) should be 'nor Europe'.

13. b 'Countries' is plural, so option (b) should be 'at Bonn were'.

14. c 'Provinces' in option (a) is plural and hence, the plural 'their own' should be used.

15. c 'Writing' used in option (c) is not consistent with the past tense 'built' used in option (a). Therefore, the correct sentence should have - 'but wrote the fabulous cult book'.

16. d 'a globe fashion empire' does not make sense. It should instead be 'global fashion empire'.

17. c 'between' should be used instead of 'among' in option (c). 'Between' is for two whereas 'among' is for more than two.

18. c Tense is not consistent throughout the sentence. It should be 'thinks and writes' in option (c).

19. d 'newest of people' is more appropriate in the given sentence.

20. b 'Countries' should take the plural – have. Therefore, option (b) should be - 'have ever seen'.

21. c 'constitutionally' is the word to be used in option (c). It means sanctioned by, or permissible according to the constitution.

22. c In option (c), the singular verb 'makes' should be used.

23. c This is a case of parallelism and the correct parallel structure is – 'feel the place, visit the ashrams, know the people'.

24. b The relative pronoun 'who' is used for living beings. So, in option (b), the more appropriate relative pronoun will be 'which'.

25. b 'Many more' is incorrect. It should be replaced with 'more'.

Exercise – 2

1. b 'instinctively sympathetic' is the correct answer. It works as an adjective phrase that describes British parent (noun).

2. a 'Everyone' is an indefinite pronoun which is taken as singular. Hence, the appropriate verb structure that should follow it is 'has received bad feedback'.

3. d 'what to wear at' is the correct expression. Here, 'at' functions as a preposition of place.

4. a 'Overruled' is the correct word to be used. It means to disallow a certain action, especially by virtue of higher authority.

5. b Plural verbs should follow plural nouns and pronouns. Hence, 'are' should be used for 'they' and 'children'.

6. d The event has already happened hence everything should be in past tense. So the correct phrase to be used is 'earlier place bids'.

7. c Plural verbs should follow plural nouns. Hence, the verb 'moves' should be used for 'investors'.

8. c Correct phrase is 'controllers of Indian foreign policy'. We should use the preposition 'of'.

9. a The correct phrase should be 'have silently worked .... to uplift human values. 'The plural word 'have' is used to denote plural pronoun 'some'. Also 'to uplift' is the correct verb form to be used.

10. d The plural 'drugs' should be used. Also, 'developing world' is the correct phrase.

11. b 'Winning policy debates and then losing elections' forms the correct parallel structure is the sentence.

12. b The quality of the car has to be 'noiseless', and the appropriate possessive pronoun to be used is 'whose' and not 'who'.

13. c Plural verb 'are' should be used to modify 'ideas' (plural noun) and singular verb 'ends' should be used to modify 'party' (singular noun).

14. a The correct parallel structure is given in option (a).

15. b The words 'neither...nor' should be used together.

16. b 'Between' should be used when two people are involved. Hence, option (b) is the correct answer.

17. a The correct verb is 'begins' because the subject is singular i.e. 'The search'.

18. d 'Series' indicates that the plural 'attacks' should be used along with the plural verb 'threaten'.

19. a The correct prepositional phrases to be used are 'of hope' and 'to disaster'.

20. b The correct parallel structure has to be used in this sentence – 'from looting to food shortages'. Also the adjective 'many' should be used to describe 'dangers'.

21. b Singular verb should follow singular noun. Hence 'is' must be used.

22. c The qualities described in the sentence have to be nouns in order to have the correct parallel structure.

23. d Correct verb 'is' and 'far' should be used. 'Far lesser' is an incorrect degree of comparison.

24. c Government is a collective noun and takes a singular verb here. Moreover, 'economical and political' forms the correct parallel structure.

25. c Quality has to be a superlative adjective. Hence 'least ideological' must be the appropriate choice.

CHAPTER 9

Sentence Completion

This Unit is a very important section for any CUCET entrance examination preparation. It is the building block for all your basics in the English language and a useful handbook to help you score well in the paper. Questions pertaining to the usage of the language are asked in almost all examinations and you need to understand the types of questions that could be asked. Completing sentences in grammatically correct English, improving a given sentence or even transforming a sentence into another form without changing its meaning, content or tense can be a very challenging task.

Going through this unit will help you in a big way. However, you can master this art, if you:

(a) Do all the worksheets on the given section.

(b) Read, read and read English every day – a good newspaper, newsmagazines, which will help you in your preparation for General Knowledge too, fiction, non-fiction, etc.

Sentence Completion

First things first; before we begin with the sentence completion section, you must have knowledge of how a simple sentence in English is constructed.

A sentence is a group of words that makes complete sense.

A **phrase** is merely a group of words that gives a meaning when used in a sentence.

E.g. "in the morning". The sun rises **in the morning.**

"of great beauty" – It was a sunrise **of great beauty.**

Thus, a phrase is a part of a sentence. A sentence has a subject, a verb and conveys full meaning.

We can classify sentences according to their **clause structure**. A group of words, which forms a part of a sentence, and contains a subject and a predicate, is called a **clause.** Sentences containing more than one clause are **complex or compound.**

The major types are:

1. Simple sentences (one main clause* and no subordinate clause**)

The people spoke about the leader's inefficiency. (main clause) (no subordinate clause)

2. Complex sentences (one main clause and at least one subordinate clause)

Although I passed the examination, I was not very happy.

('*Although I passed the examination*' is an example of *subordinate clause*).

3. Compound sentences (two or more main clauses)

My father called me in the morning (main clause) **and** I told him (main clause) that I would meet the Principal immediately (sub clause). 'And' is the conjunction that connects the two main clauses.

* A **main clause** is an independent clause that has a subject and a predicate and which can stand by itself as a statement.

** A **subordinate clause** is a part of a sentence and has a subject and a predicate but needs a main clause to make it a complete statement.

With these sentence patterns in mind, we can look into the Sentence Completion questions, commonly referred to as "fill in the blanks," which usually have a sentence with one or two blanks, which you are required to fill in with appropriate word(s) from the choices given.

You must keep in mind that you have to choose the "best" word from a list. So even if more than one word would fit in the sentence grammatically, you must choose the word that is most appropriate or the one that best expresses the meaning and suits the context of the sentence.

While your vocabulary is of prime importance, here you have a context. This is a blessing because it is possible to read an incomplete sentence, and guess, knowing the context, what kind of word *should* be in the blank. Therefore, it allows you to use your natural knowledge of English, the instinctive "feel" which tells you whether a given answer is correct or not.

It is possible to read a sentence through and think of what word or word type you should substitute. Let us work with the sentence:

"In temperament they were a complete contrast: the older man was quiet, courteous, and slightly______, the younger man was talkative, _______, and quite gregarious."

And your choices are:

    (a) reserved, brash
    (b) garrulous, asocial
    (c) agitated, friendly
    (d) extrovert, introvert

There will be **clue words**; words that suggest the correct answer choice. Looking at the second blank first, we can see we need a word that denotes a social, outgoing person. We know this because the words "complete contrast" indicate that the second blank should be a word for someone diametrically different from "quiet and courteous"- someone who is talkative and outgoing. Also, one must infer clues from the context - the second blank should be filled with a word that goes with talkative…similarly the first blank must be filled in context, meaning something along the lines of "quiet and courteous". Hence, option (a) is correct.

Sometimes the sentence that requires completion may be a difficult one and you will need to delve into the words to understand the tone / the mood that is coming through and use that as a clue to make your choice. Take this sentence: "He boasts that he is a man without prejudices; this ______ itself is a very great ______."

And your choices are:

    (a) realisation; accomplishment
    (b) statement; achievement
    (c) fact; concession
    (d) concept; feat
    (e) pretension; prejudice

Even if a sentence seems difficult, you can't look at it that way. You've got to consider it and say that there must be clues in those words or phrases which you could infer from, to deduce the correct answer. Here, the word "boasts" is a key word, as is the word "itself" in the latter part of the sentence. So you start by saying that the sentence has a tone of negativity - the person is considered boastful; it is unlikely that the completed meaning will be one of congratulation or respect. Then, there is the word 'itself' that gives a clue that there is likely to be a repetition of something said in the first part. Let us take each of the options, one by one:

(a)   Has a positive tone, not what the word 'boast' would go well with. We will have to reject it.

(b)   Again, a positive tone that is not fitting.

(c)   While 'fact' may seem probable, 'concession' means to give in or an allowance and that does not work well with boasting.

(d)   Here, feat gives a positive tone, so we reject it.

(e)   This option seems to fit best – there is a negative meaning of 'pretension' and 'itself' refers to prejudice in the first part… likely to be the right choice.

So we are correct in selecting the option (e) by the process of eliminating the wrong ones based on the tone and mood we picked up.

Clue Words to Remember

Clue words indicate the direction and purpose of a sentence, and help you to guess what kind of word(s) may be put into the blanks in a given sentence.

Typically, clue words are "connecting" words, which link two parts of a sentence, as listed below:

1.   they can connect/link **similar ideas**,

2.   they can connect/link **opposing ideas**, or

3.   they can show **cause** and **effect** in the two parts of a sentence that they link.

Knowing the purpose, or nature of a sentence in this manner is vital for deciding what kind of a word will fit a blank in a given sentence.

1.   When two parts of a sentence express similar ideas, you will find words like 'and', 'additionally', 'furthermore'. These suggest that the same idea / mood / opinion is being carried on. You should look for words in the choice list that support the same.

    One type of sentence with similar ideas is the "**synonym sentence.**" In this type of sentence, you must identify the word for which you will choose a synonym from the answer choices. Your common sense and an understanding of vocabulary are essential.

    E.g.

    Outgoing and ______ by nature, Urmila became even more gregarious at the company party.

    (a) reclusive   (b) solitary
    (c) belligerent   (d) affable

    Notice the word "and." This is a signal that this may be a synonym sentence (although you could just use common sense). In the above sentence, you must choose the word that is a synonym to 'outgoing'. 'Reclusive' and 'solitary' are opposite of 'outgoing'; and 'belligerent' does not go with 'gregarious'. If you know your meanings, you know that 'affable' is the only word that even comes close to 'outgoing', therefore it is the answer.

    Similar or parallel ideas or synonyms are indicated by words like:

and	also	furthermore	besides	moreover
as well	again	always	never	each
every	must	all	the fact that	in addition
too	additionally	moreover	as well as	indeed

    Practice: Make a sentence using each of the words given above.

2.   If there is a sentence with two parts, connected with "but," then you know that the ideas expressed in the two parts of the sentence must be

contrasting. Therefore, if the first part of the sentence describes the man as good looking, and the second part has a blank to fill in about this man, you will know that the blank must be filled by a word that describes the man **negatively**, since the clue word "but" tells us that contrasting ideas are expressed in the two parts of the sentence. Words such as "**but, in spite of, yet, despite, nevertheless, ironically, whereas, on the contrary, although, by contrast, however, unfortunately, and on the other hand**" are all examples of words of contrast. Whenever you see such words, your antennae need to go up. They are flipping / changing the direction of that sentence.

Therefore, in a sentence where one of these phrases is used, suppose you are inclined to fill in that word, before you see the "word of contrast", then chances are that, if the word of contrast is present, the meaning of the sentence will be flipped around, and you will have to use a negative word, and vice-versa.

For instance, in the sentence: "Musharraf was a great looking guy, but he hadn't taken a bath for a while; so he smelt ________." The "but" flips around the meaning of the sentence completely. Without the "but" and the second part of the sentence, you would have probably filled in a positive word, such as "divine", but now you **know** you have to fill in a negative word. Something like "foul" would be a good choice in this context. And of course, in questions of this type where answer choices are given, your task is much easier, because you can get some idea of what the answer is likely to be without even looking at the choices - as described earlier, then once you look at the answers, you can probably eliminate most of the choices, leaving only one or two likely to be the right answer.

An antonym sentence is solved in the same way as a synonym one, except that you have to keep in mind that the words in the blank will be opposites of the other idea in the sentence, not synonyms.

Opposing or contrasting ideas are indicated by words like:

although	however	but	nevertheless	in contrast
in spite of	on the contrary	usually	if	instead
despite	rather than	whereas	yet	even though

Practice: Make a sentence using each of the words given above.

Take this sentence: Although Mrs. Peters________ an interest in the spiritual well being of the parishioners, in actuality her concern for their welfare was so ________ as to be practically non-existent.

(a) manifested…exemplary
(b) simulated…profound
(c) confessed…circumstantial
(d) feigned…negligible

Which words give you a clue of the relationship between the first part and the second part of the sentence? Yes, the word, 'although' and 'in actuality'! These tell us that something that we read about in the first part is contradicted 'in actuality'.

Option (a) gets eliminated outrightly as a 'manifested' interest would be 'exemplary' and there is no contradiction in it.

Option (b) is also inappropriate for the same reason, as a simulated interest that is profound does not bring out any contradiction. Option (c) or option (d) needs to be considered. The word 'confessed' has a tone or feeling of honesty while 'feigned' indicates deceit and duplicity, which correctly begins the sentence to later reveal the low or negligible actual interest. Therefore, option (d) is correct.

3.   When two parts of a sentence have a cause and effect relation, it is easy to guess the possible answer.

This type of problem is fairly simple - you will be given either the cause and you have to figure out the effect, or you will be given the effect, and you will have to figure out the cause.

Let us work this out:

The Health Ministry rejected the experimental medicine after conducting tests for toxicity because the patients who used it experienced ________ effects.

(a) non-toxic   (b) refreshing
(c) harmful   (d) toxic

Notice that the sentence supplies you with the effect, "The Health Ministry rejected the experimental medicine..." Now ask yourself, "What would cause them to reject the medicine?" By using common sense, you can figure out that whatever it is, it must be negative. Now go through the words. You'll find that the only negative words are "harmful " and "toxic". Since the tests were for toxicity, "toxic" is more relevant than "harmful". There is the possibility that more than one negative word is given in the list of choices, in which case you must use your common sense to figure out which word best fits the given context.

Cause and effect relationships in a sentence are indicated by:

in fact	certainly	of course	surely	by all means
undoubtedly	Similarly	as a result	because	in order to
hence	therefore	consequently	Thus	was caused by
due to	since			

Practice: Make a sentence using each word given above.

Other tips for Sentence Completion

Structural clues - or clues which you can infer by studying the way the sentence is constructed have been discussed. You have learnt to look for sentences which:

- Link two phrases with support words and phrases ("in addition" and "also"),

- Show contrast or shifts in direction ("instead" and "despite"),

- Signal a turn of events or the unexpected ("ironically" and "surprising"), and

- Show cause and effect.

Let us study some finer points that will make the exercise easier for you:

1. **In Sentence Completion questions with only one blank, if you see exact synonyms among the answer choices, they have to be wrong so eliminate them!**

   This is so, because if two words in the choices are exact synonyms, they mean the same thing. That means if one is a correct answer, so is the other. Since you can't have two correct answers, both of them are wrong! Keep in mind that similar words are **not** synonyms. Frequently, different answer choices contain words that are **similar** in meaning, not exactly the same. This is to confuse you - if they are synonyms, both cannot be correct, but if they are **similar** in meaning, then you cannot eliminate both - either of the two answer-choices might be correct.

   Take this sentence: Mr Natwarlal is ________ for his evil deeds.

   (a) notorious   (b) famous
   (c) popular   (d) emotional

   In the answer choices, all options are in the adjectival form saying something about the subject. Options (b) and (c) are positive in connotation; the word 'evil' in the sentence contradicts the answer-choices. The option (a) 'notorious' fits the blank and (d) is totally out of context as 'evil' and 'emotional; have no relation.

2. **A comma before and after a group of words implies that those words either define or elaborate a point made prior to it. Use this explanation to your advantage.**

   In the sentence: Rahul found that Bangalore's infrastructure, its transport system and electric supply, were severely inadequate.

   From this sentence, you can deduce that infrastructure includes the transport system and electric supply. So if one of them was a blank, for instance there was a blank in place of 'transport system' or 'electric supply' you would know that the blank has to be filled by something that is a part of city infrastructure.

3. **In a two blanks sentence, the choices given can confuse you as in the choice pair, one word will be right (it could fit in) and the other wrong (it could not fit in).**

   This is done deliberately. Take each pair and work thoroughly through.

   Take this sentence: The law suit was resolved after many years of ________ litigation and the defendant was ordered to pay ________.

   (a) bitter, charges
   (b) acrimonious, restitution
   (c) futile, salaries
   (d) unnecessary, wages

   Here, at first glance option (a) has 'bitter' that relates well with 'litigation'; 'acrimonious' in (b) also means ill feeling; 'futile' in (c) also speaks of a wasted battle since the defendant had to pay back something; and the word 'unnecessary' is out of context.

   The second pair of options will help you in focusing on the right choice. While 'charges' in (a) refers to a price, the defendant ordered to pay charges make no sense. The words 'salaries' and 'wages' in (c) and (d) are misleading clues. 'restitution' in (b) means returning or restoring something to its rightful owner. Therefore, if read in this light, we understand that after years of acrimonious litigation, the accused was asked to return or restore something to its rightful owner.

   Thus, to answer such questions, each pair of words in the answer options has to be worked upon.

4. **One of the smart tactics that can be applied while attacking sentence completion questions is that you predict an answer when you are doing practice questions.**

   You need to mentally fill in with your own words before you see as to what words the test writer has provided. The idea behind this is to give you some idea of what the answer is likely to be - it helps narrow down, eliminate answer choices and save time. For example, in a given sentence, if you decide that the blank must be filled with some word before you look at the answer choices, you can scan the word choices to find the positive word/s there.

   Take this sentence: The heat was so intense that people ________ various remedies.

   In this example, while reading the sentence itself you can mentally visualize that due to the intense heat people resorted to various means of finding respite. With this picture in mind, words that we can think of to fill the blank could be "tried", "needed", "sought", etc.

   Answer options are:

   (a) sought   (b) brought
   (c) seek   (d) working out

   But since the sentence is in the past tense, (a) is the appropriate option.

Collocation

There is a special sentence completion type where you are given a number of sentences and a list of words to complete them. The words given are synonyms or near synonyms, with similar meanings. In English, certain words go together. For instance while you may "make" a mistake, you cannot "make" a crime but can "commit" a crime. Your knowledge of "appropriate" word choice is being tested, only here the options are so close in meaning that you have to pay attention to the precise use of words, understanding of the nuance of a word and the appropriateness of its use.

Practice: Complete the sentences given below with words from this list:

performed	practised	laboured
enacted	transacted	

(a) The state recently _______ a law banning cow slaughter.

(b) In all his free time, Leander Paes _______ his serve.

(c) The business was _______ early in the morning as a power failure was expected.

(d) Poornima _______ the operation with minimal nursing support.

(e) Shiv _______ over his assignment, despite being very ill.

To tackle this question you must first fill in the ones of which you are absolutely sure. This will leave you fewer words to choose from. Then, read every sentence with each of the available options, and judge which one suits best.

Next, as shown earlier, look for 'clue words' in the sentence. Your reading should give you an idea of which word is associated with another, such as 'enacted' and 'law' as in No.1.

Leander could not have "performed" his serve – he would have "practised" it. Poornima could not have "laboured" the operation but "performed" it. You know that business is "transacted" and not "laboured" or "performed". The last word is "laboured" and it fits well in (e) as Shiv was ill.

Let us work out another collocation exercise:

Try and solve it before you read the explanation. That way you will learn from your mistakes, if there are any.

Abolished, eliminated, erased, evaded, circumvented

1. The speech was no longer available as it had been _______ by mistake.

2. Even though dowry has been _______ by the law, in practice it still exists.

3. He has _______ paying his taxes for so long, when the law catches him he will have to pay a heavy price.

4. The team was _______ from the series after they lost to Bangladesh.

5. Any law can be _______ but you cannot always get away with it.

All the words have meanings centred on being '**cut off**' **or being** '**avoided**'. The first sentence has implied in it the fact that the speech was on tape- that is a way a speech can be 'available'. Otherwise a speech is made or delivered. So you should be able to safely say that '**erased**' would be the fitting word as removal of taped material is called erasing.

In the second statement, use of 'abolished' is appropriate as it refers to doing away with laws, regulations, customs, etc. Hence, it is appropriate to use it for the practice of dowry. 'Evading' refers to getting around or shirking the law, a duty, etc. Hence, it is appropriate to use it as evading taxes in the third statement. 'Elimination' refers to removal from consideration by defeating, as in a contest. Hence, its use is correct in the fourth sentence. 'Circumvent' means to avoid by artfulness or deception. Its use is appropriate in the last statement as a law can be avoided by deception at times but not always.

This chapter is a revision of what you have done till know. In these type of questions an incomplete sentence is usually given and you have to complete the sentence based on correct grammar usage. Practice the exercise given below.

Exercise

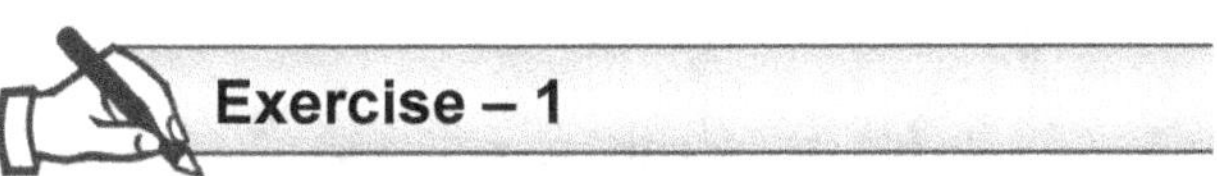

Exercise – 1

Directions for questions 1 to 15: Choose the world or phrase which best completes the sentence. Rely on the choice that would complete the meaning of the sentence.

1. Having finished dinner, ___ .
   (a) the elders retired to bed
   (b) they slept
   (c) the bed was used by the elders
   (d) a group of elders finished bed

2. I was not the only one, there were people who suffered ___ .
   (a) more than I can possible imagined
   (b) more than I can possibly
   (c) more than can possibly imagine
   (d) more than I can possibly imagine

3.   Shyam has returned ___ .
     (a) a vehicle back to its original owner
     (b) to its original owner the vehicle
     (c) the vehicle its original owner
     (d) the vehicle to its original owner

4.   Some scholars stressed the study of grammar, rhetoric, ___ and poetry.
     (a) historically
     (b) learning about history
     (c) history
     (d) studying history

5.   Lalitha ___ that she could not attend classes next week.
     (a) told to her professors
     (b) said her professors
     (c) said to her professors
     (d) told her professors

6.   Everybody ___ a ticket should stand in line.
     (a) who have not purchased
     (b) who has not bring
     (c) who has not purchased
     (d) who has not

7.   A number of applicants ___ interviewed.
     (a) are already been
     (b) has already been
     (c) have been
     (d) who have been

8.   Anna did not do well at all because ___ .
     (a) she was not good studywise
     (b) she studied bad
     (c) she was a worse student
     (d) she failed to study properly

9.   The more he shouted, ___ .
     (a) the less he achieved
     (b) he achieved insufficiently
     (c) he did not achieve enough
     (d) he was achieving less

10. ___ , the best car to buy is Maruti.
     (a) Because of its design and economy
     (b) Because it has a sleek shape, and it is very economical
     (c) Because of its design and it is economical
     (d) Because design and economical wise it is better than all others

11. People all over the country are starving ___ .
     (a) great in numbers
     (b) in more numbers
     (c) more numerously
     (d) in great numbers

12. Anil entered college ___ .
     (a) when he had 16 years
     (b) when 16 years were his age
     (c) at the age of 16
     (d) at 16 years age

13. The doctor insisted that the patient ___ .
     (a) that he not work too hard
     (b) taking it easy
     (c) take it easy
     (d) take some vocations

14. I understand that the government is considering a new proposal ___ .
     (a) what would clear files rapidly
     (b) who wants to clear files in a rapid manner
     (c) that would help in clearing files rapidly
     (d) to cause files cleared rapidly

15. Srinivas would have studied medicine if he ___ to a medical college.
     (a) could be able to enter
     (b) was admitted
     (c) had been admitted
     (d) were admitted

Exercise – 2

Directions for questions 1 to 20: Choose the world or phrase which best completes the sentence. Rely on the choice that would complete the meaning of the sentence.

1.   It is very difficult to stop Parthenium because ___ .
     (a) of it grows, carelessly
     (b) it doesn't care much to grow
     (c) of its growth without attention
     (d) it grows well with little care

2.   Manufacturers often sacrifice quality ___ .
     (a) in place of to earn more money
     (b) for a larger profit margin
     (c) to gain more quantities of money
     (d) and instead earn a bigger amount of profit

3.   She ___ before handing it to the director.
     (a) must retyping the report
     (b) is retype the report
     (c) must retype the report
     (d) should retyping the report

4.   Of the two new workers, one is experienced and ___ .
     (a) the other are not
     (b) another is inexperienced
     (c) the other is not
     (d) other lacks experience

5.   The facilities of the older canteen ___ .
     (a) is as good or better than the new canteen
     (b) are as good or better that of the new canteen
     (c) are as good as or better that the new canteen
     (d) are as good as or better than those of the new
          canteen

6.   ___ , he would have been able to pass the SAT.
     (a) If he practised more
     (b) If he were practising to a great degrees
     (c) Practising more
     (d) Had he practised more

7.   Here ___ notebook and paper that I promised you
     last week.
     (a) is the   (b) are the
     (c) was the   (d) is a

8.   Rao contributed Rs. 10, but he wished he could
     contribute ___ .
     (a) one other Rs. 10   (b) the same amount also
     (c) another 10   (d) more Rs. 10

9.   The manager of this organisation must know ___ .
     (a) money management, selling and able to satisfy
          the shareholders
     (b) how to management, selling his idea of being
          able to satisfy the shareholders
     (c) money management, selling the idea of being
          able to satisfy the shareholders
     (d) how to manage money, sell his product, and
          satisfy the shareholders

10. Steel production in the country ___ .
     (a) have take slumps and rise in recent years
     (b) has been rather erratic lately
     (c) has been erratically lately
     (d) are going up and down all the time

11. The sight of her in green silk mounted on a tractor
     ___ more newsworthy ___ .
     (a) was considered ... than anything said inside
          the House
     (b) when said ... when inside the House consider
     (c) was considered ... that said inside the House
     (d) were considered ... of inside the house

12. Neither the ministers ___ appear to have noticed
     that the Indian farmer has already been killed.
     (a) nor the environmentalist
     (b) or the environmentalists
     (c) nor environmentalists
     (d) nor the environmentalists

13. Nothing demonstrates the depth of prejudice so
     starkly ___ .
     (a) as marriage as
     (b) marriage
     (c) as married
     (d) as marriage

14. The women are disgusted when they find ___ living
     on pensions.
     (a) her new husbands are
     (b) their new husbands is
     (c) their new husbands are
     (d) their new husband are

15. Sarah came across as a decent person and ___ .
     (a) my instinct was to trust her
     (b) my instinct to trust her
     (c) my instinct was to trusted her
     (d) my instinct was to trust she

16. We will be unable to eliminate poverty if we ___ .
     (a) can control our population more effectively
     (b) cannot control their population more effectively
     (c) cannot control our population more effective
     (d) cannot control our population more effectively

17. Our ministers ___ when it comes to finding reasons
     to travel to foreign countries at taxpayers' expense.
     (a) are very imaginative
     (b) is are very imaginative
     (c) is very imaginative
     (d) are very imagination

18. The Congressional debate showcased how sharply
     divided ___ .
     (a) Americans is about China
     (b) Americans are about of China
     (c) Americans are about China
     (d) American are about China

19. You can never be America's friend ___ .
     (a) if you murder people as they do in China
     (b) if murder people as they do in China
     (c) if you murder was they do in China
     (d) if you murder people and persons as they do in
          China

20. The details vary, but the cases ___ .
     (a) has a common theme
     (b) have common theme
     (c) have a common theme
     (d) have a common thematic

Exercise – 3

Directions for questions 1 to 20: Choose the world or phrase which best completes the sentence. Rely on the choice that would complete the meaning of the sentence.

1. Upon hearing the ___ words from him, she left the place ___ .
    (a) wrongful ... abashed
    (b) misuse ... immediately
    (c) obnoxious ... abashed
    (d) acrimonious ... amicably

2. How can the plans of the government ___ the poor, if they are totally ___?
    (a) educate ... illiterate
    (b) help ... impractical
    (c) benefit ... selfish
    (d) enrich ... penniless

3. The ___ that 'A bird in hand is worth two in the bush' is ___ in the present context.
    (a) metaphor ... cavil
    (b) adage ... inappropriate
    (c) talk ... evil
    (d) sentence ... anomalous

4. The thought of a nuclear ___ sparked off by a misunderstanding poses an awesome___ .
    (a) device ... reverberation
    (b) holocaust ... spectre
    (c) liasion ... probability
    (d) explosion ... calamity

5. A ___ person is not ___ .
    (a) dishonest ... untrustworthy
    (b) handsome ... presentable
    (c) talkative ... precise
    (d) healthy ... robust

6. The ___ reached between the enemies won the ___ of the observers.
    (a) treaty ... accolade
    (b) victory ... decoration
    (c) peace ... hearts
    (d) pitch ... enimity

7. ___ persons are ___ .
    (a) careful ... circumspect
    (b) violent ... peaceable
    (c) despondent ... intrepid
    (d) garrulous ... gluttonous

8. The rebels sought to overcome the ___ of strength of the police forces by engaging in ....tactics.
    (a) lack ... divisionary
    (b) augmented ... peaceful
    (c) preponderance ... guerilla
    (d) power ... foolish

9. Science fiction is a literary ___ which postulates a change from conditions as we know them and follows the implications of these changes to a ___ .
    (a) piece ... beginning
    (b) imagination ... fantasy
    (c) sub-genre ... logical end
    (d) masterpiece ... logical end

10. It is extremely difficult to produce a legal definition clear enough so that a ___ could work with it.
    (a) lawyer   (b) cook
    (c) dancer   (d) bartender

11. When I left school, I saw it as a temporary move — I assumed I'd ___ .
    (a) go back   (b) return back
    (c) go forth   (d) go back and come

12. For young people today, there are business opportunities unlike any that have existed ___
    (a) after   (b) before
    (c) now   (d) then and here

13. She had been apprehensive initially, not about her work, ___ the audience.
    (a) and about   (b) but about
    (c) but about the   (d) but roundabout

14. I don't believe that crying on television is the best way to ___ an interview.
    (a) given   (b) give take
    (c) give out   (d) give

15. The boy's death wrenched the hearts of parents ___ the world who easily understood the love that would lead a father to ___ his child from bullets with his own body.
    (a) round ... shield
    (b) around ... shield
    (c) around ... shielded
    (d) around ... shield out

16. The army admitted its mistake, but ___ .
    (a) graceless   (b) gracefully
    (c) gracelessly   (d) grace

17. Considering the ___ cost attached to each application forwarded, the student is constrained to apply to a ___ number of universities.
    (a) high ... unlimited
    (b) low ... limited
    (c) high ... though limited
    (d) high ... limited

18. The most important element that provides one student an edge over the rest is how his application form ___ his personality.
    (a) reflect   (b) reflects
    (c) reflect off   (d) reflects the

19. The fashion industry has long been ___ for the exclusion of black models.
    (a) criticize   (b) criticism
    (c) criticized   (d) critic

20. Benazir said that the regime's decision to allow Sharif to walk ___ could ___ be part of a larger game plan or just another corrupt act.
    (a) free ... or   (b) free ... neither
    (c) freed ... either (d) free ... either

Exercise – 4

Directions for questions 1 to 20: Choose the world or phrase which best completes the sentence. Rely on the choice that would complete the meaning of the sentence.

1. The military is unable to comprehend the ___ of democratic functioning.
    (a) impotent   (b) important
    (c) importance   (d) importing

2. Taxi driver's brains are ___ to help them store a detailed mental map of the city.
    (a) adapt   (b) adapting
    (c) adapted   (d) adopted

3. Keeping in view your ___ state of mind, it's with a rather ___ heart that I'm penning down this letter to you.
    (a) distress ... heavy
    (b) distressed ... heavy
    (c) distressed ... heaviness
    (d) distressing ... heavy

4. The mess that you have created is entirely your ___ doing.
    (a) owned   (b) owning
    (c) own   (d) own up

5. Unknown to her mother, she kept meeting him on the ___ .
    (a) sly   (b) sty
    (c) cry   (d) sloth

6. Do you think all this is a ___ of my imagination?
    (a) fig   (b) figmentation
    (c) figment   (d) figment leaf

7. When the Board came down ___ on him after his disastrous performance against Australia, he knew that it would ___ him his captaincy.
    (a) heavily ... cost
    (b) heavily ... costed
    (c) heavily ... costing
    (d) heavy ... cost

8. I don't need to take lessons in ___ and ethics from such a liar.
    (a) moral
    (b) morality
    (c) immorality
    (d) modality

9. Indecency is when you humiliate and cheat people emotionally, when you use and ___ the people you love, when you lie with a ___ face to everyone when it suits you.
    (a) disabuse ... straight
    (b) abuse ... straight
    (c) abused ... straight
    (d) abuse ... straightened

10. In an article that ran across five pages, you found only two paragraphs objectionable, so I gather that you ___ to my thoughts in the rest of the feature.
    (a) prescribe   (b) subscribe
    (c) subscribes   (d) subscribing

11. Scientists say that we are almost certainly the ___ of our own destinies.
    (a) master   (b) mastering
    (c) mastered   (d) masters

12. Some people ___ with all sorts of adversities.
    (a) dope   (b) doped
    (c) coping   (d) cope

13. Luck is a triumph of nurture over ___ and people's personalities influence how they are treated by ___ .
    (a) natured ... fate
    (b) nature ... ill-fate
    (c) natural ... fate
    (d) nature ... fate

14. Internalists believe there is a ___ between them and what happens to them.
    (a) connection   (b) connect
    (c) connections   (d) connected

15. Children from ___ backgrounds are more likely to become externalists than children from poor ___, who have had to overcome adversity to succeed.
    (a) rich ... background
    (b) poor ... backgrounds
    (c) poor ... background
    (d) rich ... backgrounds

16. People who categorize themselves as lucky tend to be optimists, extroverts and ___ .
    (a) risk-taker
    (b) risk-takers
    (c) risk-makers
    (d) risky-takers

17. Eventually, if you ___ at enough of the right people under the ___ circumstances, one will smile back at you.
    (a) smile ... right
    (b) smiling ... right
    (c) smile ... wrong
    (d) smile ... rightly

18. I don't socialize with the people I work ___, I have my own set of friends and I intend to keep some sort of ___ between my friends and my work.
    (a) on ... differentiation
    (b) off ... differentiation
    (c) with ... differentiate
    (d) with ... differentiation

19. I have my own set of friends, who have access to my home and my ___ thoughts and feelings, I don't let just about anyone invade that ___ .
    (a) inner ... privacy
    (b) outer ... privacy
    (c) inner ... private
    (d) inane ... privacy

20. When I joined college, I was ___ at the lack of discipline, I saw a lot of kids bunk and go to discos. Why ___ to parents to go and have a good time? And why during study hours?
    (a) shocked ... lied
    (b) shocked ... lying
    (c) shock ... lie
    (d) shocked ... lie

Answer Keys

Exercise – 1

1. (a)	**2.** (d)	**3.** (d)	**4.** (c)	**5.** (d)	**6.** (c)	**7.** (c)	**8.** (d)	**9.** (a)	**10.** (a)
11. (d)	**12.** (c)	**13.** (c)	**14.** (c)	**15.** (c)					

Exercise – 2

1. (d)	**2.** (b)	**3.** (c)	**4.** (c)	**5.** (d)	**6.** (d)	**7.** (b)	**8.** (c)	**9.** (d)	**10.** (b)
11. (a)	**12.** (d)	**13.** (d)	**14.** (c)	**15.** (a)	**16.** (d)	**17.** (a)	**18.** (c)	**19.** (a)	**20.** (c)

Exercise – 3

1. (c)	**2.** (b)	**3.** (b)	**4.** (b)	**5.** (c)	**6.** (a)	**7.** (a)	**8.** (c)	**9.** (c)	**10.** (a)
11. (a)	**12.** (b)	**13.** (b)	**14.** (d)	**15.** (b)	**16.** (c)	**17.** (d)	**18.** (b)	**19.** (c)	**20.** (d)

Exercise – 4

1. (c)	**2.** (c)	**3.** (b)	**4.** (c)	**5.** (a)	**6.** (c)	**7.** (a)	**8.** (b)	**9.** (b)	**10.** (b)
11. (d)	**12.** (d)	**13.** (d)	**14.** (a)	**15.** (d)	**16.** (b)	**17.** (a)	**18.** (d)	**19.** (a)	**20.** (d)

Solutions

Exercise – 1

1. a Option (c) and (d) are absurd. (a) is the appropriate option.

2. d Option (a) is incorrect due to the usage of 'possible imagined'. Option (b) and (c) are incomplete. Thus, option (d) is correct.

3. d Options (a) and (b) are incorrect grammatically and option (c) is incomplete. Correct option is (d).

4. c The sentence mentions some subjects like grammar poetry etc. So the best option to fit in here is (c).

5. d There is incorrect usage of 'to' in (a) and (c). (b) is incomplete. The correct option is (d).

6. c (a) is wrong as it has plural verb form.

7. c Here 'applicants' is the subject which is plural. The sentence is in passive voice and hence, 'have been' should be used.

8. d Options (a), (b) and (c) are absurd. The correct option is (d).

9. a (a) is the correct option because it starts with 'the'- parallelism.

10. a According to the rules of parallellism, the best option is (a).

11. d All the options apart from (d) are grammatically incorrect.

12. c Options (a), (b) and (d) are all absurd options. Correct option is (c).

13. c Option (a) does not make any sense. Option (b) sounds incomplete. The most appropriate option is (c).

14. c In option (a) use of 'what' is wrong and same is the case with (b) where 'who' is wrong. Option (d) is totally absurd and grammatically incorrect. Option (c) is the correct option.

15. c Correct usage is 'had been'.

Exercise – 2

1. d Option (a) sounds absurd and incorrect. Option (b) and (c) do not fit in the sentence. (d) is the correct option.

2. b In (a) 'in place of to' is wrong, while in (c) it says quantities of money which is wrong. The best option is (b).

3. c In (a) and (c) the word 'retyping' is used which is incorrect usage here while in (b) it says is 'retype' which is also incorrect usage. The correct option thus is (c).

4. c (a) is incorrect because in the sentence it is singular while here it signifies plural. Option (c) is correct.

5. d In options (b) and (c) better that is used which is grammatically incorrect. The appropriate option is (d).

6. d Option (b) is very absurd as it is totally incorrect grammatically. Option (d) is the correct option.

7. b (b) is the correct option. Options (a) and (c) are incorrect because they use the singular 'is' for the plural subjects.

8. c (a) is incorrect because it uses one with ten rupees. Similarly, (b) is incorrect because of the use of also. Correct option is (c).

9. d (d) is the correct option - parallelism.

10. b (c) is absurd because of the usage of 'erratically lately'. The option that fits best is (b).

11. a 'Was' has to follow 'tractor' because of being singular and after 'newsworthy', 'than' has to follow because it implies comparison.

12. d Option (a) is not fit as it uses 'environmentalist' which is singular. Option (b) is not correct because 'or' cannot be used with 'neither'. Thus the correct option is (d).

13. d Option (a) ends with as so is incorrect. Option (b) is incomplete and option (c) uses the wrong tense. So the correct option is (d).

14. c   Option (a) is incorrect because it uses here which is singular. Same is the case with (b) which uses 'is'. In option (d) husband is singular that also being incorrect. Thus, the correct option is (c).

15. a   Option (b) sounds incomplete while option (c) uses trusted so is incorrect. In option (d) the case of the pronoun has been changed thus making it incorrect. The correct option is (a).

16. d   Option (a) is incorrect because it starts with 'can'. Option (b) is wrong because it uses 'their' with 'we'. The correct option is (d).

17. a   Option (b) is absurd as it uses 'is are' together. Option (c) uses 'is' which is singular thus making it also incorrect. The best option is (a).

18. c   In option (a) it uses 'is' which denotes singular which is wrong here. The correct option is (c).

19. a   Options (a), (c) and (d) are absolutely absurd and meaningless. Correct option is (a).

20. c   Option (a) starts with 'has' which is singular and does not go with 'cases'. The correct option here is (c).

Exercise – 3

1. c   In the first blank the word that best fits is 'obnoxious' as it means unpleasant and the word that fits in the second blank is 'abashed' as it means ashamed or embarrassed.

2. b   The word that best suits with 'plan' here is 'impractical'. Thus, the correct option is (b).

3. b   (b) is the correct option as 'an adage' is an old saying which fits well in the first blank.

4. b   The best word that fits here in the first blank is holocaust as it means great destruction or loss of life. Also the second word spectre fits appropriately as it means mental image of something unpleasant or menacing.

5. c   The pair of words that fits best are talkative and precise because a talkative person is not precise.

6. a   Because the word between is used in the sentence so the best word that fits here is treaty. Thus, the correct option is (a).

7. a   Options (b) and (c) are antonyms so are ruled out. While in option (d) garrulous means talkative while gluttonous means greedy so that does not match. Thus, correct option is (a) as both of them are synonyms.

8. c   The correct option is (c) as preponderance means 'greater in force, weight or influence' so it very well goes with strength.

9. c   Genre means a category of artistic work. So sub-genre is the best option that fits here. Thus, (c) is the correct option.

10. a   As the sentence mentions the word 'legal' so we can easily deduce that the answer is 'lawyer'.

11. a   (b) is wrong because return and back means the same thing. (c) is logically wrong and (d) is incorrect. Thus, the correct usage is (a).

12. b   The sentence uses 'have existed' which means past tense thus the correct option would be 'before'.

13. b   (c) is incorrect because 'the' would be repeated twice. The correct option is (b).

14. d   (b) cannot be used because both the words are antonyms and cannot be used together.

15. b   The most appropriate words that would fit in both the blanks are 'around' and 'shield'.

16. c   The correct option is (c) because there is a 'but' in the sentence which signifies negative. That is why the option is (c).

17. d   Because of the word 'constrained' used in the sentence we can easily infer that the cost is high. Because of the word 'a' before the blank 'unlimited' and 'though limited' cannot be used.

18. b   Grammatically the correct option is the singular 'reflects'.

19. c   The past form of the verb - 'Criticised' is the best option that fits here.

20. d   'Free' fits in the first blank and because 'or' is used in the sentence we cannot use 'neither'. The right words to be used is 'either'.

[Exercise – 4]

1. c   (a) cannot be used here because it has altogether a different meaning.

2. c   The most suitable word that fits in the blank is 'adapted'- which means 'fit for a specific situation or use'.

3. b   The words that fit best in the sentence are 'distressed' and 'heavy'.

4. c   Logically and grammatically the best option is 'own'.

5. a   The correct option is 'sly' because 'on the sly' means in a secretive manner.

6. c   In daily use we use the term 'figment of imagination'.

7. a   Option (d) is eliminated because the adverb 'heavily' fits in the first blank perfectly. For the second blank 'cost' is the most appropriate word. Therefore, the correct answer is option (a).

8. b   'Morality' is the best option that fits here.

9. b   The word 'abuse' is usually used with 'use'. And usually when people lie they lie with a straight face. Thus, the correct option is (b).

10. b   The appropriate option is (b) - 'subscribe' which means to 'feel or express hearty approval.

11. d   'Masters of our own destinies' is the correct phrase. So, option (d) is the answer.

12. d   The word 'dope' has altogether a different meaning and it means 'drug'. So it cannot be used here. The correct word that fits here is 'cope'.

13. d   The words that fit here are 'nature' and 'fate'.

14. a   'Connection' is the right usage of the word 'connect' that should be used here.

15. d   The first blank would be 'rich' because there is a comparison given and the compared word is 'poor'. So the other word has to be its antonym. Regarding the second blank 'backgrounds' has been mentioned in the line before so it will again be used.

16. b   Because the other descriptions given are in their plural form that is why the answer would also be in the same format. Thus, the answer is (b).

17. a   The form of the word used here for the first blank is 'smile' while for the second blank 'right' is appropriate.

18. d   We socialise 'with' people and not 'on' or 'off'. Thus, the correct option for the first blank is 'with'. The correct option for the second blank would automatically be 'differentiation'.

19. a   Thoughts and feelings are always inside a person that is why the correct option is 'inner'. The correct option for the second blank is 'privacy'.

20. d   Because it talks in past tense 'was' that is why correct option is 'shocked'. And the second option is 'lie'.